Christian Attitudes towards the State of Israel

MCGILL-QUEEN'S STUDIES IN THE HISTORY OF RELIGION

Volumes in this series have been supported by the Jackman Foundation of Toronto.

SERIES TWO   In memory of George Rawlyk
Donald Harman Akenson, Editor

Christian Attitudes towards the State of Israel

PAUL CHARLES MERKLEY

McGill-Queen's University Press
Montreal & Kingston · London · Ithaca

© McGill-Queen's University Press 2001
ISBN 0-7735-2188-7

Legal deposit third quarter 2001
Bibliothèque nationale du Québec

Printed in Canada on acid-free paper

This book has been published with the help of a grant
from the Humanities and Social Sciences Federation of
Canada, using funds provided by the Social Sciences
and Humanities Research Council of Canada.

McGill-Queen's University Press acknowledges the
financial support of the Government of Canada through
the Book Publishing Industry Development Program
(BPIDP) for its activities. It also acknowledges the
support of the Canada Council for the Arts for its
publishing program.

Canadian Cataloguing in Publication Data

Merkley, Paul Charles
    Christian attitudes towards the State of Israel

    Includes bibliographical references and index.
    ISBN 0-7735-2188-7

    1. Israel—History—Religious aspects—Christianity.
    2. Christian Zionism.   3. Palestine in Christianity.
    4. Christianity and other religions—Judaism—1945–
    5. Christianity and other religions—Islam.   I. Title.

DS126.5.M476 2001   956.9405   C00-901687-2

Typeset in 10/12 Baskerville by True to Type

Contents

Preface

A few days after the manuscript for this book was taken out of my hands and turned into page proofs at the end of September 2000, the second intifada broke out. I believe that the behaviour of all the parties since then has borne out the main features of my argument. Yassir Arafat began at once to declare openly what he previously declared only to audiences of faithful Muslims: that *jihad* (holy war) had begun and must continue until all of Palestine and all of Jerusalem were under Palestinian rule. The International Christian Embassy went ahead with its Feast of Tabernacles gathering in Jerusalem (October 14–20) at the very height of the riots in Jerusalem; it was attended, despite official US travel advisories, by some five thousand Christian pilgrims and was addressed by Likud leader Ariel Sharon, Mayor Ehud Olmert, and Rabbi Michael Melchior, a cabinet minister. The World Council of Churches followed its long-standing practice of adopting as its own the Declarations of the Middle East Council of Churches, which immediately assigned the whole responsibility for the violence to Israel and called upon "sister western churches [to] bring pressure to bear upon their governments, in particular those governments which play a decisive role in the affairs of the Middle East, to cause the Israeli government to halt these criminal activities and grant full and unqualified recognition to Palestinian rights, particularly the right of Arab sovereignty over occupied Jerusalem" (MECC Statement on the situation in Palestine, 2 October 2000). In the early weeks of the second intifada the rate of exodus of

Christians from the Palestine Authority multiplied; there are now many fewer Christians in the Holy Land than when I wrote the pages that follow.

February 2001

Acknowledgments

One major source for this book was the series of interviews I carried out, mainly in 1995 and 1998. I thank the following people and ask their forgiveness if it seems to any of them that I have not accurately reported his words: In Ottawa (by phone), Rev. Robert Assally, formerly priest at St George's Anglican Cathedral in Jerusalem (1995); and in Toronto (by phone), Douglas Ducharme, Canadian Council of Churches, 1995.

In Bethlehem, November 1995: Dr Geries Khoury and Dr Adnan Musallam, of *Al-Liqa' Journal*, published by the Center for Religious and Heritage Studies in the Holy Land, and Rev. Dr Mitri Raheb, pastor of the Lutheran Christmas church, Bethlehem.

In Jerusalem, November 1995: Ulf Carmesand, Director, Swedish Christian Study Centre, Jerusalem; and Dr Martin Bailey, Acting Director, Jerusalem office of MECC.

In Bethlehem, May 1998: Mitri Raheb; Mr Zoughbi Zoughbi, Palestine Conflict Resolution Centre (*Wi'am*); Mr Bishara Awad, President, Bethlehem Bible College; Mr. Salim Munayer, Academic Dean, Bethlehem Bible College and Director of *Musalaha* (Ministry of Reconciliation);

In Jericho, May 1998: Dr Sami Musallam, Jericho Office of the President of the Palestinian National Authority.

In Jerusalem, May 1998: Douglas Dicks, MECC office in Jerusalem (who also graciously and efficiently arranged many of these interviews for me); Dr Bernard Sabella, Executive Director, Department of Service to Palestinian Refugees (MECC); Mr Joudeh Majaj, Director, YMCA, East Jerusalem; Mr Jack Khazmo, Chairperson, St Mark's Welfare Society (Syrian Orthodox Church); His Grace Bishop Munib

Younan, Evangelical Lutheran Bishop of Jerusalem; Dr Mahdi Abdel Hadi, Director, Palestine Academic Society for the Study of International Affairs; Mr Ghassan Khatib, Publisher, *Palestine Report* (Jerusalem Media and Communication Centre); Mr Uri Mor, Director, Department for Christian Communities, Ministry of Religious Affairs, State of Israel; Mr Daniel Rossing, Friends World University (former Director, Department for Christian Communities); Mr Stan Goodenough, editor of *Middle East Intelligence Digest,* International Christian Embassy, Jerusalem; Mr David Pileggi, Shoresh Ministries; Mr Clarence Wagner, Jr, Director, Bridges for Peace.

As a Christian and a reasonably involved churchman, I wish I were able to report that I have always encountered a charitable, or at least an irenic, spirit in my dealings with the various churches and Christian organizations that I describe and quote in these pages. I have learned, however, that in some corrridors of the Church there is no patience at all with the concept of scholarly inquiry. I have found again and again that good-natured conversation will end the moment it is discovered that you are not a friendly partisan. I have tried not to let this experience colour my judgment, but no doubt it has.

I am indebted to Dr Gordon Young for reading and correcting the section on his father and the story of the Institute for Holy Land Studies; to Stan Goodenough, for reading and correcting the section on ICEJ, and to Clarence Wagner, Jr, for reading and commenting on the section on Bridges for Peace and at generous length on my project as a whole.

I find in many of the sources that are normally regarded as authoritative a variety of of spellings of the transliterated English equivalents of proper names, parties, and concepts belonging to the Arabic and Hebrew languages. I hope I have not offended anyone by making the wrong choices.

Twenty-five years ago, Joan Harcourt was the copyeditor for my first book. Now she is the editor of the same McGill-Queen's University Press. It has given me great personal satisfaction to be presenting to her this, my fifth book. She has been as patient and as thoughtful in her present role as I remember her being in that earlier one. I must also express my thanks to Claire Gigantes who meticulously edited this present manuscript. I look forward to doing this again when *she* is the editor of McGill-Queen's University Press, twenty-five years from now.

I am indebted again to the good people of St Andrew's Church of Scotland in Jerusalem and to the gracious staff of the Hospice at St Andrew's for their hospitality.

As always, my greatest debt is to my wife Gwen. Specifically, I thank her for accompanying me on some of my research and teaching visits to Israel, and for supporting me morally when I travelled alone.

Abbreviations

AIPAC	American Israel Public Affairs Committee
ACPC	American Christian Palestine Committee
AFME	American Friends of the Middle East
BFP	Bridges for Peace
CCI	Christians Concerned for Israel
CCP	Christian Council on Palestine
CC	*Christian Century*
CI	*Christians in Israel* (publication of Association of Christians and Jews in Israel)
CFI	Christian Friends of Israel
CIPAC	Christians' Israel Public Action Campaign
CIA	Central Intelligence Agency
CJPHL	Committee for Justice and Peace in the Holy Land
CT	*Christianity Today*
CZA	Central Zionist Archives, Jerusalem
EMEU	Evangelicals for Middle East Understanding
HSTL	Harry S. Truman Presidential Library
ICEJ	International Christian Embassy Jerusalem
JPost	Jerusalem Post
ME	Middle East
MECC	Middle East Council of Churches
MED	*Middle East Intelligence Digest* (renamed *Middle East Digest)* newsletter of ICEJ
NCC	National Council of Churches, US
NCLCI	National Christian Leadership Conference for Israel

NYT	*New York Times*
PA, PNA	Palestine Authority, Palestine National Authority
PASSIA	Palestine Academic Society for the Study of International Affairs
PFLP	Popular Front for the Liberation of Palestine
PLC	Palestine Legislative Council
PLO	Palestine Liberation Organization
PPF	Pro-Palestine Federation
WCC	World Council of Churches
ZAL	Zionist Archives and Library, World Zionist Organization, New York

NOTE: All references to Hebrew and Christian Scriptures are from Revised New King James Version unless otherwise noted. All references to Qur'an are from The Holy Qur'an, translated and with commentary by A. Yusuf Ali (Brentwood, Maryland: Amana, 1983).

Christian Attitudes towards the State of Israel

Introduction:
Israel's Reappearance in the
Company of Nations

For as soon as Zion was in labor,
She gave birth to her children.
"Shall I bring her to the time of birth, and not cause delivery?"
says the LORD?
Shall I who cause delivery shut up the womb?"

Isaiah 66:8-9

The State of Israel is a surprise, yet the modern mind hates to be surprised. Never before has a nation been restored to its ancient hearth after a lapse of 1,897 years. This extraordinary aspect is bound to carry some shock to the conventional mind, to be a scandal to the mediocre mind and a foolishness to the positivists. It requires some reordering of some notions.

Abraham Joseph Heschel[1]

NOVEMBER 1947: ATTITUDES OF THE NATIONS OF THE WEST TOWARDS THE PROSPECTIVE STATE

On 29 November 1947, in a moment of time, the nations of the world recorded their conclusion that the Jews of the world could be entrusted with the responsibility of building a state, which should thereafter be the homeland of the Jewish people. For nearly nineteen hundred years previous to this moment, the people of Israel had persevered without a homeland. Though stripped of their territorial posessions and humiliated by the destruction of their Temple, scattered to all the corners of the globe, the people called "Israel" clung to their prayer, recited three times a day: that they would all be reunited "next year in Jerusalem." This prayer had prevented them from disappearing as a people – as all other communities suffering comparable experiences before and since ultimately have done. For half a century, Zionists had sought to persuade the world that this record of persistence entitled the Jews to be re-established as a people where they had begun. The world listened, and in November 1947 the world parliament agreed.

As the United Nations was approaching its decision in 1947, most of the speechmaking of politicians and diplomats, and most of the arguing of editorialists, was couched in the rhetoric of "justice." In the long background of this perception that the cause of the Zionists was "just" was the two thousand years of Jewish Diaspora, characterized by many kinds of deprivation and persecution. In the immediate background was the Holocaust. In the foreground was the reality of several hundred thousand homeless European Jews. Given that the alternative to a Jewish state in Palestine was the absorption of these hundreds of thousands of displaced Jews into gentile lands, it was not difficult to see what "blessing" Israel required at this moment, nor to appreciate that in so blessing Israel, we too – the nations of the West – would also be blessed.

As the years passed, the basic requirements of patriotism were met and exceeded by the new people of Israel (the Israelis). No longer could anyone doubt that the fundamentals of national patriotism could be quarried from the Jewish legacy (the legacy of recollection and anticipation of nationhood while living in Diaspora on the edges of everyone else's national life and culture) and fashioned into a Jewish equivalent of other people's patriotism. Many who had previously only condescended gradually developed authentic admiration for the Jews. For some, this admiration grew further as the years went by, becoming, in extreme cases, a powerful pro-Israelism – indeed, a kind of second patriotism for many non-Jews.

But there were many others whose picture of the Jews was not improved by Israel's persistence. Resentment began to intrude into many hearts where condescension had reigned before. There were many who simply never came to terms with the picture of the triumphant Jew. This company included those whose anti-Semitism had not been set aside when the question had been "Should the Jews be allowed to try to make a State in Palestine?" but was only momentarily forgotten, or repressed, or denied, or transmuted tentatively into condescension. As the years passed – as the Israelis drove out their enemies and expanded their boundaries, making life less than everything it might be for Arabs who were reluctant to leave or unable to leave and unwilling to accept the status of a minority – anti-Semites began to resort to old habits of mind, simultaneously coining new vocabulary to conceal their primitive disdain for the Jews. In this new world – where "Israel" was not a thing of the past or a thing of the future or a "metaphor" for all kinds of things, but a living, breathing state – anti-Semitism took on new life as "Anti-Zionism."

CHRISTIAN ATTITUDES TOWARDS
THE CREATION OF THE STATE OF ISRAEL

For most Christians, the argument-from-justice for the creation of a Jewish state had been, in 1947–48, as compelling as for most others, but not necessarily more so. For some Christians, it was, in one sense, harder to decide in favour of Zionism than it was for the non-Christians or post-Christians. Once the world acknowledged the existence of the Jewish state, it would be welcoming back onto the track of world history a national polity with the same name and the same religion as that which had been ushered off that track by the concerted effort of the Roman Empire nearly nineteen hundred years previously. At that earlier moment, when the nations had dismissed Israel into political oblivion and the Jews had entered upon their apparently perennial destiny as a scattered people, the Church was ready with the explanation that this state of affairs had been predicted by Jesus of Nazareth: the scattering of the Jewish people was God's judgment on their rejection of their Messiah, and proof of Christianity's claims to succession to the promises made to Abraham in the Book of Genesis. Thus, when Israel reappeared among the nations in a moment of time in the character of a State, the problem of the relationship between the destiny of the Jews and the destiny of the Church had to be restated. From one point of view, it became simpler; from another, more complicated.

Many Christian people in 1948 said that the logic that brought the State of Israel into being that year ran much deeper than any of the causes and concerns espoused by the politicians in their national political counsels or at the UN – deeper, even, than any of the causes or concerns that the politicans knew the names for. These were the Christian Zionists. To them it was no coincidence that in the earliest months of the Cold War it was on that issue, and only on that issue, that the superpower antagonists were agreed. Nor did it come as a surprise *to them* that the consensus among the nations that originally "legitimized" the creation of the state broke down immediately afterwards and never returned. If the nations united behind this cause in 1947–48 it was because their politically self-interested arguments and their ephemeral rhetoric were really serving a cause that had always been the drivewheel of history, if only one had the eyes to see. If the nations fell to gnashing their teeth against the State of Israel once it came into the world and began to demonstrate a capacity for self-preservation that other nations envied but could not fathom, then it proved that the friendship of the nations was not an essential element in Israel's strength – that the nations were helpless to defy the announced will of God. To these Christian Zionists, no less than to many religious Jews, Israel's coming-to-being constituted proof of the faithfulness of Scripture. Likewise, Israel's ability to survive without the goodwill of the nations must be understood as something foretold in Scripture, and thus impossible for the nations to prevent.

In 1947–48, that part of the Church in the West that is today called "fundamentalist" or "evangelical" was overwhelmingly supportive of the Zionist solution to the Jewish problem. The rest of the Protestant church (what is generally spoken of today as "the mainstream") was mostly well disposed, but with many dissenters. The Roman Catholic church had powerful objections but did not feel able, in the light of the general humanitarian advantage that the Jewish cause briefly held in the immediate wake of the war, to compel nations with Roman Catholic populations to oppose.

Yet almost immediately after the initial decisions were taken, these latter two constituencies (mainstream Protestants and Roman Catholic) shifted into the ranks of those denouncing the new state – and eventually became overwhelmingly hostile. Had the voting on the partition of the Palestine Mandate taken place five or ten years later, the Jewish state would not have come into existence.

Even in 1947–48, when the desperate circumstances of the European Jews disposed most American politicians and most Church leaders to endorse the Zionist solution, there was formidable opposition. In the forefront were spokesmen for the Protestant missionary societies that had worked with creditable success among the Arab populations of the Middle East for over a century. In the United States, they were allied with anti-Zionist Jewish organizations, notably the American Council for Judaism. Virginia Gildersleeve, then President of Barnard College and a member of the board of the American University in Beirut, was perhaps the most influential leader of this Christian anti-Zionist lobby. In her memoirs, Professor Gildersleeve recalls: "It was not until the middle of World War II, that I began to realize the critical strategic importance of the Middle East to my country from a military and political point of view," and she thereupon concluded that it was essential that the US not be won by the cause of Zionism, "a movement which was to plunge much of the region into war, sow long-lasting hatred and make the Arabs consider America not the best-liked and trusted of the nations of the West ... but the most disliked and distrusted."[2] In 1948 she helped found the Committee for Justice and Peace in the Holy Land and became its chairman.[3] Later, the CJPHL was merged into the American Friends of the Middle East, which remains an active anti-Israeli lobby. The AFME spoke bitterly of the leverage that Jewish money had over public opinion and policy making in the US but was not above accepting subsidies from Aramco, the Saudi-US oil combination. Senatorial Investigations of CIA activities undertaken in the 1970s disclosed that AMEF was among the many volunteer organizations of the Cold War years that had been secretly subsidized by the intelligence agency. This should not have been hard to guess, given that its executive secretary at the time was none other than Kermit Roosevelt, known to be the CIA's principal operative in the Middle East. Over the next few years, Gildersleeve appeared before congressional committees and lobbied policy makers, in which efforts she was joined by several other prominent Protestant figures, including Harry Emerson Fosdick, Henry Sloane Coffin, and Dorothy Thompson. In the face of all this pressure, President Harry Truman and his principal political advisers remained committed to Israel. Notwithstanding the embarrassing fact of Arab refugees and stories of Israeli harshness in dealing with Arab terrorists, the Arabs lost the contest for public opinion because of their unwillingness to compromise – indeed, their refusal even to talk to Israelis. The anti-Zionists were simply outgunned in those early contests for public support. And down to 1967 their credibility seemed to decline further as Arab hostility to Israel persisted.

1 The Birth and Early Adventures of the State of Israel

> The final goal is a State which fulfills the prophecy, heralds salvation and is a guide and example for all men.
>
> From the "Charter of Independence of the State of Israel," 14 May 1948

JEWS AND ARABS

The UN Partition decision of 29 November 1947 had the support of two-thirds of the member nations, including the United States and the Soviet Union, leaders of the two antagonistic world blocs. It was heralded throughout most of the Western world as well as the communist world as proof of the ability of nations to solve problems together – to put ancient quarrels aside and get on with the shaping of a new world. It called for a Jewish state and an *Arab* state (*not* a "Palestinian state"), both to be created "in Palestine." These two states were to be quite apart from the Arab Kingdom of Jordan (which had been created under the original mandate of Palestine in 1922). The new Arab state would have included the areas that Jews call by their biblical names of Judea and Samaria, as well as Gaza and most of the Galilee. The Zionists accepted the terms of the proposal, with great reluctance. But the Arab states that neighboured on Israel (all of them newly carved out of League of Nations mandates, colonies, or protectorates of the empires of Britain, France, and Italy) refused to accept the decision of the United Nations to permit the creation of a state of Israel – a miniature state, that would have been about one-tenth the size of the original Mandate of Palestine, having about 1/500th of the land-mass of the Middle East, and about 1/250th of the population – the only non-Arab state in the Middle East.[1] As most Zionists had expected, the Arab nations immediately set about to crush it.

Since the 1920s, Arab refusal to contemplate the creation of a Jewish state in any part of the Middle East had never wavered. Although a minority of Palestinian Jews had professed to believe that expressions of Jewish goodwill and mutual recognition of the economic benefits of coexistence would eventually overcome Arab hostility and make possible a "binational" state, something along the lines of Switzerland, most recognized that the Jewish state could only come into being when the Jewish people became strong enough to enforce their right to a state. The question was never "Can a solution be found that satisfies the Arabs of Palestine" but rather "Can a *just* solution be found?"

When the dust settled on the Arab war to prevent the birth of Israel, Israel's boundaries were more secure than they would have been had the Arab states accepted the UN's decision. According to Jewish estimates, 530,000 Palestinian Arabs (the UN estimate was 720,000), or about seventy percent of the Arab population of Palestine, fled their homes. Of these, some 300,000 settled in Abdullah's enlarged kingdom of Jordan – about 250,000 west of the Jordan River (on the "West Bank"), the other 50,000 east of the river. The remainder settled elsewhere in the Arab world, mostly in refugee camps in Gaza (ruled by Egypt), in Egypt proper, in Lebanon, Syria, and Iraq.

The Second World War had caused massive dislocation of populations in many parts of the world. Perhaps fifty-five million people, of whom forty million were civilians, had lost their lives during the war; when it ended, some forty-eight million more were reckoned as refugees in Europe, and thirty-one million in Asia. Between 1945 and 1957, another fifty-seven million became refugees throughout the world. There were Koreans, Indochinese, Jews, Hindus, Sikhs, Moslems of India, Hindus of Pakistan, Chinese, Germans, Poles, Italians, et cetera. In all these cases, the refugees were eventually repatriated or relocated or simply ceased being regarded as refugees. West Germany absorbed nearly ten million Germans from the East. Italy absorbed about 600,000 Italians, following territorial changes in favour of Yugoslavia and Albania and the loss of its empire in Africa. In general, great misery was endured by these refugees, whose story is today remembered by almost nobody. When it proved impossible to divide Britain's colony of India in such a way as to separate Muslim and Hindu populations, there was an outright exchange of Muslims who found themselves in predominantly Hindu India and Hindus who found themselves in predominantly Muslim Pakistan, so that India could be partitioned. This involved the dislocation of fifteen million people. Yet, the world eventually came to accept that when the problem was of such dimensions, and where no basis for agreed community could be found, the best solution was relocation of minority populations. Then, with a sigh, the world turned to other matters.

Only the Palestinian refugees have been exempt from this healing effect. Some 400,000 to 600,000 Palestinian Arabs have languished for up to half a century in refugee camps in Jordan and nearby Arab lands on welfare provided for the most part by the United Nations, and in some cases continuing to the present. The fifty million Arabs of the neighbouring states have continued to insist that they could not possibly absorb so many people (less than two percent of the total Arab population of the Middle East); and fifty years later they still have not done so – this despite their possession of vast unsettled lands and (except for Lebanon) population deficits.

For a brief while in the late 1940s and early 1950s, the plight of Palestinian-Arab refugees temporarily lost its newsworthiness as the press abroad turned its attention to stories of the Jewish state's herculean job of absorbing its own refugees. Between 14 May 1948 and the end of 1951, 685,000 Jews were admitted to Israel from seventy countries, thus doubling the Jewish population of the state. Survivors of the Holocaust came from displaced persons camps in Europe, or from the British detention camp in Cyprus. Most of the Jewish population of Yugoslavia and about half of the Jewish population of Czechoslovakia made their way to Israel. In Poland, Romania, and Hungary, there was official restriction of Jewish emigration; but even so, many thousands were able to come. Middle Eastern Jews (Sephardim) fled from Moslem countries: 30,000 from Turkey, about 5,000 from Persia (Iran), and 35,000 from North African countries. Five thousand came from China. One hundred and twenty-one thousand came from Iraq, taking advantage of a law permitting immigration for one year only, providing that all assets were left behind. Forty-eight thousand were airlifted from Yemen. Not all immigrants were refugees fleeing from homelessness or repression, although the vast majority were. Smaller numbers came from affluent corners of the Diaspora, including 1,711 from the US between 1948 and 1951, bringing financial assets with them.

Despite the general perception today, the number of Jews expelled from Arab and Muslim countries greatly exceeds the number of Arab Palestinians who left Israel. Most of those from Muslim lands, having been stripped of their assets by the Muslim populations from which they fled, arrived utterly destitute. This new citizenry, drawn from all corners of the globe and roughly equal in number to the whole population of the Jewish state at the time of its declaration in May 1948, was fed, sheltered, educated, and eventually provided with employment by the Jewish state, assisted by Jews of the Diaspora.[2] No one ever referred to them again as "refugees." Instead, they were now part of the whole Israeli population, turning to the task of absorbing the many hundreds of thousands who subsequently entered the state as they had done, from Yemen, Ethiopia, Sudan, Egypt, Iraq, Syria, Iran, and beyond. In the 1980s and 1990s a new dimension was added to this story by the absorption of about a million and a half Jews from the collapsed communist empire. Israel's population was estimated in May 1948 at 600,000; in late 1999 the estimate was nearly 7,000,000 – a tenfold increase. Not a penny of assistance came from the UN for any of these Jewish refugees.[3]

Israel's proclamation of 14 May 1948 had guaranteed equal rights to the Arabs of Israel and professed to welcome those who might wish to stay. But the arrival of Arab armies and the flight of Palestinian Arabs from Israel changed all that. On 1 August 1948, Prime Minister David Ben-Gurion advised the UN:

When the Arab states are ready to conclude a peace treaty with Israel this question will come up for constructive solution as part of the general settlement, and with due regard to our counterclaims: in respect of the destruction of Jewish life and property, the long-term interest of the Jewish and Arab populations, the stability of the State of Israel and the durability of the basis of peace between it and its neighbours, the actual position and fate of the Jewish communities in the Arab countries, the responsibilities of the Arab governments for their war of aggression and the liability for reparation, will all be relevant in the question whether, and to what extent, and under what conditions, the former Arab residents of the territory of Israel should be allowed to return.[4]

And that, essentially, is where the matter still stands today.

THE NATIONAL CHARACTER TAKES SHAPE

In Israel's Charter of Independence of 14 May 1948, we find the founders' understanding of the task ahead: "Eretz Israel was the birth place of the Jewish people. Here their spiritual, religious and political identity was shaped. Here they first attained to statehood, created cultural values of national and universal significance and gave to the world the eternal book of Books ... The State of Israel will be open for Jewish immigration and for the Ingathering of the Exiles; it will foster the development of the country for the benefit of all inhabitants; it will be based on freedom, justice and peace, as envisaged by the prophets of Israel ... Placing our trust in the Rock of Israel, we affix our signatures."[5]

On 25 January 1949, elections were held – the first, and for many years to come the only, democratic elections to be held in the Middle East. The Israelis had settled on a multiparty proportional system of voting, which in effect continued practices already tested through many years of the Jewish Agency (whose members, elected both in Palestine abroad, represented the interests of the Jewish inhabitants through the years of the Mandate), but which Americans found diffi-cult to grasp and alien to their taste and experience. The new state's "Basic Laws," written in these early months, and the initial legislative decisions made in the realm of domestic policy confirmed the demo-cratic and liberal credentials of the regime while equally affirming the Jewish character of the nation. Government soon established a large role for itself in education, housing, health, transportation, regulation of industry, and so on. Like the contemporaneous left-of-centre demo-cratic regimes of Western Europe, Israel's Labour government was despised by the Soviet Union, which denounced its spurious "social-ism" and accused it of being a lackey of the United States; the Israeli government was thus inoculated against any suspicion of pro-commu-nism, which would have been fatal to the goodwill of the American public.

Through all the years that Christian politicians had been wrestling with "the Palestine question," there had been a formidable cohort of Jews who would come to them with arguments *against* the creation of a Jewish state. One string to the bow of these anti-Zionist Jews was the argument that a Jewish state would create a dual loyalty for Diaspora Jews – or at least the impression of a dual loyalty – and would thus jeop-ardize their standing as citizens in the lands where they lived. This argument did not much impress non-Jews; it was essentially an argu-ment within the family, and for a gentile to countenance it might be taken as an admission of anti-Semitism. A more effective argument was that a Jewish state would inevitably become a theocracy; its constitu-tion would have to give a privileged position to the religion of the Jews, and its practice would deviate from the model of separation of religion and state that most Americans believed was engraved in their own con-stitution. This argument gave pause even to the best friends of Zionism. Harry Truman often spoke of this possibility and admitted that it worried him. What would happen to the Christians who lived in Israel, expecially those in Jerusalem and Bethlehem? How would visit-ing Christians be affected? What would become of Christian mission-aries and their missions?

The Zionist movement had always been divided bitterly over the question of acknowledging a religious basis for the nation's identity and for its cause. In her memoirs, Golda Meir, Israel's prime minister from 1969 to 1974, describes the fiery debate that she witnessed within the group that was about to declare itself the Provisional Government of Israel on the morning of 14 May 1948:

> The very last sentence, as finally submitted to the small subcommittee charged with producing the final version of the proclamation, began with the words "With trust in the rock of Israel, we set our hands in witness to this Proclamation ..." Ben-Gurion had hoped that the phrase "Rock of Israel" was sufficiently ambiguous to satisfy those Jews for whom it was inconceivable that the document which established the Jewish state should not contain any reference to God, as well as those who were certain to object strenuously to even the least hint of clericalism in the proclamation.
>
> But the compromise was not easily accepted. The spokesman of the religious parties, Rabbi Fishman-Maimon, demanded that the reference to God be unequivocal and said that he would approve of the "Rock of Israel" only if the words "and its Redeemer" were added, while Aaron Zisling of the left wing of the Labor Party was just as determined in the opposite direction. "I cannot sign a document referring in any way to a God in whom I do not believe," he said. It took Ben-Gurion most of the morning to persuade Maimon and Zisling that the meaning of the "Rock of Israel" was actually twofold: While it signified "God" for a great many Jews, perhaps for most, it could also be considered a symbolic and secular reference to the "strength of the Jewish people." In the end Maimon agreed that the word "Redeemer" should be left out of the text.[6]

Few of the Zionist leaders, in the early days at least, were observant Jews. Christian Zionists were often distressed by the expressions of atheism or agnosticism that occasionally issued from their mouths. But what really puzzled Christian Zionists, as people whose religious beliefs were prior to their political commitments, was to find these same leaders in so many of their public addresses, and later in their memoirs, expressing personal philosophies that contained elements of religious sentiment, which were inconsistently, though apparently inextricably, bound into their political commitments.

One classic example is Chaim Weizmann (1874–1952), head of the World Zionist Organization, pre-eminent leader of the movement in the quarter-century prior to the creation of the Israeli state, and the man who became its first president. Over the years, when addressing audiences of British or American citizens, or the General Assembly of the United Nations, or the various commissions and inquiries of Great Britain or the League of Nations, Chaim Weizmann would draw upon prophetic sections of the Hebrew Scriptures in defence of the creation of the State of Israel; and he would do the same later in justification of its policies. Abba Eban describes himself and his colleagues at work in a New York hotel room, preparing a text for Weizmann to read to the General Assembly in October 1947. Before Weizmann would accept their text, he said: "We'll make this do – but how about a *posuk* [biblical verse] for an ending?" They looked for a Bible, Eban recalled, "and eventually found one supplied by the hotel in the bedside table. Spent half an hour on Isaiah, looking for [a] 'Return to Zion' passage." Eventually they located a passage in Isaiah: "The Lord shall set His hand for the second time to recover the remnants of His people and He shall set up an ensign for the nations and shall assemble the outcast of Israel and gather the dispersed of Judah from the four corners of the earth."[7]

Norman Rose, Weizmann's biographer, gives little attention to religious matters but summarizes Weizmann's religious situation thus: "He thought of himself as "a deeply religious man, although not a strict observer of the religious ritual ... He was observant, conforming to the traditions he had learned as a child, but he interpreted them in an individual, common-sense way as befitted a nineteenth-century liberal, a product of the Enlightenment ... Toward the end of his life he wrote to Harry Truman that it was never the intention 'that Palestine should become a "religious" or "theocratic" state.'"[8] Summing up impressions gleaned from Weizmann's published letters, Chaim Raphael says: "[He was] a rationalist and humanist to the core but with an element in his make-up that sees a God in the shadows, a Jewish God, a Being left over from childhood ... a God of *history* ... Jewish experience would never have the assurance, and the clarity, that a Christian – or at least an Englishman – inherited as a matter of course. That was a heritage linked to a national soil and a simple faith. The Jewish character was so much more complex."[9]

Serious Orthodox Jews find this attitude very trying. They know that it is not because they lack "complexity" that they embrace the faith and the practice of Judaism," but rather because they possess integrity; and they resent this condescension on the part of the secularized official Zionists. Equally, serious Christians do not think of themselves as having "inherited" *anything* as a matter of course; if they possess "assurance and clarity" about what they believe, these things were not given to them as a gift, without cost, handed down by their ancestors. They worship the God of Israel, and they admire the Jews as fellow worshippers of this same God. Their religious heritage is no more, but also no less, "perplexing" than that of the Jews. Their faith is neither more nor less "simple."

In all of Weizmann's letters, there are few clear-cut references to his religious faith. Yet here and there we find words that would cheer the

most fervent Christian Zionist heart. For example, in October 1914 –
in the first weeks of the Great War – Weizmann writes to his Zionist col-
league Shmarya Levin: "With feverish anxiety I am watching events
which have for me a deep hidden meaning; it is the struggle of the
pagan Siegfried against the spirit of the Bible, and the Bible will win"[10]
– a perfect expression of the Christian Zionist understanding of
history!

As president of Israel, Weizmann held strong views about the place
of religion in the public life, views more or less in line with those to
which the Ben-Gurion government was committed, by reason of its
coalition agreement with the "Religious" parties:

Whereas the State will treat with the highest respect the true religious feelings
of the community, it cannot put back the clock by making religion the cardinal principle in the conduct of the state. Religion should be relegated to the
synagogue and the homes of those families that want it; it should occupy a
special position in the schools; but it shall not control the ministries of State
... I foresee something which will perhaps be reminiscent of the *Kulturkampf*
in Germany, but we must be firm if we are to survive; we must have a clear line
of demarcation between legitimate religious aspirations and the duty of the
State towards preserving such aspirations, on the one hand, and on the other
hand the lust for power which is sometimes exhibited by pseudo-religious
groups.[11]

Much the same thinking is to be found in the case of David Ben-
Gurion (1886–1973), the first Prime Minister of Israel. Like most of
the leaders of the new state, Ben-Gurion started life in a Central European *shtetl* and had been thoroughly immersed in Orthodox Judaism.
Like Weizmann, he had as a boy something of a reputation for preco-
cious religiosity, which he began to shed in his teens. The way "political" and "religious" experiences combined in this milieu is illustrated
by the way Ben-Gurion was introduced to Zionism. His biographer,
Shabta Teveth, writes: "One day during prayers in the New Synagogue,
he overheard something that cast an immediate binding spell on him.
It was 1896 [when he was ten], the year Theodor Herzl's *The Jewish
State* was published. From the excited talk he gathered that a messiah
had appeared, 'a miraculous man, head and shoulders taller than
other men, with beautiful features and a luminous face adorned by a
long beard ... In a certain foreign town a messiah named Herzl had
arrived.'" Ben-Gurion remembered this episode all his life, and
repeated his account of it time and again, always in the same words, as
if it were a melody he loved to hear. He knew that he was destined to
be the messiah's alter ego, a second Herzl.[12]

To the Council of the Jewish Agency Ben-Gurion wrote in October 1935: "We live in the days of the Messiah."[13] What could he have meant by this? Is this piety, or is this blasphemy? Another biographer, Dan Kurzman, explains Ben-Gurion's words: "Jewish redemption was destined to be 'intertwined with universal human redemption.' Thus, the Jewish state would forgo the luxury of being 'normal' and become 'a light unto the nations,' as prophesied by Isaiah (42:6), with a mission to bring salvation to mankind."[14] Ben-Gurion's mature belief is expressed in these words, spoken many years later in conversation with Richard Nixon: "Since I invoke Torah so often, let me state that I don't personally believe in the God it postulates. I mean that I cannot 'turn to God,' or pray to a superhuman Almighty Being living up in the sky ... I am not religious, nor were the majority of the early builders of Israel believers. Yet their passion for this land stemmed from the Book of Books ... [The Bible is] the single most important book in my life."[15]

SECULAR ZIONISTS AND RELIGIOUS JUDAISM

The relationship between secular and religious Zionism is not easy to summarize. It is certainly more complex than Richard Nixon seemed to grasp. It cannot be reduced to the consideration that they all read the Bible. Secular Zionists, from Theodor Herzl forward, were aware that to embrace their message was to embrace a transcendent possibility. It required believing in something that already had the authority of realized fact, although it belonged to the future, and although it was impossible! Religious people believe that such thinking is both possible and necessary because there is God and there is eternity; *per contra*, they argue that without God, such thinking is desperate nonsense.

In some moods, the secular Zionists despised their religious brethren. In better moods, they reflected and even sometimes publicly conceded that their own processes of thought had something in common with religious ones and sought to find words to express the commonality – as in Ben-Gurion's comments to Richard Nixon. Since, like most of us, they were usually in neither their best nor their worst mood, they preferred to pass over the claims of religion with a giggle and get on to other things. It is not difficult to find examples, privately expressed, of such nervous, light-hearted judgments on the religion of their fathers. While he was a minister in the government of Menachem Begin, Ezer Weizman had an encounter with Miriam Levinger, wife of Moshe Levinger, leader of the settlement that the Orthodox religious movement called Gush Emunim had established in Hebron. "'Last night,' she told me, 'as I was dreaming, I heard the voice of King

David. He said that you, Ezer, will be greatly blessed if you work for the settlement of Jews in Hebron.' On hearing her words, someone else might have laughed. I was appalled at the thought of our senior political echelons being led and influenced by such fanatical dreamers. On top of that, David is not one of my favorite biblical characters. He rose in rebellion against his annointed king, goading and humiliating him; later, having gained the throne, David coveted the wife of one of his own military commanders and sent the man to his death to get her. All the same, the Bible sings hymns of glory to his name – which probably proves that King David controlled the media of his time."[16] When Weizman became president of the state in 1993, this reputation preceded him; and so the religious politicans were waiting for signs of his irreligion. They did not have long to wait. His inaugural speech, they found, was entirely without religious references: none to God, none to "heaven " – not one biblical verse. Knesset member Rabbi Avraham Ravitz said: "Even if Weizman considers himself as a non-believing Jew, he is at least under obligation to use the phrase cited in the Charter of Independence – the Rock of Israel, as it was his duty to use, at least, the unimplicating verse in which Isaiah says: 'They shall beat their swords into plowshares and their spears into pruning hooks.'"[17]

When exasperated, Labour government leaders would slip into careless or flippant expression on religious matters – a habit that frequently got them in trouble with those of their political colleagues who were elected as spokesmen of the Jewish religious tradition, and upon whom, to varying degrees but always to some degree, the Labour party's continuation in power depended. Prime Minister Yitzhak Rabin was heard to dismiss the Bible as "an antiquarian land registry book."[18] Shimon Peres, Foreign Affairs minister in the Rabin government, caused a brief parliamentary crisis by expressing a judgment similar to Ezer Weizman's regarding King David. Defending his government's dealings with Yassir Arafat of the Palestine Liberation Organization against the complaint that he was giving away the legacy of King David, Peres shrugged: unlike David, *his* concept of the good of Israel did not require "occupation and ruling another people." After all: "Not everything that King David did, on the ground, on the roofs [see 2 Samuel 11], is acceptable to a Jew or is something I like." The remarks provoked a no-confidence motion at a most awkward time for the government, which was dependent on a portion of the "religious vote" if it was to command a majority in the Knesset without the Arab bloc. The next day Rabbi Yohanan Fried, head of the Education ministry's Torah Culture Department, said that King David was holy, and therefore "the rabbis say that whoever says that King David sinned does nothing but err." An even more shocking occasion had occurred a little previously when Yael Dayan, a Labour member and daughter of the late Moshe Dayan, suggested, on the basis of 2 Samuel 1:26, that "David was gay." But Dayan was not a Cabinet minister. After Peres's remarks about King David, intense negotiations were necesssary between the Labour leaders and the "religious" partners to avert an early election.[19] Thereafter, Peres was noticeably chastened and, during his own brief tenure as Prime Minister (November 1995–June 1996), sought out the religious leaders in the broad light of day for advice on public matters.

For all their commitment to the secular world-view, the Labour party leadership have always been prevented by their indebtedness to the religious parties in the Knesset from trying to make Israel a secular nation in fact. At the same time, the parties of the right, eventually coalescing as Likud, made clear to the electorate from the beginning that they were readier to accommodate themselves to the programs of the religious partners; and after they formed their first government in 1977 they proved this to be the case. Always conceding that, as Queen Elizabeth I said, "we cannot open windows into men's souls," it is clear that there have always been more "observant" Jews in the ranks of the Likud leadership than in the ranks of Labour. But the North American media have tended to make too much of this relative distinction. The fact is that no Israeli government has ever been formed without making some concessions to the "Religious parties" – concessions that compromised the secular commitments of most Labour leaders but also complicated priorities for Likud leaders when they came to power. During the whole of his brief term as prime minister (1997–99), the Likud leader Binyamin Netanyahu was constantly harassed by leaders of the religious parties, upon whose support his government depended, for his failure to respond adequately to the "religious community" in such matters as the closing of certain roads on the Sabbath, the right of Jews to pray on the Temple Mount, maintaining the monopoly of Orthodoxy in the matter of conversions to Judaism, and beefing up the laws restricting Christian missionary activities. The national election of 17 May 1999 reduced the strength of the two mainline parties – Likud to nineteen seats and Labour (now renamed One Israel) to twenty-six seats – and of all of the religious parties except Shas, the voice of the Sephardic Jews – which won seventeen of 120 seats. At the same time, it brought to the prime minister's office a secular-minded One Israel leader, Ehud Barak. Pursuing his election commitment to draw into his governing coalition all sections of the electorate, he won the allegiance of Shas and other religious parties while attaching all but the tiniest of the parties of the left – except for the uncompromisingly anti-religious Shinui (which had only six seats.)

In mid-1999, it seemed possible that the *kulturkampf* that so many politicians had been predicting might be averted. In reality, it had merely been postponed. By the end of the summer of 2000 the coalition was in shambles and by the end of that year it had collapsed. The political weight of religious differences now seemed greater than ever before.

2 Christian Attitudes towards the State of Israel, 1948–1960s

The ecumenical movement is driven by the Spirit of the Lord. But do not forget, there is only one really important question: Our relations with Israel.

Karl Barth, 1966[1]

REACTIONS OF AMERICAN CHRISTIANS TO FIRST IMPRESSIONS OF THE RELIGIOUS CHARACTER OF THE STATE

Christian Zionists would have preferred, other things being equal, to find believing Jews at the helm of the new state. But this was not to be. As we have seen, the leading figures in Mapai – the main faction in the Labour alliance, and thus the leading figures in the new government itself – were all secularists. Some retained a modicum of loyalty to the religious faith of their childhood (which in most cases had been lived in Central or Eastern Europe), but others did not.

What, for instance, would a Christian Zionist make of the story, told in chapter 1, of Weizmann's search for a *posuk* with which to adorn his speech to the UN? What would strike him immediately, of course, was that none of the leaders had a Bible in his possession. Worse still, none of them knew, by chapter and verse, any of the key scriptural passages with which Christian Restorationists had been supporting both their teaching on behalf of the cause of restoring the Jews to Israel (for many centuries) and the program of Zionism (for many decades.) Then, once a Bible was acquired – a Gideon Bible, presumably, provided free to hotels by a Protestant-evangelistic organization – it took them half an hour to find a text.

What should a Christian Zionist make of the spiritual situation of such men? And what was one to think of their appeal to Scripture on behalf of their politics? Was this a reflection of something real, or just a cynical tactic? There is no doubt that Christian Zionists were disappointed by the secularism of the leaders of the state of Israel. They cringed at the politicians' insensitivity to the transcendent meaning of Israel's history, and their ignorance of the eschatalogical dimension – the meaning of the rebirth of Israel as a stage in God's Plan for History. On the other hand, most saw that this situation was consistent with what Christian Restorationists had always preached: that Israel would be restored "in unbelief."

Political exigency forced the secular Zionists to establish a much larger place for the Jewish religion in public life than any of them had wanted. But what were the prospects for Christianity in this Jewish state?

Christian Zionists for the most part were much less exercised by this question than were anti-Zionist Christians – which might seem paradoxical, given that most Christian Zionists were on the "evangelical" side of Protestantism and thus cared deeply about the freedom to preach and disseminate the gospel. But most Christian Zionists were philo-Judaic and trusted that the best face of Judaism would prevail in the new state, and that Christians, and for that matter Muslims, living within the state would suffer no loss of religious freedom. Jewish sovereignty over the Holy Land could not possibly be as unhealthy for the free exercise of Christian faith as would the sovereignty of a Muslim authority. This has certainly proved to be the case.

Despite recurring flare-ups of anti-missionary spirit, culminating from time to time in pressure for legislation intended to restrict missionary activitity, missionary work remains perfectly legal in Israel and goes on in the bright light of day. Since the State of Israel has come into existence, both Roman Catholic and mainstream Protestant churches have renounced missionary intentions towards the Jews, as part of their policies of "reconciliation" with the Jewish people; thus, such Christian missionary activity as exists in Israel is entirely conducted by evangelical Christians, most of them of American, or perhaps British and Canadian, origin. The only local missionary effort with any significant organizational basis is that conducted by the group of Messianic Jews who are a congregation affiliated with Christ Church, Anglican, inside the Old City at Jaffa Gate.[2]

Both Labour and Likud governments have avoided enforcing the existing anti-missionary laws, which in any case do little to cramp the style of serious evangelical missionaries. At this writing, the only significant legal constraint on missionary activity is a law of 1978 that makes it illegal to offer monetary enticements to secure conversions (something that virtually never occurs anyway.) In recent years, evangelical Christian church properties have occasionally been vandalized by Jewish anti-missionary zealots. But these incidents, which contribute, unfortunately, to the image of religious "fundamentalists" as bomb throwers, usually backfire, since they immediately engage the Israeli public's contempt for religious zealotry. The image of the evangelicals, normally perceived by secular Israelis as part of the problem, is toned up for a while by incidents that offer them the temporary glow of victimhood. Every such incident is followed by speeches from politicians and editorials in the major papers denouncing religious bigotry. An important factor here is that major politicians in both blocs recognize that victimizing of evangelicals will not be well received in those circles in the United States that have always provided the most constant Christian friends of Israel.[3]

The key to the attitude of most evangelical Christians is that neither the religious character of the Jewish leadership nor their provision for Christian worship in the Holy Land had ever been their central preoccupation. To the Christian Zionist, the purpose of the project had always been to bring the Jewish people back to Israel. Taking all in all, Christian Zionists have always been more sympathetic than mainstream Protestants or Roman Catholics to the world-view of observant Jews, notwithstanding that it is mainly from the Orthodox Jewish camp that the recurring political pressures come for setting limits to the activities of Christian missionaries. (We shall return to this complex story in chapter 8.) Most Jews might return "in unbelief"; but a sizeable minority has returned in order to establish authentic Jewish religious practice in Zion. To many evangelicals, this implies that in due course the Temple will be rebuilt – a necessary precondition, many believe, to Christ's return. It is difficult to envisage any of this happening if the Jews were ever to abandon their religious practice, or allow it to be marginalized in a secular state. Typically, evangelical Christians see the practice of Judaism as more crucial, for the time being, to this unfolding scenario than the fortunes of the Christian communities.

Liberal Protestant journals (notably, the *Christian Century*)[4] were oddly inconsistent in their approach to the question of religion and religious practice in Israel. On Mondays, Wednesdays, and Fridays, over the years, the *Christian Century* has denounced Israel for irreligion. But on Tuesdays, Thursdays, and Saturdays, it has denounced the people of Israel for their reactionary religiosity, speaking of the "reactionary religious bloc" as "a serious obstacle to Western, especially American policy in the Middle East" and calling on "the rabbinate of the West" to set before the population of the new state an interpretation of the Jewish religion" that is "compatible with modern thought, and a challenge to the higher ethical levels of living by man in the modern world." The Jewish friends of liberal Protestants were likely to be enrolled in Reform or Conservative congregations; not surprisingly, therefore, their own critique of Israel echoes the complaints of these two constituencies against the monopoly of the public role of religion by the Orthodox. If, on Mondays, Wednesdays, and Fridays, Israel's "irreligion" explains "the immorality of Israel's dealings with Arabs," on Tuesdays, Thursdays, and Saturdays it is its "Old Testament thinking" that "lies behind her brutal dealings with fedayeen [i.e., Arab terrorist] attacks."[5]

Not only liberals but many of evangelical background note the unfortunate fact that the leaders of the Jewish state, on the day of its creation, did not see fit to invoke the God of Israel, settling instead for a reference to the Rock (see page 14 above). Looking back some forty-five years later, Gary Burge, an evangelical Christian, traces the beginnings of his anti-Zionism to this moment: "I found this to be remarkable. If indeed this was a nation claiming some continuity with its biblical heritage, surely a reference to God would be acceptable."[6] Critics who make this point usually neglect to mention that upon the signing of the document the founders stood while Rabbi Fishman-Maimon pronounced *Shehekhayanu*, the traditional benediction (" ... that we have lived to see this day ...)."[7]

It is ironical that liberal Christians, who deny theological meaning to the creation of the State of Israel, have felt so free to criticize the people of Israel for the way they have implemented their religious practice in their public life, while evangelical Christians generally have generous or positive attitudes towards the same scene. This should be seen as evidence that on the whole evangelicals generally approve of Israel's performance as a nation over the first half-century. While liberals tend to dwell on the injustices and inequities that have befallen the Palestinian Arabs, evangelicals have rejoiced in the survival of the nation over its unremitting enemies. While liberals dwell on the political embarrassments and the scandals and agonize about the many divisions that continue in the land beween Ashkenzim and Sephardim, between rich and poor, between observant Jews and secularists, evangelicals prefer to accentuate the positive: the authentic democracy, the miracles of absorption and acculturation, the hard-earned prosperity. Most evangelicals regard the history of the last fifty years as a marvellous accomplishment, and many made a point of being present in May 1948 to join in the celebration of the *Jubal* (jubilee) at the creation of the state. Liberals avoided the *Jubal*, preferring to take note instead of the *Nakba* – the Palestinian Arab observance of fifty years of disaster. It has come to the point where many liberal Protestants feel free openly to question the wisdom of bringing Israel into existence in the first place.

There are always exceptions, of course. The most eminent American theologian of the post-war years, Reinhold Niebuhr, remained out of step with the liberal company that he generally kept by displaying his firm pro-Israelism to the end of his life (1971), even though he felt uncomfortable about some elements of "religious obscurantism" that he detected from time to time in Israel's public life. On the other side (as an example of an exception to the pro-Zionism we expect among fundamentalists and evangelicals) we note O.T. Ellis, Professor of Old Testament at Princeton Theological Seminary, who wrote in 1956: "What other people in the world would venture to demand that the clock of history be put back two millennia for their benefit? ... There are many open spaces in the world, many friendly nations, in which oppressed Israelites can find a refuge and a home without imperiling the peace of the world ... Does the Israeli cause deserve to succeed? ... We believe the verdict of history will be, No!"[8]

Hertzl Fishman concludes his valuable review of American Protestant attitudes towards the State of Israel in these formative years with the judgment that the "basic contradiction" in attitudes towards Jews as individuals and Jewish people collectively has "a theological root." Although, in the normal way, National Council of Churches publications avoid resort to doctrinal-theological language, an exception is made of pronouncements on Israel, where we find full-blooded expressions of the Replacement doctrine that characterized the thinking of the early Church. This theological position, Fishman shows, has issued in "consistently negative policies towards the concrete expression of Jewish collective existence" that we find expressed in the journals that speak for liberal Protestant intellectuals. Abetting the fundamentally *theological* bias in American Protestantism against Jewish Restoration and against Zionism is the fact that Protestant missionary efforts in this part of the world have been successful only among the Arab population, so that the churches generally have become accustomed to see the local situation from the perspective of their clients. (I have more to say on this theme in chapter 7.) The outcome of all of this, as Fishman has shown, is that "American liberal Protestantism has fought against Jewish national and ethnic interests."[9]

THE FOUNDING OF THE STATE OF ISRAEL AND THE FOUNDING OF THE WORLD COUNCIL OF CHURCHES

The State of Israel and the World Council of Churches came into the world in that same *annus mirabilis*, 1948. In fact, their birthdays are within a few weeks of each other, on 14 May and 22 August respectively.

The creation of the World Council of Churches received very little press attention – one might say a minuscle amount in comparison with the story of the State of Israel. This disproportion of attention has grown ever since. Today, Israel has one of the world's largest contingents of foreign news gatherers encamped in its midst. It is, for example, many times larger than the cohort assigned to China or India, countries of 1.3 billion and 1 billion citizens. Few Israelis regard this as an honour. There is no doubt that the World Council of Churches would like a great deal more attention and the State of Israel a good deal less. Not even the septennial General Assembly meetings of the wcc make the front pages, (except, perhaps, in the papers of its temporary host city). The newsmagazines have little interest in the council, and the journals of opinion have none. The current college textbooks that I have consulted on us or world history do not so much as mention the wcc in their indexes; neither does the *World Almanac and Book of Facts* (1999). In its thousand-odd pages, the popular reference book *Chronicle of the Twentieth Century* never mentions the wcc, not even in the twenty-page section on the year 1948.

Yet many Christians had been working nearly as long and some at least as hard for the birthday of the wcc as Zionists had been working for the birthday of their state. Many Christians regard the former as no less a miracle than the latter.

Many instructive comparisons can be made between these two stories. First, in each case the invention of the new body was meant to solve an age-old dillemma of identity within a far-flung community – the Jewish people, on the one hand, and the Universal Church on the other. Thus, Zionists had always claimed that the creation of a State of Israel would make clear at last, to individual Jews and to the world, how the individual Jew was to relate the two sides of his legacy: the "religious" and the "national." Simultaneously, creation of the State of Israel was meant to alter radically the status of the Jews as a people in the world: henceforth, the Jews as a people would stand in a "normal" relationship to other peoples who had nation-states of their own. This has not happened as predicted. Instead (most people will agree) it simply raised the decibel level of the argument.

Similarly, the enthusiasts of "ecumenical Christianity" had always claimed that creation of a World Council of Churches would clarify – perhaps permanently define – the nature of the Christian's belonging to his Church and help those inside and outside the Church to see the true character of the Church as it lived its life in the world. This has not happened as predicted either.

In each case, a large portion of the religious community on whose behalf the invention was professedly undertaken regarded the exercise as something of a fraud, or worse. Thus, anti-Zionist Jews, both "religious" and "secular" ones, struggled for many years to prevent the invention of Israel, and after they failed, many were never reconciled. Many "secular" Jews eventually gave up their Jewish identity because (they said) they could not identify with or condone the behaviour of the body that alleged to represent them in the world. Many "religious Jews" denounced Israel then and denounce it today for having fatally compromised the legacy of Moses and the Prophets. Similarly, large portions of the world community of Christians lamented the creation of the World Council of Churches at the time, and in recent decades substantial blocs of Christians have turned upon it, denouncing it as an illegitimate voice of the Church of Christ.

On the other hand: much as the creation of Israel assisted Jews throughout the world in clarifying their identity as Jews and encouraged the habit of thinking of themselves as a world body (Jewry), so the creation of the World Council of Churches has advanced in a practical way the habit of cooperation among many of the churches. In fact, there is today such a degree of practical cooperation between the WCC and the Roman Catholic hierarchy, from the Pope down, that many of the leaders of both these major wings of the church believe in the possibility of complete ecumenical reunion in the foreseeable future. The World Council of Churches did not achieve a reunion of the whole community of the Church of Christ. Far from it. But then, neither has the State of Israel, even yet, brought all the Jews of the world within its borders. The leaders of the State of Israel and of the WCC feel entitled to say that the shortcomings of their respective institutions, such as they may have been, are owing to the weak-hearted or malicious reluctance of those outside to come inside and make the community (whether "Israel" or "the Church") whole.

Just as Zionists promised their followers that creation of their state would promote self-identification of Jews everywhere in the world while simultaneously advancing respect for Jewish values, so promoters of the concept of a World Council of Churches claimed all along that their project, once complete, would provide to all Christians a clear understanding of their Christian identity, a rewarding new dimension of fellowship with all other Christians, and a powerful medium for expressing the purposes of the Church in the world political arena. But just as the existence and activity of the State of Israel have not achieved a unity of opinion on major matters among the Jews of the world – not even those matters that directly touch the security of the state – so the existence and the activity of the WCC have not achieved unity of opinion among Christians on the most basic of matters. In fact, there are many who say that this very effort to find a concensus of the whole Christian community on large matters has only caused tension and even consternation within the Church of Christ, while doing nothing to raise the moral level of decision making that takes place in the company of the politicians of the world.

Adding to the fascination of this exercise of comparing and contrasting the accomplishments of Zionism and the WCC is this stark truth: that the one issue on which it has proved most difficult for the WCC to encourage unanimity among Christians has been the issue of Israel.

Painful though it is for Church historians to admit, the *ecclesia* has never been truly unified in matters of cult or of teaching or discipline. During the forty years, roughly, prior to the destruction of the Second Temple, the early Church experienced many divisive episodes. As one easily discovers by reading the Book of Acts and the Letters of the apostles, the Church was always blaming itself in those early years for its failure to maintain its unity, and always seeking to find ways to reconcile the factions. The broadest definition for the term "ecumenism" would, therefore, be the desire for and the effort to achieve that unity of the Church that has always been sought but never achieved.

Yet as in the case of Zionism, there is a narrower and more practical definition, one more patient of historical examination. It can be found in the vision of those Christian leaders who actually lived to see the establishment of the World Council of Churches in August 1948.

One landmark in this story is the founding of the International Missionary Council in Edinburgh, 1910. Activists seeking "Church unity" had won their first practical victories in the missionary fields, where practical efforts at cooperation among denominations were virtually imposed by the requirement of presenting a cooperative face to unfriendly populations and authorities. Out of this exercise came various experiences in Church union (notably, in India), and a habit of finding a common denominator of expression regarding theological and ecclesiological differences. When this was reported back to the parent denominations in Europe and America, the seed of the idea of "ecumenical unity" was planted.

Quite a different impulse was at work among another set of Christians in those years before the First World War. Certain Protestant leaders, clerical and lay, wanted to make the Christian conscience a force in the public life of nations by promoting organized expressions of the Christian viewpoint on great public matters. To follow a distinction made by the historian Darril Hudson, in the history of the ecumenical movement there has always been one set of leaders whose primary vision was Church unity, and another whose primary vision was Church action. Thus, on the one hand, we can speak of the ecumenical movement as an effort to bring the many separate churches together in community, as the Body of Christ, in order to make all Christians aware of the many strands of Christian community and enhance their appreciation of different understandings of Christian duty and Christian devotion. On the other hand, we can speak of the ecumenical movement as one that looks towards the promotion of organized expressions of the "Christian conscience." Today, as at the beginnings of the story in the years around the First World War, there is a line that runs through the Church dividing those whose first love is the vision of the Church United and those whose first love is the vision of the Church in Action in the World. A very rough-hewn truth, but a truth nonetheless, is that clergy, full-time church workers, and intellectuals tend to belong to the "action" camp, while the bulk of the laity are more drawn to the "unity"camp. It is not surprising, therefore, that policies announced in the name of the World Council of Churches tend to reflect the "action" rather than the "unity" side of the agenda.

The 1920s and 1930s saw many conferences of leaders of the churches in pursuit of the ecumenical dream. For my purpose it suffices to note that in 1937 two great conferences were held, one at Oxford on "Life and Work" (basically, the "action" side of the movement) and the other in Edinburgh on "Faith and Order" (basically, the "unity" side). These two conferences moved quickly, drawing up blueprints for an ecumenical apparatus, wishing to mobilize the churches to play their part in heading off a great war. Still, Hitler acted too quickly for these Christian leaders, as for everybody else; and thus the actual formation of a World Council was still pending when the Second World War ended in 1945.

After Hitler's tyranny was crushed, the world did not enter onto those "broad, sunlit uplands" that Winston Churchill had foreseen. Instead, there ensued the Cold War, which was at a particularly nasty stage when the opening session of the First Assembly of the World Council of Churches began on Sunday, 22 August 1948 at Nieuwe Kerk, Amsterdam. Ecumenical leaders had hoped that the achievement of Christian unity would help to end the Cold War. At very least, they expected to keep it off the agenda in the opening meeting. They did not reckon with John Foster Dulles, however – the principal foreign policy adviser to Republican Presidential candidate Thomas Dewey – who was there to warn fellow delegates that the Christian way of life was doomed if the Church did not categorically denounce atheistic communism. Organizers had already assured the various Church leaders who lived under communist regimes that no such thing would happen. In any case, Eastern Orthodox churches within the jurisdica-

tion of the Moscow Patriarchate had been forbidden by their governments to attend. Senior Orthodox clergy attached to Constantinople,
including some from North America, did attend but were noticeably
cautious about making life difficult for fellow Orthodox Christians
behind the Iron Curtain. Professor J.L. Hromodka of Prague was
present to explain that socialist systems were currently the best embodiment of the teaching of Christ. But the American theologian Reinhold Niebuhr wasn't having any: there at Amsterdam, and repeatedly
throughout his remaining years (until 1971), he warned the Western
Churches that they were falling into the trap of exaggerating the sins
of the "capitalist" world, relativizing the issues at stake between West
and East, turning their backs upon the fact that freedom of religion
had been snuffed out behind the Iron Curtain.[10]

The wcc constitution, adopted in 1961, describes the council as "a fellowship of churches which confess the Lord Jesus as God and Saviour
according to the Scriptures and therefore seek to fulfill together their
common calling to the glory of the one God, Father, Son and Holy
Sprit." At its formation in 1948, there were 144 member churches,
coming from forty-four different countries. By 1996 the wcc had
expanded to 320 member bodies. Today, the wcc contains almost all
the major Church bodies of the Western world (with the exception of
the Roman Catholics and Unitarians), nearly all the Eastern Orthodox
churches, and about two hundred other churches in the non-Western
world. Since 1961 the Vatican has sent accredited observers to wcc
meetings. Later, a Joint Working Group was established between the
Roman Catholic church and the wcc and later still a joint Secretariat
for Society, Development and Peace (SODEPAX), which speaks for both
the Vatican's Pontifical Commission for Justice and Peace and the wcc
on issues of justice and peace. Thus, single positions are taken and
single, unified statements are made on certain issues in the name of
virtually the whole Christian world. Cardinal Jan Willebrands can
write: "The great problems and tasks that now confront the Churches
are seen by the wcc and the Catholic Church in the same way, indeed
they are also formulated in the same way."[11]

Every seven years, a wcc General Assembly is held in a different location: Evanston in 1954; New Delhi in 1961; Uppsala, 1968; Nairobi,
1975; Vancouver, 1983; Seoul, 1990; and Harare, 1998. Between
Assembly meetings, authority resides in a 150-member Central Committee, elected by the Assembly. wcc headquarters at Geneva is run by
a large bureaucracy. There are innumerable subgroups and much over-
lapping; but those that have had the most to say about Middle Eastern

issues are the Commission on Church and Society; Commission on Interchurch Aid; Refugee and World Service; and Commission of the Churches on International Affairs (CCIA).

In many Western countries different Protestant churches had formed groups for "inter-church" action long before the first steps were taken towards the creation of the World Council of Churches. This was particularly true in the United States, famous as the land of voluntary associations, where interdenominational bodies for various purposes date from the days of the Great Revival early in the nineteenth century. In 1908 several separate bodies that had previously met at local levels were grouped into the Federal Council of Churches. Thirty-odd years later, an exploratory meeting was held for the purpose of establishing closer collaboration on 7 December 1941. But this activity was overshadowed (to put it mildly) by other events that same day. After the war, work resumed towards the establishment of the National Council of Churches, which was formally inaugurated in Cleveland on 28 November 1950. Scheduled appearances by Secretary of State Dean Acheson and President Harry Truman were cancelled because of a severe snowstorm in the region. Critics of the movement were tempted to see a pattern here: first Pearl Harbor; now a record-breaking snowstorm. Were these clues to the attitude of Providence?

The NCC originally brought together twelve interdenominational agencies and twenty-nine denominations. By 1990 there were thirty-three denominations, four of them Orthodox. Outside the NCC today are Roman Catholics and Southern Baptists, as well as most Pentecostal and Fundamentalist churches.

THE WCC AND INTERNATIONAL POLITICS

The first formal report of a WCC Assembly is called "The Church and the Disorder of Society: A Report from the Amsterdam Assembly of the World Council of Churches, 1948."[12] Here we read that the presently disordered world has to be transformed into "the responsible society" by accepting "God's design." After a few years had gone by, however, the hearts and minds of Protestant churchmen began to turn more to recognition of the inhibiting effects of "order": WCC position papers tended now to see "order" and "disorder" in creative mix. By 1968 the Theology of Order was out, and the Theology of Liberation was in.

Among other factors at work in this evolution there was the desire to appear more relevant in academic-intellectual circles. In the late 1960s the universities of the West found themselves under seige by radical student movements, ostensibly the result of the anti-Vietnam movement but ultimately stemming from a crisis of self-esteem that took place in the traditional civilization of the West. Courses in Western civilization were driven to the periphery of the curriculum. The Third World was discovered. Black activists announced that their revolutionary movement was part of a cause that included all those in Africa, Southeast Asia and Central and Latin America who had been oppressed by European colonialism. Unlike American universities, the wcc actually had very large and increasing numbers of Third World people in its ranks. Still, Ernest Lefever says, "This shift of focus was ... not simply the result of increasing representation in the wcc from Asia, Africa, and Latin America. The Third World outlook and constituency ... had been developed largely in the United States and Europe; then it was exported to the Third World."[13]

One defining moment in this story came at the Uppsala Assembly in 1968. Here, the "Program to Combat Racism" was adopted: it called for educational efforts, political and social action, economic sanctions against "racist" regimes, and moral and material support for groups "fighting racism"[14] This new program caused much offence in conservative ranks because of its explicit adoption of Third World rhetoric and Marxist-Leninist insights on imperialism. Yet not even the most suspicious of conservatives anticipated what followed: on 10 August 1978 the World Council of Churches announced a grant of $85,000 to the Patriotic Front guerrillas who by violence were seeking to overthrow the interracial interim regime in Rhodesia that preceded Mugabe's victory in the 1980 elections. This liberation movement was one of the most vicious on the scene. To that date it had murdered 207 white civilians and about 2,000 black civilians. Especially galling to many Western Christians was the knowledge that among the victims were several entire missionary families.[15] As this sank in, several churches suspended their wcc membership in protest.[16] Unchastened, the council proceeded to announce grants to other guerrilla movements. One favourite recipient was the notoriously bloody minded guerrilla movement swapo, the South West Africa People's Organization, which received altogether $498,500 from the wcc before the end of 1978.[17] A wcc document, "Violence, Non-violence and the Struggle for Justice," published by the central committee in Geneva, 1973, provided examples of oppression and violence in South Africa, various Latin American counries, and Northern Ireland, among many other countries, but none from any communist country. It charged the us with exercising "massive, obvious violence" in Vietnam and "economic domination and political interventions, sometimes openly violent, in Latin

America." The WCC saw the sometimes violent behaviour of certain protest movements in the US (like the Black Panthers) as a necessary response "against a systematic oppression armed with weapons both brutal and subtle."[18]

These initiatives in the realm of political action cried out for rationalization. Accordingly, the WCC sent out a call for scholars to provide an appropriate theology.[19] The "liberation theology" that emerged from the Nairobi Assembly drew upon Marxist, Leninist, Maoist, and so-called neo-Marxist vocabulary, from such fashionable left-wing commentators as Franz Fanon, and from Roman Catholic liberation theologians resident in Latin America, such as Gustavo Gutierrez, Jon Sobrino, Leonardo Boff, and Jose Miquez Bonino.[20] The author of *Christians and Marxists* (1976), Bonino was at one time one of the six members of WCC's executive, and he appealed to Marx to explain "the obvious political motifs and undertones in the life of Jesus." Following this clue, Christians should understand the Resurrection as "the death of the monopolies," and as proof that "a world revolution is necessary." These insights, Bonino noted, are common in Cuba, where we find "the creation of a new man, a solitary human being who places the common good before his own individual interest."[21] Unlike the secular philosophers from whom they drew their primary insights, liberation theologians (both Roman Catholic and WCC) made frequent use of short biblical passages. But, like the secularists, they made no reference whatever to historic schools of theology. On this point, Ernest Lefever echoes the judgment of Pope Paul VI on the Church's "loss of confidence in the great masters of Christian thought [which leaves a vacuum] too often filled by a superficial and almost servile acceptance of the currently fashionable philosophies."[22] Peter Byerhaus, Director of the Institute of Missiology and Ecumenical Theology at Tubingen University, speaks of WCC's "political theology" as "a camouflaged atheistic humanism, in which the names of God and Christ are simply cyphers for the real nature and destiny of man."[23]

WCC declarations ensuing in the 1970s and 1980s not only confirmed the commitment of the WCC intelligentsia to leftist ideology but revealed a substantial adherence to the Soviet view on current world issues. "Western capitalism" and "the profit motive" were seen as the fundamental forces tending to war. In Central America, pro-Soviet, pro-Cuban Nicaragua was a beacon of hope, while pro-US Salvador and Guatemala were irredeemably oppressive and in need of overthrowing. When Moscow invaded Afghanistan in December 1979, the WCC echoed the Soviet Union's explanation that it was all done to restore order. After the US left Vietnam, the WCC turned a deaf ear to the colossal persecutions that followed in Vietnam itself and in Cambodia.

WCC general secretary Philip Potter praised the communist victory in Vietnam as "the most dramatic manifestation of hope in our time." South Korea (but not North Korea) and Taiwan (but not China) were regularly denounced for their oppressiveness.[24]

Inevitably, the WCC and NCC faced criticism from within and without their ranks for their theological liberalism and social radicalism, and for their accomodations to Marxist philosophy and the communist world-view. In the early 1980s unhappiness with NCC policies was reflected in drastic reductions of financial support from many member congregations, leading to equally drastic budget cuts, including reductions of staff. In the later 1980s both the WCC and NCC began to respond to these complaints by choosing less-radical leaders and toning down their left-leaning policy statements. Some of the zeal for denunciation was redirected into the past, where WCC intelligentsia found allies among the fashionable anti-European deconstructionists. The aboriginal angle on the history of the world since 1492 was eagerly embraced: in a statement of 1990 Columbus was denounced for his contributions to "genocide, slavery, and ecocide, and the exploitation of the wealth of the land."

One of the harshest critics of the WCC is an English evangelical, Bernard Smith. Smith quotes a WCC document – "We recognize the importance of cooperating at every level with the Roman Catholic church, with other non-member churches, with non-church organizations, adherents of other religions, men of no religion, indeed with men of goodwill everywhere" – as proof that the council is driven by the spirit of Antichrist – the ambition to "break free from the restraints of a specifically Christian identity." Thus, the WCC "abandons the uniqueness of the gospel and , in the face of secularism, it abandons the gospel itself."[25]

In theory, WCC policy statements do not bind the member churches or the various national groupings. Member churches study WCC position papers at their conventions; and national interchurch groups (like the NCC, or the British Council of Churches) likewise study WCC papers at their meetings and almost invariably adopt them or express support, in deference to their expert knowledge.[26] The United Nations has been dealing with the WCC for more than half a century. It is one of the oldest of the international non-governmental organizations (NGOs) that, in effect, piggy-back upon UN humanitarian and educational operations, serving, in return, as an allegedly disinterested gatherer of information in various fields.[27]

Few individual Christians give much thought to the WCC. One might find a reference to a WCC or NCC statement about something or other in a daily newspaper or denominational paper and fire off a letter of approval or dissent to the editor. Political leaders of the world see it as an organization that conveniently provides them with a wholesale product – the Opinion of the Church. But politicians in democratic countries who take this bargain at face value are likely to find themselves in trouble at the polls, where the customers show up one at a time.

TWO DECADES OF CHANGE IN THE JEWISH STATE, 1949–67

Anyone who had visited Israel in 1949, at the end of its war of Independence, and then again in 1955 would have seen many striking changes. Mainly because of immigration, the Jewish population had doubled between 15 May 1948 and 30 June 1953. This had caused a conspicuous change in the "racial" makeup of the state. With the naked eye one could see the relative decline of Western (Ashkenazi) Jews as result of the dramatic increase in numbers of Eastern (Sephardi) Jews from Arab countries of the Middle East and Maghreb, from greater Arabia, and even from Asia. Constant turmoil marked the poltical scene. Between 1949 and 1960, Israel had had nine different governments; all were "Labour" coalitions, with Mapai at the centre, and (except for the brief tenure of Moshe Sharett, 1954–55) all with David Ben-Gurion as Prime Minister. On the opposition side, several ill-defined right-wing groups, whose stars (notably, Menachem Begin and Yitzhak Shamir) were ex-terrorists, somehow affiliated with Orthodox religious leaders who stood outside (or perhaps above) the political bargains that were keeping the Labour coalition in power. These extra-government parties represented so many disparate interests and ideological colorations, however, that there was no prospect of their congealing into a "shadow government," let alone undertaking to replace the government.

The early years were marked by a virtually continuous political crisis over "religious issues." Liberal Christians in the United States spoke reproachfully of "theocratic politics," of the triumph of "obscurantism." Yet those of more conservative theology and social views were intrigued by the vitality of religious forces in Israel – indeed, were tantalized by the success of Israeli religious leaders in securing a place for religious education in the public realm. There were state subsisides for religious schools and a place for religion in the curriculum of the state schools. Religion was represented front and centre in the ceremonial life of the nation and had a stake in the state-owned information media and the armed forces. Despite the expressed unhappiness of the "secularists" and of those adhering to the non-Orthodox house of Jewish religion (a tiny minority in Israel), none of this was apologized for.

In Israel, government was given a role in restraining some of the license of the popular media (whose most licentious products, needless to say, were imported from the United States, or from Europe). To the envy of many Christian churchmen abroad, the religious authorities of Israel succeeded in forbidding theatres to carry movies that were judged to be offensive to the religious sensibilities of Christians – as, for example, *The Life of Brian* (1978), the work of the English satirists known as "Monty Python," which crudely mocks the sacred themes of Christianity. Particularly interesting to American Christians was the fact that provision for a prominent role for religion in the public life was not limited to Judaism. A broad range of what would in most Western states be regarded as civil matters, including family law, were assigned to the religious jurisdictions – to the rabbinical courts, the various Christian churches, and the Moslem courts. A ministry for Religious Affairs was established in the government, with separate departments for dealing with Muslim, Christian, and Druze religious communities.

Many Christians now began studying Israeli politics with greater care. They discovered that a number of political parties had always been squarely based on religious programs, and several were playing substantial roles in government – involving themselves not merely in "religious" issues, narrowly defined, but in issues of finance, education, settlement policies, immigration, etc. Their efforts had won state subsidies for a distinct stream of "religious schools" as well as religious instruction in the "secular" system. All this, American Christians noted, was going on at the same time that the US Supreme Court, in a sequence of decisions today regarded as irreversible, was severely limiting the public role of religion.

In the 1970s American commentators began noting that "out of nowhere" had appeared political activists motivated by the desire to bring "Christian" or "Judaeo-Christian" values back into the public life of the United States. The most conspicuous of these were to be found among evangelicals and fundamentalists who (conventional wisdom had always said) were little interested in the political sphere of things and could safely be ignored by political powerbrokers. After some assiduous apprenticeship, usually in the service of Republican candidates from the South, religious conservatives began to master the techniques of political mobilization, and in the 1980s they would become a force of very great significance in the political arena. They were one of the major elements in the Reagan victory of 1980. I shall have much more to say about this in chapter 8. For now I note only that in this early stage of the politicization of Christian conservatives in America, one can already see the role played by sympathetic interest in the political situation in Israel. Many in the conservative Christian camp were working to establish a community of interest with "religious" (i.e., Orthodox) Jews in Israel and in the US. This surprised many of the conservative Christians themselves, most of whom had been raised in a milieu where (to put it mildly) Jews were not ordinarily held up as role models. But now a new sort of philo-Judaism was becoming common in evangelical and fundamentalist ranks. Evangelical and fundamentalist educators moved to Israel to set up facilities for learning the Hebrew language and the history of Israel and the Jews. Bible colleges in the US increased their offerings on the Hebrew language and Judaism. Evangelical bookstores carried a wide range of books whose authors argued that the fullest understanding of the origins of the Christian faith was open only to those who had some informed appreciation of the Jewish religious forms and symbols and cult. This sympathetic interest in Judaism and Israel continued to grow through the 1970s and 1980s, reinforced by another trend of the 1980s: the proliferation of "End Times" literature.

1967: CHRISTIAN OPINION AND THE SIX-DAY WAR

The events of June 1967 constitute the watershed in the story of Christian attitudes towards the State of Israel. From this moment there is rapid movement towards the present polarization between Christian Zionists – generally, but not exclusively, on the right wing, theologically speaking, of the churches – and Christian anti-Zionists – generally, but not exclusively, on the left wing.

American Jews were distressed, even appalled, at the lack of sympathy for the Israeli situation shown by official spokesmen of the churches, as Israel's Arab enemies closed in on the Jewish state in the spring of 1967. Egypt brazenly defied the UN and tore up the pledge it had made to permit international supervision in the Sinai and the Gulf of Aqaba. The Middle Eastern air was full of the threat of an imminent war of annihilation against the Jews declaimed by Egyptian president Gamal Abdul Nasser and other Arab statesmen. But the Protestant and Roman Catholic churches had next to nothing to say.[28]

There were exceptions. A number of Roman Catholic and Protestant clergy in the Boston area, led by Richard, Cardinal Cushing, signed a "Declaration of Moral Principle," in which Americans were asked to recognize that Israel might well be destroyed, as Arab voices hoped and believed it would, if her rights to free passage through the Suez Canal and the Gulf of Aqaba were not sustained by the UN.[29] Several friends of Israel among Protestant and Catholic clergy (including J.C. Bennett, Robert McAfee Brown, Martin Luther King, Jr., Franklin Littell, and Reinhold Niebuhr), published a joint statement that called upon "our fellow Americans of all persuasions and groupings and on the Administration to support the independence, integrity and freedom of Israel."[30] But the Christian press did not take up this note. Despite their unremitting efforts throughout the month of May 1967, American Jewish leaders were unable to persuade either the National Council of Churches or the National Conference of Catholic Bishops to issue a straightforwad declaration of support for Israel's right to exist, which might have steadied the nerves of Israelis groaning under the effects of the declarations coming from Arab states.[31]

Israel was surrounded by hostile countries whose armies vastly outnumbered her own. Nevertheless, on 4 June the Israeli army launched a pre-emptive war, initially targetting Egyptian air power. The moment the war began it was obvious that Nasser had miscalculated. Thereupon a rush of statements came from Church bodies reminding everyone that war has never solved anything. Among liberal Protestants, there was almost universal readiness to blame Israel for the outbreak of the war. Particularly harsh was Dr Henry Pitt Van Dusen, president of Union Theological Seminary, who spoke of "Israel's assault on her Arab neighbours." He elaborated: "All persons who seek to view the Middle East problem with honesty and objectivity stand aghast at Israel's onslaught, the most violent, ruthless (and successful) aggression since Hitler's blitzkrieg across Western Europe ... aiming not at victory but at annihilation – the very objective proclaimed by Nasser and his allies which had drawn support for Israel ... Israel has consistently refused collaboration with the UN in maintaining peace. Every square mile of Arab homeland appropriated by Israel, every additional Arab subjugated or driven into exile will merely exacerbate the smoldering desire for revenge. Our grandchildren, if not we, may witness an even more murderous and tragic holocaust."[32]

Among many other repercussions, the Six-Day War marks a momentous juncture in the history of the influential Protestant journal *Christianity and Crisis,* founded 10 February 1941 by Reinhold Niebuhr. As poor health loosened his domination of the journal's editorial board, Niebuhr was reduced to protesting, like any other contributor, to the change in direction that was coming over the journal's policy towards Israel. Gone forever was the journal's original commitment to Israel as an outpost of Judaeo-Christian civilization and democracy; most of the articles now echoed the unfriendly line that had always dominated the pages of the journal *Christian Century*.[33] Niebuhr's longtime associate at the journal, John C. Bennett, expressed the view that "we cannot proceed as though Israel as a nation has a biblical deed to Jerusalem as so much territory. Nothing that was true in an earlier century in regard to the relation of Israel can sanctify the right of conquest in the twentieth century." As *Christianity and Crisis* turned towards the "Palestinian" camp, Israel lost its last friend in the ranks of respectable mainstream Protestant journals; and Niebuhr, very shortly, lost his interest in *Christianity and Crisis*.

Not only in evangelical and fundamentalist ranks but among most Christians of conservative theology, the creation of Israel in 1948 had seemed thrilling proof of the reliability of prophetic scripture. Nonetheless, many of those who saw the founding of Israel in this light had reservations. One prominent fundamentalist theologian wrote: "The nation of Israel has been formed, they have all the likeness of one of the nations of the earth; they have their government, their postal, coinage, and banking system, but there is no God. They have come together as a nation of Israelites, without the God of Israel."[34] Similarly, Charles Feinberg, while welcoming the State of Israel as "remarkable fulfilment of the the ancient prophecy of Joel 3:2 (last clause),"[35] warned: "They are not being prospered because they are now in the will of God, but in spite of their being out of His will through personal and individual rejection of Christ as Messiah and Savior ... Israel is doomed to sad and dismal disappointment as they place their trust in the United Nations ... God Himself will regather Israel to the land in the last days (Isa. 27:13; Matt. 24:31) to accomplish His consummating purposes with the nations there."[36] Similarly, John Walvoord, in his book *Israel in Prophecy* (1962), wrote: " Heart-rending as it may be to contemplate, the people of Israel who are returning to their ancient land, are placing themselves within the vortex of this future whirlwind which will destroy the majority of those living in the land of Palestine." [37] A Southern Baptist spokesman was quoted with approval by the *Christian Century*: "The new nation Israel is a miracle. In honesty, I must add that it is an 'immoral miracle.'"[38]

In most instances, however, the events of June 1967 served to revive and even amplify the Restorationist zeal of 1948, sweeping away doubts and reservations that many conservative Christians had had originally, or had developed in the meanwhile. To see the Western Wall taken from Jordanian hands and returned to the possession of the Jewish people, to witness the religious outpourings that this inspired, and then to be told that the more zealous were now talking out loud about restoring their Temple – all of this magnified respect for "prophetic teaching" among Christian laity. People who had previously been open to persuasion on the matter of the internationalization of Jerusalem now closed their minds on the issue forever, concluding that God's hand was in the victory that had given the Jews possession of their Holy City.

The politicians, however, were not amused. Through all the years (1949–67) when Israel held West Jerusalem and Jordan held East Jerusalem (including the Old City), the UN upheld the vision of a "unified" and "internationalized" Jerusalem. To protest Israel's declaration of Jerusalem as its capital on 23 January 1950, most nations doing business with Israel had located their embassies in Tel Aviv and now refused to budge. Now Jerusalem was unified, which simplified the situation on the map and, in the minds of the Israelis and the friends of Israel, advanced the prospect for a normal life for its citizens. Unimpressed by this thinking, the Western statesmen announced their intention to keep their embassies in Tel Aviv. (The Soviet bloc had withdrawn recognition of the state altogether.) The possilibilty of coaxing Israel towards the official UN solution (called "internationalization") was now virtually hopeless.

To most evangelicals and fundamentalists, these matters were far from the real considerations. To them, the six-day war was powerful proof of the authority of the prophetic sections of the Bible. Following in the tradition of Christian Restorationism and Christian Zionism, they proclaimed that history's clock had been dramatically advanced: all mankind was much closer to the events of the Last Days that are described both in the Old and New Testaments. In this, as in so many other matters, we find a significant gulf between the attitudes of laity and clerisy. Most official Church spokesmen eschewed a biblical interpretation of the events; in fact it became a point of honour in ecumenical-Christian circles to condemn such fundamentalist interpretations of current events. Yet many Christians were drawn by these events into study of biblical prophecies about how it will all end. "End Times" theologians flourished, and most Christians were to some degree affected by the End Times excitement that surrounded the events of June 1967. Once the conflict over Jerusalem had moved from the front pages, most observers probably set these exciting thoughts back on some remote shelf of their imaginations, but many would return to them as further events unfolded.

Among evangelicals and fundamentalists, the events of June 1967 made it seem necessary to accept in more literal terms than ever before that the Restoration of Israel stood at the head of a sequence of literal fulfilments of Old and New Testament prophecy that would culminate in Christ's return.[39] Two issues of the *Moody Monthly* in the summer and fall of 1967 were devoted to "Bible Prophecy and the Mid-East Crisis." The consensus of the contributors, as summarized by John F. Walvoord, was that they had just seen "one of the most remarkable fulfilments of biblical prophecy since the destruction of Jerusalem in 70 AD."[40] For Christians of conservative theology – not only "evangelicals" and "fundamentalists" but many whose churches were located in the "mainstream," as well as many Roman Catholics – the events of 1967 made clearer the significance of the events of 1947–48. The editor of *Christianity Today*, I. Nelson Bell, a former missionary-doctor who was active in evangelical leadership (and father-in-law of Billy Graham), wrote: "That for the first time in more than 2,000 years Jerusalem is now completely in the hands of the Jews gives the student of the Bible a thrill and a renewed faith in the accuracy and validity of the Bible."[41] Soon there were many books developing this theme. Hal Lindsey's *The Late Great Planet Earth* (1970) eventually became not only the most popular of such books, selling seven and half million copies, but the biggest-selling non-fiction book of the entire 1970s, regardless of theme or field.[42] (By the end of 1999, 28 million copies had been sold, according to *Newsweek*.)[43] Early in 1971, fifteen hundred delegates from thirty-two countries attended a Prophecy Conference in Jerusalem. Former Prime Minister David Ben-Gurion welcomed them, and speakers included almost all the important voices in the End Times field.

Of inestimable value to Israel over the years has been been the friendship of Billy Graham, without doubt the most influential figure in world Protestantism during the entire half-century that Israel has been in existence. In Graham's book, *His Land*, published in 1969 and later made into a film, he explained to his enormous following that the re-instatement of the Jews in Israel and in their ancient capital, Jerusalem, was an indisputable part of God's Plan. Biographer William Martin describes Graham's quiet lobbying over the years on behalf of Israel with all those presidents to whom he has enjoyed access, but notably with Richard Nixon and Ronald Reagan; and he cites many examples of Israeli and Jewish-American leaders acknowledging Graham's role.[44]

At the beginning of the week of His Passion, Jesus had gathered His disciples on the Mount of Olives. Directing their attention across the Valley of Jehosephat to the site of the Temple, He said: "And they [the population of Jerusalem] will fall by the edge of the sword, and be led away captive into all nations. And Jerusalem will be trampled by Gentiles until the times of the Gentiles are fulfilled" [Luke 21:24] – after which, he said, the supernatural signs of the end would occur. [Luke 21: 25–36; Matt. 24]. With Zion now entirely in Jewish hands, was it not obvious that the "Times of the Gentiles" had been completed? Certainly most Israelis, at that hour of triumph, believed that this was so – without, needless to say, assuming that the signs that fundamentalist Christians were anticipating would follow, or that the authority of Jesus of Nazareth had any bearing on the matter. From this moment on, we begin to find expressions of interest among evangelicals and fundamentalists in preparations being made by some Jews for the building of the Temple.[45]

Israel's incredibly swift victory was not without its drawbacks, however. At the end of the six days of fighting in June 1967, Israel found itself in control, for the first time, of large territories densely and exclusively populated by Arabs – an estimated 600,000 in the West Bank and an estimated 400,000 in Gaza. Commentators who prided themselves on their sensitivity to the brutal uses of power now turned on the Israelis for no better reason, in many cases, than that they, the Israelis, had been getting away all these years with appearing vulnerable. Now the Arab nations had captured the underdog position. In several communities, it was noted, Christian representatives who were scheduled to appear at emergency rallies for Israel withdrew when it became clear that an Israeli victory was in the offing.[46] Those few Jews who made it their business to be well informed about the various currents within American Protestantism were especially shocked when they read in *Christianity Today* (normally thought to be a friendly source, the voice of moderate evangelicalism) that Israel alone was to blame for the war: "The Balfour Declaration has been the major cause of the three wars whereby the Jews have stolen so much of Palestine from the Arabs who have owned it for centuries ... Ever since Israel made a military conquest almost twenty years ago, she has refused to have anything to do with the refugees upon whose land she now lives. To her, Arabs are simply dogs ... There is a deep horror about all this history in the fact that great numbers of Christians in the United States applaud Israel's crimes against Arab Christians and Arab Muslims. How can a Christian applaud the murder of a brother Christian by Zionist Jews?"[47] The author of these words was Rev. James L. Kelso, a former Moderator of the United Presbyterian Church. This was not, however, the dominant note in *Christianity Today*, which seems to have been roughly as inclined towards the Israeli side in 1967 as the *Christian Century* was towards the anti-Israeli side. Still, the comments of James Kelso were shortly to be echoed by several other contributors to the journal, and in the years that followed, the anti-Zionist note grew.[48] By the 1980s, editorials and articles in both the liberal *Christian Century* and the evangelical *Christianity Today* reflected increasing enthusiam for the Palestinian cause and increasing hostility, shading into hatred, towards the various Christian Zionist organizations.

Beginning in June 1967, the anti-Israel posture of mainstream Protestantism became more overt with each passing month. The *Christian Century* now questioned whether Israel should ever have been given statehood: "The Christian Century was among the journals that 20 years ago questioned the wisdom of translating the Israel that had been a faith and a folk into the Israel that became a state ... [A]s the word Israel becomes increasingly identified with a special geography and a particular political entity, it will inevitably lose some of its meanings heretofore most precious to Jews and Christians. As the word moves from general, abstract meanings to a specific concrete focus, it inevitably loses its broad and deep spiritual significance ... Christians owe to Israel the faith – the heritage, the community – a debt they can never fully discharge, but history has not made the state of Israel the collector of that debt."[49] It should be noticed, in fairness, that while this line of thought dominated the pages of the *Christian Century* at the time,[50] the editors gave substantial space to several pro-Israeli articles as well.[51] Both Fishman and Banki have conveyed too monolithic a picture of the Protestant liberal viewpoint in 1967. It is true, nonetheless, that events of those months brought forth expressions of hostility towards Israel that had hitherto not found expression in the liberal journals, setting precedents, as we shall see, for an anti-Israeli tone that became more strident as the years went by. It is especially striking that commentators who denounced Israel for her "aggressions" seemed unmoved by Jewish losses. (During the course of the Six-Day War, eight hundred Israeli soldiers died.[52] Total Arab losses were many times the Israeli number.) Afterwards, there was no shortage of statements expressing concern for Arab refugees and supporting the Arab line that finding a solution to this refugee problem must be a precondition for talks with Arab governments; but there was little appreciation of Israel's argument that recognition of the State of Israel must precede all concessions from Israel's side.[53] Discovering this strange bias and recalling that few Christian leaders had shown any alarm at the imminent threat Israel faced in May, many Jews felt bitterness towards Christian organizations. At the same time, they noted that public opinion polls showed much stronger support of Israel's position among the general American public than among Church spokesmen.

THE WCC AND ISRAEL TO 1967

Even before the World Council of Churches came into being, one could have deduced from the attitudes of its predecessor organizations that there was not likely to be a warm relationship between a Jewish state and organized, ecumenical Christianity. When the Federal Council of Churches of the United States presented its official view to the Anglo-British Joint Committee of 1946 (the official body that was seeking a solution to the problem of Palestine and of the Jewish refugees), it refused to commit itself on the question of a Jewish state, claiming that this was a matter that divides Christians and on which there was no clear theological direction. Within the mainstream American Protestant ranks, an influential pro-Zionist body, the American Christian Palestine Committee, did play a significant part in manoeuvring American public attitudes in a pro-Zionist direction. When their turn came to speak at the hearings of the Anglo-British Joint Committee, their designated spokesmen were Daniel Poling and Reinhold Niebuhr. Dr Poling claimed that an overwhelming majority of Christians were in favour of the partition of Palestine and the creation of a Jewish state, but he gave no proof. Reinhold Niebuhr did not endorse the claim, but merely stated: "I belong to a Christian group in this country [the American Christian Palestine Committee, or ACPC] who believe that the Jews have a right to a homeland. They are a nation, scattered among the nations of the world. They have no place where they are not exposed to the perils of minority status." In response to the complaint that this solution would work some injustice for the Arabs of the region, Niebuhr said: "There is in fact no solution to any political problem; the fact, however, that the Arabs have a vast hinterland in the Middle East, and the fact that the Jews have nowhere to go, establishes the relative justice of their claims and their cause ... Arab sovereignty over a portion of a debated territory must undoubtedly be sacrificed for the sake of establishing a world homeland for the Jews."

Spokesmen for the ACPC described the Roman Catholic church and other Church bodies that did not support the Jews as being guilty of some cynicism, or at the very least a lack of proportion, fixated as they were on the issue of "Christian rights and interests in the Holy Places." The League of Nations mandate and the Balfour Declaration "stipulated that the Holy Places be fully protected, a stipulation which has been meticulously observed by the Jews of Palestine. As Christians, we protest this effort to create an issue out a situation which has never been a problem; and thus obscure the real issue at stake which is not only to create a haven for homeless Jews, but to build a national home for a homeless people ... The Jews as a people have an ethnic consciousness which makes their relationship to Palestine unique.[54]

At its First Assembly in August 1948, meeting just a few weeks into Israel's first war for survival, the wcc let it be known that its heart went out to the Jews: "No people in His one world has suffered more bitterly from the disorder of man than the Jewish people. We cannot forget that we meet in a land [Holland] from which 100,000 Jews were taken to be murdered. Nor can we forget that we meet only five years [*sic*] after the extermination of 6 million Jews ... In the design of God, Israel has a unique position. It was Israel with whom God made His covenant by the call of Abraham. It was Israel to whom God revealed His name and gave His law. It was to Israel that He sent His prophets with the message of judgement and of grace. It was Israel to whom He promised the coming of His Messiah ... We have therefore, in humble conviction to proclaim to the Jews , 'the Messiah for Whom you wait has come.'" At the same time, however, the new world parliament of ecumenical Christianity could not take a position on such a controversial issue as Israel's right to exist: "On the political aspects of the Palestine problem and the complex conflict of 'rights' involved we do not undertake to express a judgment. Nevertheless, we appeal to the nations to deal with the problem not as one of expediency – political, strategic or economic – but as a moral and spiritual question that touches a nerve center of the world's religious life ... The establishment of the state 'Israel' adds a political dimension to the Christian approach to the Jews and threatens to complicate anti-Semitism with political fears and enmities." If that last sentence means anything at all, it must be that Israel has only itself to blame if more "anti-Semitism" should now appear in the world.[55]

Invariably in wcc documents,[56] the creation of the State of Israel appears as a complication, never as an answer to a problem. "Having no judgment" to make on the "political aspects of the Palestinian problem" is, of course, a political judgment, to the effect that there is parity between the historical claims of the two sides. Never in wcc documents do we find any hint of recognition that Israel came into existence in response to the decision of the world's parliament, taken in November 1947, and that, therefore, the dilemma of the other side follows from its steadfast and illegal rejection of the *legitimacy* of this decision. Legitimacy, as this term appears in the classical literature on international relations, has never been a thing close to the heart of the wcc, since it first began to turn away from its preference for "order" and "responsibility" (expressed in its earliest declarations on world affairs) in order to exercise its preferential option for disorder and "liberation."

As we shall see in chapter 8, in the 1980s the wcc formally pronounced as "heresy" any attempts to use theology to justify the existence of Israel. Prior to this, the wcc was officially uncommitted on the theological question whether the creation of the state was a fulfilment of the purposes of God as expressed by Old Testament prophets. At the Second World Assembly in 1954, where the official theme was "Jesus Christ, the Hope of the World," a group of prominent theologians proposed including in the proceedings a statement to the effect that Israel was among many recent signs of hope. This proposal was voted down, 195 to 150, after Charles Malik, a Christian political leader from Lebanon and a figure of importance in those days in un circles, urged the delegates to say nothing that would alienate Arab Christians.[57]

This provoking refusal at the highest reaches of the wcc to take a position on such a vital theological issue did not go unnoticed in the churches. Several national church bodies within the wcc took a bolder line.[58] An interesting example is a report, "People, Land and State: Suggestions for a Theological Evaluation," issued by the General Synod of the Reformed Church of Holland in 1970, in which we read that the Israel "of which the bible of ot and nt speaks has not disappeared. The Jewish people, as it appears in our time, is its continuation." The authors of this report were aware that in wcc circles it was routinely said that, whatever Old Testament prophets may have said and meant, the expectation of the Jews' future possession of a land is not any part of Jesus' message. It is true, they reply, that this expectation is not actually expressed in the New Testament: "On the other hand, nothing is to be found there which denies it ... The situation of the people of Israel regarding salvation is the same as it was in nt times. They are still, even in their alienation, the special people to which God has bound Himself. Their election remains valid, and through this election they are determined and marked."[59] The authors of this Dutch Reformed report were not unaware of the moral ambiguity in Israel's behaviour, or of the dimensions of Palestinian Arab suffering and the legitimacy of the Palestinians' cries for justice. Nor did they hesitate to criticize Israel for not acceding to some form of "internationalized" status for Jerusalem (in line with the thinking of the un, the wcc, and the Roman Catholic church). Nonetheless, the report affirms that Christians should be defending the right of Israel to exist, not just passively conceding it; they should consider support for Israel as a duty that follows from the recognition that God is the master of the historical process, and that He has put Israel in place as the fulfilment of His promise to the Jews.

THE WCC AND THE ISSUE OF JERUSALEM

When the dust settled after Israel's War for Independence in 1948–49, the UN took note again of its commitment to the virtues of internationalizing Jerusalem and its immediate vicinity, as was provided for in the partition declaration of November 1947.[60] A Palestine Conciliation Commission was sent to look at the changed situation on the ground and came back with a slightly modified version of the original declaration. Arab states, other than Jordan, now expressed support for this solution (which they had previously rejected); but it was no longer acceptable to Israel. The WCC and the Vatican likewise supported the UN proposal, as did the United States, the Soviet bloc, and all the Arab states except Jordan. The American Christian Palestine Committee, the pro-Zionist body that had played so large a role in moving Christian opinion in the United States towards support for the creation of the state in the first place, favoured a compromise solution: "international curatorship" of the holy places while leaving the Old City and Bethlehem under international supervision, and acceptance of the annexation of the "New City" of Jerusalem to the State of Israel.[61] This position, with a little finessing, could have been accepted by the Israeli government in the years 1948–67 but was not acceptable to Jordan and thus not acceptable to her patron, Great Britain.

The issue of Jerusalem took up much of the UN's time in 1949. In the words of the Jewish historian Howard Sachar: "The Catholic nations generally followed the lead of the Vatican in endorsing ... *corpus separatum.* An extreme propaganda against Israel was launched throughout the Catholic world. In this campaign, Transjordan was ignored, although Abdullah's forces controlled the great majority of Jerusalem's holy places." Sachar suspects that the Vatican feared that Christians would not wish to find themselves living in a Jewish state, and thus the city would soon come to lack a base of Christians sufficient in number to sustain the churches there. "For centuries an intense rivalry had festered between Orthodox and Latins in the Holy city. Generally, the Latins had been outnumbered there by Eastern and other non-Latin Christian groups. In the United Nations, on the other hand, the non-Catholic element possessed no spokemen at all, while the Latins were represented by a substantial bloc of delegates. With this diplomatic influence available to widen their bridgehead in the city, the Catholics understood that it was not the time for minimalism in defining the United Nation's role in a *corpus separatum.*"[62]

On 16 December 1949 Reinhold Niebuhr wrote to Frederick Nolde, director of the WCC's Commission on International Affairs: "If the

Protestant Church is disposed in any way to support anything like the Vatican plan, I will feel bound to break ranks and try to organize a group to opppose it."[63] The WCC was not deterred by this threat and went on record at the first opportunity as being in favour of internationalization.

Many anomolies appear in this story – not least that on 9 December 1949 the Soviet bloc sided with delegations from Roman Catholic and Protestant nations in supporting the Vatican's proposal for a *corpus separatum*. The Government of Israel was not moved, however: on 13 December the Knesset unanimously voted to move to Jerusalem, and on 1 January 1950 the entire Israeli government operation, except for defence, police, and foreign affairs, was transfered from Tel Aviv to the parts of Jerusalem that were then in Jewish hands. On 23 January 1958 the Knesset declared that Jerusalem had "always been" the capital of the Jewish people.[64]

The American government saw little profit in keeping this issue alive after the end of the 1940s. And, truth to tell, leaders of the churches found little interest among the rank and file. Thus, while the Vatican and the WCC continued to pour down resolutions in favour of "internationalization" upon the heads of UN officials and delegations, the UN dropped the issue from its active agenda in 1952 and did not raise it again for 15 years – that is, until immediately after the Six-Day War in June 1967.[65]

By the time of the WCC assembly meeting in Nairobi in 1975, the Council's position ran as follows:

1 For many millions of Christians throughout the world, as well as for the adherents of the two great sister monotheistic religions, namely Judaism and Islam, Jerusalem continues to be a focus of deepest religious inspiration and attachment. It is therefore their responsibility to cooperate in the creation of conditions that will ensure that Jerusalem is a city open to the adherents of all three religions, where they can meet and live together. The tendency to minimize Jerusalem's importance for any of these three religions should be avoided.

2 The special legislation regulating the relationship of the Christian communities and the authorities, guaranteed by international treaties (Paris 1856 and Berlin 1878) and the League of Nations and known as the Status Quo of the Holy Places must be fully safeguarded and confirmed in any agreement concerning Jerusalem. *Christian Holy Places in Jerusalem and neighbouring areas belong to the greatest extent to member churches of the WCC.* On the basis of the Status Quo none of the church authorities of a given denomination could represent unilaterally and on behalf of all Christians the Christian point of view, each church authority of a given denomination representing only its own point of view.

3 Many member churches of the WCC are deeply concerned about the Christian Holy Places. However, the question of Jerusalem is not only a matter of protection of the Holy Places, it is organically linked with living faiths and communities of peoples in the Holy City. Therefore the Assembly deems it essential that the Holy Shrines should not become mere monuments of visitation, but should serve as living places of worship integrated and responsive to Christian communities who continue to maintain their life and roots within the Holy City and for those who out of religious attachments want to visit them.

4 While recognizing the complexity and emotional implications of the issues surrounding the future status of Jerusalem, the Assembly believes that such status has to be determined within the general context of the settlement of the Middle East conflict in its totality.

5 However, the Assembly thinks that apart from any politics, the whole settlement of the inter-religious problem of the Holy Places should take place under an international aegis and guarantee which ought to be respected by the parties concerned as well as the ruling authorities.

6 The Assembly recommends that the above should be worked out with the most directly concerned member churches, as well as with the Roman Catholic church [*sic*]. These issues should also become subjects for dialogue with Jewish and Muslim counterparts.

7 The Assembly expresses its profound hope and fervent prayers for the peace and welfare of the Holy City and its inhabitants.[66]

The keynote in all recent WCC documents that deal with Jerusalem is the parity of all the religious claimants. This is approached in two ways. The first is to stress the holiness of the site, and hence its indivisibility. In a document of 1982, for example, we read that "Jews, Christians and Muslims have all maintained a presence in the Land from their beginnings. While 'the Holy land' is primarily a Christian designation, the Land is holy to all three. Although they may understand its holiness in different ways, it cannot be said to be 'more holy' to one than to another."[67]

The other approach is to moralize about the human weakness for exalting mere geography (or "real estate") to spiritual status: "Various Christians, including Evangelicals, identify the historically and topographically located city of Jerusalm with 'the new Jerusalem,' described in Apoc. [Book of Revelation] 21, and 'the heavenly Jerusalem' in so many songs. Most Christians have a special feeling of belonging to Jerusalem because she is the city of the beginnings and the place of the great events of salvation. According to the Churches of the Reformation neither the fulfilment of the promise nor the reality of faith in the events of salvation are linked to geographically and historically located 'holy places.'"[68]

Either way – whether these are *Holy Places* or merely "holy places" – wcc documents always manage to establish parity of Muslim claims with those of Jews and Christians. In fairness we should note that the document just cited does give high grades to Israel for her conduct of reponsibilities towards the holy places: "In Jerusalem today under Israeli administration the monuments connected with historical events are as much as possible maintained and kept in repair with respect and care ... Freedom of religion is granted more extensively today than in Mandate times and also better than under Jordanian rule."[69]

3 Christians in the Holy Land[1]

THE HISTORICAL SETTING

I assume that most readers of this book are English-speaking Christians, resident in the US, Great Britain, or Canada. They will have practical knowledge of some part of the life of the Church, some understanding of the place that the Church holds in the social order in which they live, and some understanding of how most people relate their religious observance and belonging to the rest of their commitments as citizens. Most will have some familiarity with the history of the Church in their own country – which they will tend to read from the perspective of the particular denomination to which they belong or in which they were raised – and perhaps some understanding of how the history of the Universal Church is to be related to the history of Western civilization. Knowledge along these lines is of limited value, however, in relation to our present theme – Christians in the Holy Land. The fact is that most of the generalizations that Western Christians draw from knowledge and experience of Christianity in what used to be called Christendom do not apply in the past and present situation of Christians in the Holy Land. Indeed, some of these generalizations are useful only if stood on their heads.

To belong to the Church in the Middle East is to be the descendant of a tradition that was once all-powerful; that was for many centuries in a position to set limits to the practice of other religions by other people – people whom the Church despised. Then, abruptly, the pendulum swung, and the persecutors became the persecuted. The churches of the West and the churches of the East together underwent the humiliation of defeat in battle at the hands of the Muslim Arabs – people whose religion all Christians regarded as a demonic deviation from truth – and quickly found themselves in a semi-servile situation towards these new masters. During the centuries that followed, the Christians of the Holy Land were subjugated equally with those whose spirit and way of life and religion they had previously sought to crush – a despicable people called the Jews.

Christians who live in the West have great difficulty grasping the most salient features of the situation of the Christians who live in Israel today.

(1) Christians living in Israel are a tiny minority there and practise their various cults and organize their social life in a setting where the final decisions about religious rights and privileges are made by the Jewish state.

(2) Most Christians who live in the State of Israel prefer to pretend that they live somewhere else. In their imaginations, they live in "Palestine," or (as is prefered in some circles) the Holy Land. In conversation as well as in their writings they sedulously avoid reference to the name of the state in which, in juridical fact, they live; and they remain vigilant, day in and day out, not to take into their eyes the life and not to hear with their ears the language of the Jews.

(3) Most Christians who live in Israel display a spirit of grievance regarding the recent history of the Middle East. (In the Middle East, "recent" means the last three centuries.) As they read it, the salient theme of this history has been Europe's intrusion into their lives, with entirely baneful consequences. They blame the Western powers and the churches of the West for weakening their position relative to their neighbours (the vast community of Arab Muslims) and, in a variety of ways, weakening their social cohesion and jeopardizing their future.

(4) Most Christians who live in Israel despise everything they know about the history of the Church in Europe and America. They believe that European and American Christians are, in their own world, wilfully abetting the demise of the faith they profess by making concessions to all the most baneful spirits ruling in the contemporary world. Christians of the East despise the whole regime of "secularism" and "secularization" that Western churches tolerate and, indeed, celebrate. They despise the diabolical post-Christian popular culture upon which nominal Christians feed. Committed to the belief that social cohesion and decency require the explicit support of a religious tradition, they despise the concept of separation of Church and State, which American Christians parade before them as the beneficent outcome of generations of struggle for "freedom of conscience."

Christians living in the State of Israel are indeed subject to the laws of the state – as are Muslims, Druze, and others of many faiths, not to mention the goodly number who profess no faith at all. The same is true everywhere in the world: the limits within which one may publicly profess and actively practise one's religious faith are aways set by the state. Two documents are fundamental to all discussion of the place of religion in Israel. These are the Charter of Independence of 14 May 1948 and "The Basic Law: Religion."[2] Consulting both of these documents, we find three principles that are important to our discussion. First, Israel is "the Jewish state." Second, in it there is to be provision for "freedom of religion, conscience, education and culture." Third, the State of Israel shall "safeguard the Holy Places of all religions."

In striking contrast to the constitutional situation familiar to Americans, the State of Israel has responsibility to see to it that citizens have basic religious opportunities provided to them, while leaving it to the various religious authorities to determine the content. In legal terms, there is no one who does not belong to a religion. The religious communities recognized by the state are: Jewish (in effect, only the Orthodox version of Judaism); Muslim (predominantly Sunni Islam, but also some Shi'ite); Christian (there are about thirty recognized Christian bodies, affiliated with the Orthodox, or the Roman Catholic, or certain of the Protestant branches of the Church); Druze; and Baha'i. These arrangements derive from the legacy of the Ottoman Empire: the *millet* system – *millet* meaning in Turkish a recognized community within the empire – under which the Turkish conquerors had for centuries accommodated religious differences, playing one religious community against the other for ease of rule but also preventing the hostilities among them from getting out of hand; and the *Status Quo*: a complicated set of agreements with respect to the rights and privileges of various churches at the various holy places, worked out from the mid-eighteenth century forward, in conjunction with various European powers who regarded themselves as "protectors" of certain of the Christian communities. (Some steps in the evolution of the *Status Quo* were conducted bilaterally, but others came out of international conferences, notably the Congress of Berlin in 1878.) Under the *millet* system, religious courts were established for each principal community in which the recognized ecclesiastical leaders discharged responsibility for what we would call matters of personal status (marriage, divorce, inheritance, adoption, etc.) The distinctive creedal and cultic differences of the recognized religious bodies were permitted to continue, even though citizens of these non-Muslim communities experienced discrimination and often humiliation in their dealings with the larger community of Islam. (I have more to say on this theme in chapter 5.) The well-being of the minority communities depended on the ability of their ecclesiastical leaders to maintain reasonable levels of social peace within.

The *millet* system was to some considerable degree breached, or at least modified, by the *Status Quo* – that set of arrangements that came out of the diplomatic dealings of the steadily weakening Ottoman dynasty with the European powers, which were bent on asserting their presence inside the Ottoman realms. This set of arrangements included understandings about the rights and privileges of the various Christian bodies with respect to the holy places (the *Status Quo*), as well as recognition by the Ottoman regime of a special standing that certain of the European powers had as protectors of the interests and the welfare of Christian groups that had (or allegedly had) distinctly close historical connections to particular European powers. Thus, the French had standing as protectors of both Latin and Uniate Christians in Lebanon and what was then called the province of Damascus (including Palestine); the Russians had standing as protectors of all the Orthodox (Russian and non-Russian); and the British acquired standing as protectors of English Protestants. Complicating this picture further was a right that the British eventually tacked on uni-laterally to their original obligation as protector of the Protestants: namely, a right and a duty to "protect" the Jewish converts to their Anglican missions in Jerusalem. By cunning diplomacy, this was expanded into a right of "protection" of the Jews of Jerusalem and ultimately to the Jews of the Ottoman Empire.

Under the Ottomans, the original *millet* communities were: Pre-Chalcedonian Armenians; Armenian Catholics; Orthodox; Syrian Catholics; Nestorians (that is, Assyrians or "Chaldeans"); Greek Catholics; Melkite Christians; and Maronite Christians. To these were added the Church of England and the Evangelical Lutheran Church (whose protector was the kaiser). Under the British Mandate, and then under the Israeli government, a number of Protestant churches were subsequently brought into these arrangements. Still, there are always newcomers on the scene whose members must, if they are citizens, seek satisfaction of their civil rights in the courts of one or other of the accredited churches.

Christians resident in the State of Israel and in the Palestinian entity are overwhelmingly Arab, by self-definition – a fact that usually takes visiting European and American Christians by surprise. Furthermore, Arab Christians are monolithically anti-Zionist – a fact that visiting Christian pilgrims may not have occasion to discover but that, when and if they do, usually catches them off guard. Right from the beginning of the life of the state, Western church authorities have been loathe to alienate their friends and clients in the Arab world by conceding the existence of the State of Israel, except when strictly necessary – as, for example, when collecting funds for support of church activites from the Israeli Ministry for Religious Affairs. Until recently, maps that local church groups made available to tourists indicated that they were visiting HOLY LAND. But this usage has declined in recent years, not because it insults the State of Israel (which it does), but because it is now objected to by Palestinians.[3]

From the very beginning, leaders of the Christian Arab communities, led by their clergy, have been blaming the State of Israel for the alleged decline of the Christian communities. For example, Greek Catholic priest Elias Chacour (founder of Mar Elija college and author of *Blood Brothers*, 1984, and *We Belong to the Land*, 1990) says: "The Holy Land is being emptied of its Christians." The Holy Land Foundation (begun in Washington, DC, in 1994 by the Franciscan Custody and certain of the local churches in Jerusalem "to alert Christians world wide of the present dilemma that Christians are facing in the Holy Land") declares: "Because of a policy of systematic discrimination that impinges on every facet of daily life, Palestinian Christians along with Palestinian Moslems, can no longer live peacefully and securely in their native land. Christians are departing from the Holy land at an alarming rate and it is possible that they could one day entirely cease to exist in the very land where Christ founded His Church."[4] This conclusion is echoed by the World Council of Churches, the Middle East Council of Churches, and other Church spokesmen who depend on Palestinian sources. Members of the United Methodist Churches of the United States have been told, for example, that "Christians now comprise less than three percent of the population of Israel and of what is destined to become sovereign Palestine. Because they have had a continuous presence in the holy land since the time of Jesus and were part of the first community – the church of Jerusalem – their diminishing numbers and lack of political rights is a cause of concern to the universal church."[5] In this same vein, Bishop Baycroft of Ottawa, described to a Christmas Eve congregation at his cathedral in 1997 what he and thirty-seven other Anglicans of the Diocese of Ottawa had learned during a month-long pilgrimage during which they traced the steps of St Peter and St Paul through Israel and Turkey to Rome. His impression was that Israel was "a state built on oppression," that it therefore "stands under the divine judgements [for its] evil, wickedness, cruelty and oppression." The bishop learned from his hosts in the Palestinian Christian communitees that Israel's restrictions on the free movement of Christian clergy explain why Christians in Gaza and the West Bank (that is, within the jurisdiction of the Palestinian Authority) "are being reduced to such a minority."[6]

The testimonies offered by the Palestinian Christians are never challenged in mainline Christian circles, where the feeling exists that European or American outsiders cannot possibly know what the local Christians know of their own experience. As a result, even Western Christians who are otherwise well disposed to Israel are often convinced that in religious matters Israel has turned out to be, if not actually a persecutor, something of a bully now that the Jews have a block of their own to be a bully on.

There are no two ways about the fact that the Jews are a vast majority in the Jewish state. To provide Jews with a homeland was, after all, the reason for creating the state in the first place, as the United Nations had understood in November 1947. From time to time Jewish alarmists, pointing to such basic realities as the much smaller birthrate on the Jewish, as compared to Arab, side, have raised the possibility that Jews will eventually be a minority in their own state. Renewed waves of immigration in recent years have once again put off that day – but not necessarily to the Greek kalends. Since 1948, the Muslim population of the State of Israel has increased from 110,000 to 887,000, while the Muslim *percentage* of the whole population, despite massive Jewish immigration, has also risen: from 9.5 percent to 14.8 percent.[7] Likewise, despite the propaganda from the Palestinian side, the number of Christians resident in Israel is not declining.

To avoid sleight-of-hand, it is always useful to set a disputed statistic in a larger context – in this case, the total population of Israel. At the end of 1998, official Israeli statistics showed that there are slightly over six million inhabitants in Israel, of whom 4,756,000 are Jews (79.4 percent) (including 130,000 in Judea, Samaria, and Gaza); 887,000 were Muslims (about 14.8 percent); 190,000 were Christians (2.9 percent); and 100,000 were Druze (1.7 percent).[8] Throughout the half-century of Israel's existence, Christians have held their own as a component of the population. There were some 150,000 Christians living in the Mandate of Palestine before the UN Declaration of 2 November 1947. In the course of the 1948–49 War of Independence, some 50,000 (that is, about one-third) fled from Israel. Today, within the borders of what had been the Mandate of Palestine – that is, the whole of the present State of Israel as well as the Palestinian Authority PA – there are about 180,000 Christians.

During the period of Jordanian rule (1949–67), the Christian population in East Jerusaelm and the West Bank continued to decline. It is estimated that another 12,000 Palestinian Christians left the West Bank and Gaza between 1967 and 1992. But through natural increase, Christians have maintained their place in the whole popluation equation: in 1948 Christians made up 2.9 percent of the whole (34,000 in a total population of 1.2 million); in late 1995 there were 160,000 Christians living in Israel (still 2.9 percent of the total population of 5.7 million); in late 1998, there were 190,000, which is 3.2 percent of a total population of 6 million.[9]

One circumstance that helps to explain the perception that so many tourists have of a Christian community declining under Israeli rule is that the longest stop on their tour is likely to be in the Old City of Jerusalem. Here they visit the "Christian Quarter" of the Old City, where the guides point out the once-splendid Muristan area, and where they see many untenanted shops and other signs of decay. (A similiar sight meets them in Bethlehem, which is now governed under the Palestinian Authority.)[10] Jerusalem as a whole held 25,000 Christians in 1948, most of them in the eastern part of the city. Between 1948 and 1967, when that part of the city was under Jordanian rule, the figure declined to 10,000.[11] Since 1967, the Jewish population in the whole of Jerusalem has increased two hundred percent, and Muslim population forty percent. Unlike these two constituencies, the Christians (who are mainly Arabs) have had high rates of emigration; thus, according to Dr Bernard Sabella, a professor of Sociology at Bethlehem University, about 2,500 Christians have left the city since 1967. To add to the bleakness of the picture, commentators like Sabella, whose purpose is to highlight the plight of Arab Christians, insist that we deduct from the number of Christians resident in Jerusalem the "expatriates" (that is, the Europeans, Americans, and Africans who will, most likely, not live out their entire lives in Jerusalem) from the number of Christians resident in Jerusalem, in which case, the present number is reduced to about 11,000. But this last number is still slightly higher than the number in the days before the Six-Day War of 1967 (about 10,000). The fact is that while the number of Christians resident in the Christian Quarter (that is, the Arab-Christian Quarter) and the Armenian Quarter is shrinking, the total number of Christians in East Jerusalem has *not* declined; and it is certainly not true that there are fewer Christians in Jerusalem as a whole. Since 1967, when the city was reunited under Israeli rule, the Christian population in East Jerusalem has in fact risen by fifty percent, to stand today at some 15,000.[12]

Three other major concentrations of Christians exist: one is in Nazareth (under direct Israeli rule), and the others are in the Judean town of Bethlehem and the Samarian town of Ramallah, both now under the Palestinian Authority. The first of these three communities is growing in numbers; the latter two are declining.

In summary, the Christian population of Israel (not including Judea, Samaria, and Gaza) rose in absolute terms from about 34,000 in 1948 to nearly 180,000 in 1998 – a sixfold increase. Adding to this number the 42,000 who live in West Bank and the 9,000 who live in Gaza gives a total Christian population in the Holy Land of about 230,000 in 2000.

Taking Israel alone, the *percentage* of Christians in the whole population is virtually the same after fifty years of Israel's existence.[13] At the beginning of the Jewish New Year 5760 (late 1999), there were nearly 190,000 Christians, still making up about 2.9 percent of the whole population. That the increasing number of Christians is not accompanied by an increase in the Christian proportion of the whole is owing *mainly* to the large-scale Jewish immigration, which, in its most recent wave, is largely drawn from the former Soviet empire.[14] *Secondarily*, it is owing to the departure of many Arab Christians bound for the West.

Meanwhile, despite the large immigration of Jews, the proportion of the population that is Muslim is increasing, owing to a much higher birthrate than that of the Israeli Jews, coupled with a miniscule rate of emigration.

While the Christian population of Israel proper has increased throughout the half-century of the State's existence, it has *decreased* in the West Bank and Gaza in the same period. In 1967 the Christian population of the areas held by Jordan and Egypt was estimated at 33,000. As I have noted, this population declined steadily for about a quarter-century thereafter. When the Oslo peace negotiations began – that is, when the daily lives of Palestinian Arabs started to come under the effective rule of their own leaders – the rate of decline of Christian numbers began to accelerate further.

The beginning of wisdom, however, with respect to the present life and future prospects of Christians resident in the Holy Land is the reality that *Israel is the only jurisdiction in the Middle East where, over the past half-century, the Christian population has grown in absolute numbers and has remained stable as a proportion relative to the whole population.* To put it another way: *Everywhere in the Middle East except in Israel the Christian population is declining – in most places, precipitously.*

In the Middle East generally there has been a devasting reduction in Christian numbers in the last century. At the end of the nineteenth century, thirteen percent of population of the Middle East was Christian. Today, it is two percent – a lesser proportion than in Israel. According to Walid Phares, president of the World Lebanese Organization and professor of Political Science at Florida International University, [15] there are more than twenty-six million Christians in the Middle East: twelve million in Egypt, seven million in southern Sudan, 1.5 million in Lebanon (and another 4.5 million Lebanese Christians living elsewhere in the Middle East), and a further one million or so living under other Arab regimes. Of this twenty-six million, only about 600,000 are ethnic Arabs. Speaking at the Third Christian Zionist Congress in Jerusalem in 1996, Phares complained about the tendency of Western media to portray Palestinian Christians as the major body of Christians in the Middle East, and to picture them as suffering in an extraordinary way because they are Arabs, and because they live in the Jewish state. It is not likely to dawn on readers of American newspapers that the Christian Arabs of Israel are less than one percent of the Christian population of the Middle East, most of whom are suffering truly brutal persecution in Arab lands because they are Christian and because, for the most part, they are *not* Arabs.

THE CHRISTIAN COMMUNITIES OF ISRAEL

Keeping in mind, then, the entire Middle Eastern context, the most noteworthy feature of the situation of the Christian community in Israel is its *exceptional stability*. Of the roughly 190,000 Christians living in Israel, about 55,000 are Greek Orthodox, about 45,000 are Greek Catholic (almost all of these in the Galilee), about 26,000 are Latins (that is, Roman Catholic), and about 4,000 are Protestant (mainly Anglican and Lutheran).[16] What first strikes the Christian visitor to Israel is the variety of Christian communities there. This contrasts with the situation in Arab lands, where the few Christians remaining are typically members of the one Christian body that traces historically to the days before Islam when the region was formally a Christian land. In contrast, because Eretz Israel has always been the Holy Land, every distinct body of Christians in the world strives to have a presence there. The same cannot be said of any other land in the world.

In some cases, the representation is miniscule, consisting of *either:*

(a) a tiny number of persons of strong religious vocation appointed, in effect, to maintain the presence of a certain church, that otherwise has no place in the life of the region. This small cohort typically clings to a holy site – if possible, to the Holy Sepulchre. One example is the small Ethiopian community on the roof of the Holy Sepulchre; or

(b) a small number of persons who have come as missionaries, with or without denominational auspices, or perhaps to study, or to experience the privilege of living in the Holy Land. These, joined by a fluctuating number of visitors to the Holy Land or short-term expatriates from the US or Europe, worship together in small bodies, often in rented premises. There is such a range of small churches that there is no official or public list of them all.[17] Each of these churches, regardless of the size of its local establishment, takes itself far more seriously than it is taken at home – that is, in the region of its greatest numerical strength – because here the body is strongly infected with the spirit of urgency about all religious matters that is found everywhere in the Holy Land. The churches that are the most visible in the US are the least visible in the Holy Land. Conversely, the churches that are most visible in Jerusalem, Bethlehem, and Nazareth figure among those that are least visible in North America and have the least social importance and political effect there. It is usually the case that American or British Christian pilgrims, visiting the Holy Sepulchre, for example, will meet for the first time in their lives the Greek Orthodox or the Armenian Orthodox; and if they take the time to go up on the roof (as a few will do) they will find the Coptic and the Ethiopian churches – which they have never heard of, and which, they are shocked to be told, have been in the world for a millennium or even a millennium and a half before the church to which they themselves belong. Responses to these moments of discovery range widely. The moment might mark the beginning of a serious study of the alternative ways of Christian worship and variations of doctrine, leading to a greater ecumenical spirit. Or (one suspects, more typically) there is a stiffening of the spirit of resentment against "superstition."

CHURCHES OF THE EAST

The Christian communities whose historical roots are deepest in this region are those we call, for convenience, the churches of the East. Their subdivisions seem almost infinite in number. The principal division, however, is between the Orthodox churches and the Oriental churches. These churches, taken together, are the lineal descendants of all the churches that existed in the days of the Byzantine (that is, Eastern Roman) empire. The former (Orthodox) are the legatees of the Church that sustained the first Christian Empire (the Byzantine Empire); and the latter (the Oriental churches), much divided among themselves, are the legatees of churches that were at odds with this official Byzantine church, in matters of theology and ecclesiology, and were, with various ups and downs, subject to much discrimination and even persecution while that empire held sway.

The Orthodox churches were those on the winning side of the theological war that the Catholic church sought to conclude forever with the Trinitarian formulae worked out at the Council of Chalcedon, 451. The theologians who opted for the various losing formulae (generically called "Monophysite," or "One Nature") belonged, for the most part, to churches at the furthest geographical remove from Rome and Constantinople and continued to flourish so long as the writ of the Western church leaders did not run in those remotest parts of Rome's empire. Indeed, some of the Church communities extended into India and other parts of furthest Asia, including western and coastal China.[18] These churches are collectively called the "Pre-Chalcedonian," or, as I shall do here (since the debates about the nature of the Trinity do not affect the present story), simply the "Oriental" churches. The Oriental churches include the Armenian, Coptic (concentrated in Egypt), Ethiopian, and Syrian churches, and the Syrian church in India. The preponderance of the roughly twenty-two million members of these churches live in the Middle East, though increasing numbers of expatriate communities are appearing in Europe and America.

Under the *dhimmi* system imposed by the Muslim conquerors from the seventh century forward (which I shall discuss briefly in chapter 5), all Christians were reduced to an inferior legal situation; the Orthodox Christians now found themselves reduced to the inferior status that they had imposed upon the Oriental Christians – or even worse.

Orthodox Christian historians take the line today that the pledges made by the British, French, and Americans to the Zionists, embodied in the Balfour Declaration of 1917, were contradictory to the spirit and the letter of their pledges to the Arab nationalists. They describe Zionism as an arm of Western imperialism. Most of the Oriental churches, too, remember the Ottomans as oppressors; but they are also aware that the religious communities they belong to have subsequently been victimized to various degrees in the successor Arab states created in the twentieth century. The Armenians are an interesting case in this regard. As is well known, the Armenians retain bitter memories of the Ottoman Empire; they have a deep distrust of all Muslim regimes, and this has caused them, by and large, to be more open to persuasion about the advantages of Zionism – as, we must assume, would the Assyrian Nestorians have done, had they survived (see below, page 116).

Orthodox

All of these derive from the world of the Eastern Roman (Byzantine) Empire, and all recognize (at least nominally) the primacy of the patriarch of Constantinople. The principal groups are as follows,

(a) *Greek Orthodox.* This is by far the largest congregation in Israel today – slightly more than fifty percent of the whole Christian number. While the congregations are today overwhelmingly Arab speaking, the leadership tries (but with increasing resistance from the resident membership) to preserve the Hellenic character of the church by continuing the hegemony of the Greeks at the top of the hierarchy. There are about 120,000 members in the Holy Land today, living under either Israeli or Palestinian rule. The Government of Israel has inherited from the Ottoman Empire (via the British Mandate) the responsibility, under the *Status Quo*, of reassuring the Government of Greece of its fair treatment of the Greek Orthodox churches.

(b) A smaller community of *Russian Orthodox,* mainly tracing from Russian missions to Holy Land in the nineteenth century.

(c) Some even smaller groups (Georgians, Bulgarians, and others) consisting mainly of monks and nuns.

Since early in the nineteenth century, and through the subsequent succession of Russian regimes, down to the present post-Communist Republic of Russia, the Russian political authority has maintained a right to be consulted as the protector of the Slavic Orthodox populations of this region. Today, this means that the Ministry for Religious Affairs of the Government of Israel has to consult regularly with Moscow, assuring the patriarch of Moscow and the president of Russia that their wishes are being met with respect to the disposition of properties of Slavic Orthodox churches, their educational systems, their religious courts, and so on.

Oriental

(a) *Armenian Orthodox.* This church dates from 301, when Armenia became (so far as we know) the first kingdom to embrace Christianity officially in a moment of time. The community in Jerusalem dates from the fifth century and persisted under Muslim rule from 638. In the late nineteenth century the community grew in number, though its life became more precarious, when it absorbed refugees from the massacres in Turkey; and similarly in the middle decades of the twentieth century the community absorbed many who fled the Soviet regime. But since 1939 the community has declined from 15,000 to about 4,000 (in Jerusalem, Haifa, Jaffa, and Bethlehem.) Now that there is a sovereign Republic of Armenia, Israel consults that regime with respect to the interests of the Armenian churches.

(b) *Coptic Orthodox.* These belong to another very early Christian nation, one established in Egypt long before the Arabs arrived. They have about one thousand members living in Jerusalem, Bethlehem, and Nazareth. The Republic of Egypt is the party that Israel consults when the interests of this small religious community are at issue.

(c) *Ethiopian Orthodox.* The presence of this community in Jerusalem was noted by European pilgrims as early as the fourth century, and we know that they persisted through the Middle Ages. But their rights at the Holy Places were lost to their larger and more powerful competitors, the Orthodox and the Latins, during the Turkish period; they were not dealt into the *Status Quo* agreement of the eighteenth and nineteenth centuries. Since the establishment of diplomatic relations between Israel and Ethiopia, pilgrimage has grown greatly. In the 1990s there were several incidents – embarassing to the Government of Israel – in which individuals from Ethiopia who came as tourists then sought and won asylum in Israel, because of the political situation in Ethiopia.

(d) There are several smaller "Monophysite" churches, including the *Syrian Orthodox* (or "Jacobites"), numbering about 5,000, resident in Jerusalem and Bethlehem, Ramallah and Jericho.

Despite their many differences, I have included the church bodies mentioned so far in a single large category, the Churches of the East, because, in common, and in contrast to the Churches of the West, they were all shaped by more than a millennium of life in a Muslim empire. They share with the Muslims the mixed attitude of awe and resentment towards the cultural and intellectual accomplishments of the West. They stood apart from the Cold War. These Churches of the East were not included in the ranks of the World Council of Churches when that body was formed in 1948. However, by stages they have been introduced to its ranks over the years. Nowadays, the officers of the WCC turn immediately to leaders of the Churches of the East for expert knowledge of the Middle East situation and hand over to them the largest part of the burden of writing the WCC's position papers on related matters. There is an element of condescension in this. Western liberal Christians are attracted to the Eastern churches by nostalgia for the Western churches' own lost world. In a recent Middle East Council of Churches document, William Schwartz speaks in this romantic vein of the difference between how Western and Eastern Christians perceive Christianity: "For most westerners, Christianity is defined in individualistic, personal and doctrinal terms. Eastern Christians tend to see themselves as a community with an ethnic or cultural background and defined traditions. Continuity is a principal factor in eastern culture, while westerners often view change as equivalent to progress. These are not contradictory values, but there is little common ground between them."[19]

The Churches of the East, which portray themselves as victims of Western imperialism, speak to the European and American left's anti-colonial enthusiasm. Furthermore, the Churches of the East are always ready to assist the Churches of the West in seeing the connection – which might otherwise escape them – between imperialism and Zionism. Good taste usually restrains the editors of Church publications in the West from acknowledging this linkage explicitly; but it is constantly brought out as something that Eastern Christians, and Arab Christians in particular, understandably feel. The line is that we must be constantly alert and sensitive to the conviction among Palestinian Christians that the State of Israel is an engine of Western imperialism, a thing foisted upon innocent Arabs as compensation for the guilt feelings of Western Christians arising out of the unfortunate matter of the mistreatment of the Jews – now, happily, a thing of no immediate historical relevance. The thought always is that it would be rude to argue about this history with the people who have suffered it.

CHURCHES OF THE WEST

Roman Catholic (Latin and Uniate)

(a) *Latin*   All Western churches in the Holy Land prior to Crusades were under the Orthodox patriarchate, situated in Byzantium (Constantinople). "Latin" churches (that is, Western European, that is Roman Catholic) first appeared with the Crusaders (1099–1291). After the crusader kingdoms were destroyed, the Franciscan order remained in place to represent the Latin churches until diplomatic dealings between the Ottoman Empire and France, which began in 1847, led to their reconstitition on more or less normal hierarchical lines. Today (in 2000), the Latin church in the Middle East is headed by the Patriarch of Jerusalem (who is an Arab, Michel Sabbah) and three vicars (one in Nazareth, another in Amman, Jordan, and a third in Cyprus.) About twenty thousand Roman Catholic Christians live in Israel, and another ten thousand are estimated to live under the Palestinian Authority.

(b) *Uniate*   The picture of the Christianity in this region is further complicated, for serious students, by the existence of certain churches that have a foot in both East and West – the "Eastern Rite," or "Uniate," churches. These are certain communities of churches that came out of the Orthodox history but attached themselves to the Roman Catholic church, mainly in the late eighteenth or in the nineteenth century, entering into agreements under which they main-

tained most of the features of their separate liturgy, liturgical language, and practice (for example, permission of their clergy to
marry). A number of reasons played their part in those negotiations,
but the principal one was that attaching themselves to the Church of
Rome provided the patronage and protection of European Catholic
powers, notably France, against the Ottoman masters. With respect to
some of the generalizations I have so far developed, the Uniates are
closer to the opinion of the Orthodox than to Roman Catholic
opinion. Nonetheless, Uniate churches take their direction on the
largest matters of policy from Rome and not from any of the Orthodox patriarchs. Uniate churches include:

(i) The *Maronite* church, of Syrian origin, has been formally
attached to the Roman Catholic church since 1182; its principal forces
are concentrated in Lebanon.[20]

(ii) The *Greek Catholic* church, created in 1724 through schism in
the Greek Orthodox church in Antioch. It has absorbed some other
churches of Greek Orthodox origin and numbers about 53,000 today,
the largest proportion resident in the diocese of Galilee,

(iii) Other smaller Uniate churches include the *Armenian Catholic,
Coptic Catholic,* and *Chaldean Catholic* (Assyrian).

Protestant

No Protestant church existed in the Holy Land prior to the nineteenth
century. The first Protestants to live in the region were British, American, German, and other European expatriates involved in the work of
exploration and archaeology. They were followed by missionaries from
the same lands. The first chapter in the story of official Protestant
church presence begins with a united Anglican-Prussian Protestant
bishopric, 1841–86, which subsequently divided into Anglican and
Lutheran components in 1886.

(a) *The Episcopal Church in Jerusalem and the Middle East.* Today, there
are about forty-five hundred Anglicans in the diocese of the Middle
East, of whom three thousand, the largest Protestant community in
the Holy Land, live in Israel. The Anglican bishop has his seat in the
Cathedral Church of St George the Martyr, in the Arab section of
Jerusalem. For several years now, the senior clergy of the cathedral
have all been Arab.

(b) The *Lutheran church* has about two hundred German-speaking
members and about five hundred Arabic in its congregations in
Jerusalem and Bethlehem. Again, the senior clergy of this denomination have all been Arab in recent years. Bishop Munib A. Younan was
installed in January 1998 as bishop of the Evangelical Lutheran

Church of Jordan (which includes the congregations in Jerusalem and Bethlehem), which he leads from his post in the Evangelical Lutheran church in the Old City of Jerusalem.

(c) *Baptists* have ten churches and centres in Israel: Jerusalem, Acre, Cana, Haifa, Jaffa, Kfar Yassif, Nazareth, Petah-tikva, Rama, and Tur'an. The total membership of these essentially autonomous churches is about nine hundred, mostly Arabic.

(d) *The Church of Scotland* (Presbyterian) has had a mission in Galilee since 1840, and a church in Jerusalem since shortly after World War I. Today, a small expatriate community shares in worship with a somewhat larger number of Arabs living in Jerusalem and its environs. The long-serving lay leader of this congregation is an Arab, Rizak Abushar; but the presiding minister has always been a Scot (currently, Canon Iain F. Paton).

(e) A number of small Protestant groups meet in various places throughout Israel, mainly in Jerusalem. Of these, there are perhaps four hundred "charismatic" Christians, some with backgrounds in the American *Church of God* (Pentecostal) or the *Pentecostal Assemblies of Canada,* and others of various backgrounds, meeting in small groups, in rented facilities – such as the King of Kings Assembly, which meets in the YMCA (opposite the King David Hotel).

Mormon

In a category of its own is the *Church of Jesus Christ of Latter Day Saints* (Mormon), which has about two hundred members in Israel plus about 170 students at the Jerusalem Center for Near Eastern Studies (a branch of Brigham Young University of Utah).

Messianic Jews

Yaakov Ariel, now the foremost scholar of the subject of Christian missions to Jews in the last century and a quarter, is convinced that the fastest-growing Christian community in Israel is the Messianic Jews – that is, Jews who have formally converted to Christianity and organized themselves in groups that deliberately retain Jewish ethnic and cultural identity, and that, to various degrees, have retained features of traditional Jewish religion in their Christian worship. Ariel estimates that about three hundred people were counted as Messianic Jews in the 1960s, and about six thousand today. There is reason to believe that many thousands more Israelis quietly regard themselves as "believers in Yeshua" but have not undertaken the public stigma that follows an announced "conversion." A large number have immigrated to Israel from America and represent some part of the fruit of the latest wave of American missions to the Jews, which began in the 1970s, when "Jews For Jesus" entered the field. But the greatest growth is now among recent Russian immigrants, few of whom have had much exposure to traditional Judaism, but all of whom have been subject to the attentions of evangelical missionaries from the West since the 1970s and 1980s – well before the fall of the iron curtain. Some fellowships of Messianic Jews hold services of their own on the premises of certain denominational congregations – for example, at Christ Church, just inside the Jaffa Gate. Others have their own premises and conduct a variety of educational programs, in addition to regular worship, in a variety of languages that include Hebrew, Russian, English, and Amharic (the language of Ethiopia). Some are charismatic; others are not. What they all have in common is a strictly evangelical, conservative theology, featuring a strong literalist dispensationalist millennialism. All share their faith actively among the people of Israel. As some of their numbers are reported in the membership lists of various denominational churches, it is not clear what number one should attribute to a distinct column of "Messianic Jews."[21]

THE GOVERNMENT OF ISRAEL AND THE CHRISTIAN COMMUNITIES OF ISRAEL

The most important financial contribution that the Government of Israel makes to the work of the Christian communities comes out of the budget of the minister of Education. This is the US $50 million (roughly) that goes each year to pay about eighty percent of the salaries of teachers in Christian elementary and secondary schools. (These schools must include the curriculum that is necessary for Israeli matriculation – that is, for eligibility to higher education in Israel and, for that matter, to universities in the West.)

Within the Israeli Ministry for Religious Affairs there is a Department for Christian Communities, presided over by a director whose job might just possibly be the most challenging job in Israel, if not on the whole face of the earth.[22] While ninety-nine percent of the roughly $400 million budget of the ministry of Religious Affairs has gone to Jewish institutions in recent years, there is still enough assigned to the Department for Christian Communities to support a range of important activities. The director tries to attend all the public occasions sponsored by the churches and such occasions as the induction of bishops, etc. He welcomes at the airport virtually all of the Church dignitaries who visit Israel and helps them during their travels. He provides financial assistance towards the upkeep of certain Christian holy places. He arranges for the rebate of millions of dollars of customs duties on major items, such as the expensive automobiles favoured by the heads of the Christian congregations.

Some years ago, I had an opportunity to see the then director, Daniel Rossing, at work under circumstances that graphically illustrated the complexities of the task. Rossing, who began life as a Lutheran in Wisconsin and converted to Judaism as a young man, is well educated in Church history and theology. He is the only man I have ever met who could explain in clear language the differences between Pre-Chalcedonian (Monophysite) and Chalcedonian (Trinitarian), Ante-Nicean and Nicean, Latins and Uniate, Maronites, Jacobites, Greek-Catholics, Syriacs, Armenians, Armenian Catholics, Armenian Orthodox, and so on.

The occasion was a tour of the places of worship and the working premises of the various Christian communities in the Old City organized by the director for visiting academics at the Hebrew University, all Jewish (I and my wife were the only exceptions), and most Americans. We followed Rossing from the Greek Orthodox patriarch's residence to the Armenian archbishops' residence, then to the Greek Catholic headquarters. Each archbishop in turn gave us a little summary of the History of the Church – capital H, capital C – pausing at the points where the church of his particular tradition suffered some unspeakable affront at the hands of the church we would would be visiting next. The director's aspect of unmixed goodwill remained unaffected, even when the host archbishop delivered his pitch from beneath a portrait of the king of Jordan, then officially in a state of war with Israel. Nothing that any of these dignitaries said gave away for a moment that he recognized, let alone appreciated, that all of this was happening in the State of Israel and under its auspices. Nor did he seem to recognize that this company of correctly courteous Jewish academics might have something less than his own consuming interest in the Church history he was reciting.

The highlight came when we arrived at the Holy Sepulchre. There, dignitaries representing the three churches that have principal custody of the holy places (Latin, Armenian, and Greek Orthodox) attached themselves to us in sequence. One dignitary took the director aside and poured out to him very earnestly and firmly his complaint that one of the other occupant churches in the Holy Sepulchre had put a lampstand on a corner of the wall that belonged to his church. The director promised to look into it. The thought occurred to me that in the past, before Israel took responsibility for the Holy City, this would have been one of those incidents one finds in such abundance in books about the history of the Christian churches in the

Holy City where words would lead to shoving, and shoving to blows, and blows to demonstrations, and then to riots, and people would be left dead in job lots all around the grounds of the Holy Sepulchre.

Ever since that day, the director of Christian Relations has been carrying out his daily task of tempering hostilities between the leaders of the various Christian bodies. His daily work does not get noticed in the papers. A rare exception is an item that appeared in the international edition of the *Jerusalm Post* in March 1993:

NEW BID TO END CHURCH SPAT
The Government has appointed a new interministerial committee to try to resolve the over 20-year old conflict over Deir el-Sultan, the Monastery on the roof of the Church of the Holy Sepulchre.

In April 1970, the Ethiopian Church, taking advantage of the fact that the Coptic Christians were at their Easter rites, changed the lock on a door linking the rooftop monastery with two chapels and a stairway leading to the church below.

The Copts charged the change had been made with the collusion of the police. The Ethiopians claimed they had historical right to control access to the chapels and passageway, a right that had been usurped by the Copts. Both churches have a wealth of documents to prove their ownership of the disputed chapels and passageway. The question gained importance since the peace treaty with Egypt in 1982, since the Egyptian government backs the Copts. The Ethiopian government, meanwhile, has always stood behind its church.

In reaction to the appointment of the new committee, composed of Foreign Minister Shimon Peres [a man whose interest in religious matters was always miniscule], Justice Minister David Liba'i, and a representative of the Religious Affairs ministry, Coptic Archbishop Dr Anbva Abraham said that "millions" of Coptic pilgrims would come to the Holy Land were it not for this dispute. However, he said that there was currently no friction between his church and that of the Ethiopians.

"We and the Ethiopians [have] good relations because the problem is in the hands of the Israeli government," he said.

The Ethiopian archbishop was not available for comment.[23]

Any serious student of the history of Jerusalem since the fall of the Second Temple knows that there was never a time when there has been less resort to violence among the religious communities in their dealings with one another than now, under the sovereign auspices of the State of Israel. Jewish custody of Jerusalem is the only arrangement for keeping the religious peace of Jerusalem that has ever worked. Because there is so little knowledge of this history, even in the ranks of the educated clergy, almost everyone has the opposite impression.

Israel's liberal and self-interested (in the correct sense) efforts to establish religious peace in Jerusalem have simply been shouted down with complaints and tendentious press coverage. The situation has been considerably complicated since the Oslo process began. While Israel has not conceded anything to the Palestine National Authority's claims to Jerusalem, the regime of Palestinian president Yassir Arafat has tried, in many ways, to insinuate its authority on the ecclesiastical ground. For example: while Israel, for its own reasons, has formally handed over custody of Muslim spiritual matters to the king of Jordan, President Arafat has insisted that these matters belong to the political realm – that is, to himself; and to prove this point he has insisted on appointing the mufti of Jerusalem (the spiritual leader of the Muslim population there). At this writing, there were two muftis of Jerusalem – one appointed by the late King Hussein of Jordan, the other by Yassir Arafat; the latter (Sheikh Ikrama Sabri) seemed to have the effective allegiance of most of the Muslim population. In the same spirit, Arafat has tried to coax Christian leaders to acknowledge his regime as the morally legitimate heir to the status of protector of the holy places in Jerusalem under the *Status Quo* and to refer their differences to him. Israel has made it clear to the churches that it will not tolerate divided allegiance in these matters.

In April 1997, the owners of the Hanke mosque, across the narrow street from the Holy Sepulchre, suddenly took it into their heads to expand their premises, without getting the normal city permits, by closing the gap between their building and the Holy Sepulchre on one side and a smaller gap between their building and a Greek Orthodox patriarch on the other side. In effect, they simply annexed parts of these two buildings and made them over into facilities for their own use, including toilets. Keen to demonstrate its goodwill towards the Christians and its influence over the Muslims, Arafat's government attempted to deal itself into the dispute that followed. The leaders of the three churches with principal responsibility for the Holy Sepulchre refused to be enticed, confining their appeals for redress to the Israeli channel. The feeling in the Palestinian political community was that the churches had broken ranks with the Palestinian people by preferring not to avail themselves of Arafat's auspices.[24] But it is evident that the churches knew that to take up his offer would have been to ally themselves publicly with those who denied the legitimacy of Israel's presence in Jerusalem. The stakes were much too high. Quite apart from that, one suspects that the Church leaders, on this occasion and many like it, were voting quietly in favour of the record of fair-mindedness and relative disinterestedness with which the Israeli Ministry for Religious Affairs has handled such issues in the past.

However Arafat might have dealt with this particular matter, there could be no doubt that appeasing the Muslim population would, in the long term, have to be a greater consideration for the Palestine National Authority.

All the Christian religious notables with whom the Israeli Ministry for Religious Affairs dealt in the matter of the Hanke mosque preside over local congregations that are overwhelmingly Arab and vehemently anti-Israeli and anti-Zionist. All are members of the Middle East Council of Churches, whose officers are mostly Arab speaking and were in the pre-Oslo days publicly declared supporters of the terrorist activities of the PLO and PFLP, and, through the 1980s, of the Intifada. By way of example: in 1969 Elias Khoury, an Anglican priest from Ramallah, then Dean of the Anglican Cathedral Church of St. George the Martyr in Jerusalem, was caught and convicted by Israeli authorities for having transported explosive devices inside a medicine chest placed in his car for the Popular Front for the Liberation of Palestine, one of the subgroups within the PLO that denounced then and denounces now all negotiations with Israel, and that has carried out several assassinations of other PLO leaders. The explosive materials were later used to carry out terrorist actions at the British consulate in Jerusalem and at a supermarket in Jerusalem. Two were killed and eleven wounded. Afterwards, as part of a deal with the Israeli government (which, as always in these cases, was trying to minimize the bad publicity that follows when Israeli authority appears to be strong-arming Christian leaders), Khoury was allowed to emigrate to Jordan, where he was made bishop of the Anglican church in Amman. He was subsequently appointed a member of the Executive Council of the PLO. Later, another Arab Palestinian and champion of the PLO, the Anglican priest Samir Kafitty, took up the mantle of Dean Khoury at the Cathedral Church of St George the Martyr and later still became the bishop. In 1998 Bishop Riad Abu-Assal and Dean Naim Ateek were continuing the cathedral's tradition of anti-Zionism.

A similar case is that of the Greek Catholic archbishop Hilarion Capucci, who, throughout the spring of 1974, used his official limousine and the cover of his priestly office to personally smuggle explosives, submachine guns, and even katyusha rockets into Israel, which were then used in PLO terrorist actions accounting for the loss of many lives inside Israel. He was finally caught on 18 August 1974, tried, convicted, and sentenced to a total of fifty-seven years of imprisonment.[25] Greek Catholic patriarch Maximos Hakim summed up the reaction of Palestinian Christians: "Is this Bishop reprehensible if he thought it was his duty to bear arms or help the fedayeen or take actions that Israel does not approve?" Bishop Capucci's successor, Monsignor Lutfi

Laham, was equally puzzled by Israel's behaviour: "Bishop Capucci," he said, "liked politics. He believed that a clergyman should be active politically in his society." The Holy See did not repudiate Capucci; indeed, it pleaded publicly with Israel to understand the historical context and forgive: "This episode is a painful blow to one of the glorious Eastern Catholic communities, the Greek Catholic Church, where Monsignor Capucci has exercised for many years the episcopal function ... This verdict, unfortunately, cannot but aggravate tension in the complex situation of this territory where, notwithstanding laudable efforts, just peace is far from being established and where populations live in a climate of anguish, conflict, and uncertainty."[26] Capucci was reprieved in 1977, on the direct appeal of Pope Paul VI, who gave his personal and official assurance that no consequences prejudicial to Israel would be permitted to follow, and that Capucci would be forbidden to play any political role again. In plain words: the Holy See did not keep its word in this matter. Capucci became more visible than ever, on a wider stage. After his release, he went to Rome, where he celebrated mass in the presence of the Libyan, Syrian, and Egyptian ambassadors to the Holy See. "Jesus Christ," Capucci has said, "was the first *fedayeen*. I am just following his example." In January 1979 he attended meetings of the PLO National Council in Damascus and thereafter served as the Vatican's contact with the PLO's "foreign minister," Farouk Kaddoumi. In 1979 Pope John Paul II dispatched Capucci to Teheran to represent the concerns of the Vatican before the new regime of the Ayatollah Khomeini.[27]

At the time the State of Israel was created, the leaders of the various Churches of the West were people whose home bases were in Europe or America; they were born, raised, and educated in the West and had been sent by their mother churches to preside over congregations established in Israel. By contrast, those who presided over the Churches of the East tended to have lived always in the region; for the most part, the principal seats of authority of their churches were not in Western Europe but in the Near East or Middle East. Before the modern State of Israel came into being, the churches of the West had been generally well disposed to the Jewish cause. Most of their congregants in Europe and America had welcomed the Balfour Declaration. During the 1920s and 1930s, as the League of Nations and the Powers mulled over the problem of Palestine, they were, if not actively helpful, at least not disposed to get in the way. Then, during the two and a half years, roughly, that followed the revelation of the Holocaust, moved by the desperate plight of Jewish refugees, they generally held up the arms of the Western politicians while the UN was disposing of the Mandate (1945–48). But during the 1960s and 1970s, these same churches realigned their political position to match that of the Churches of the East, whose leaders had opposed the Balfour Declaration, the partition decision of 1947, and recognition of the state in 1948 and had proclaimed consistently throughout the half-century following that all those actions were mistakes that must be redressed.

Members of the Churches of the West who lived in the State of Israel at the beginning of modern Israel's history amounted to only a tiny fraction of the whole Christian community. The leaders of the vastly more populous Eastern Churches felt uncomfortable about the motives of these Churches of the West, given the history of their "missionary" activities among local people whose ancestors were long settled in the Churches of the East. At first, the political weight of the Churches of the West in the State of Israel owed much to the fact that their leaders could speak languages in common with the new leaders of Israel (English usually, but often French as well) and shared much else in common with them, as products of Western colleges and universities, trained in similar philosophical assumptions. Another factor was that leaders of the Churches of the West could bring to bear on Israeli politicians diplomatic pressures following from the circumstance that their churches were believed by Israelis to have the support of the citizenry of the Western powers.

With respect to our theme – Christian attitudes towards the State of Israel – the distinction just made between Churches of the West and Churches of the East, originally of great significance, is now of virtually no significance. The local leaders of the Churches of the West are for the most part no longer Europeans but Arabs. Michel Sabbah is the Latin patriarch,[28] Lutfi Laham is the Greek Catholic archbishop, Riad Abu-Assal is the Anglican bishop, Munib Younan is the Lutheran bishop. For a variety of reasons (which I shall explore in the following chapters), the Churches of the West no longer regard themselves as the Churches of the West – that is, as defenders, let alone emissaries, of what used to be called "Christendom." In the 1980s, as the World Council of Churches became more attached to the Palestinian cause and increasingly anti-Zionist, its official statements on the history of the conflict and its proposals for resolving it increasingly reflected the effects of the introduction into the WCC of the Churches of the East. The outcome is that the Churches of the West and Churches of the East are now virtually at one in their attitude towards the State of Israel – an attitude of resentment shading over into active hostility. All formal and authoritative spokesmen for the Churches of the West and the Churches of the East now agree that Israel is an oppressor of Christianity – and that this is so is because it is a Jewish state.

PALESTINIAN THEOLOGY: "THE INTIFADA OF HEAVEN"

In 1989 the Executive Committee of the Middle East Council of Churches affirmed that "it supports the struggle of the Palestinian People for reaching its justified aspirations, of which the establishment of its independent state is primary."[29] Long before this moment, the worldview of the MECC had won the hearts and minds of the official bodies that speak for European and American churches – notably the World Council of Churches, and the various national component councils of the United States, Britain, Canada, et al. Henceforth, official statements of all these bodies reflected exactly the mindset of the MECC.

This alignment of viewpoints of the Churches of the East and the Churches of the West with regard to the issue of Palestine came about in the 1970s, when the ranks of the World Council of Churches were being enlarged by inclusion of the Churches of the East. This was also the decade that saw the vogue of "liberation theology," which began with certain European theorists but was then most successfuly promoted in Latin America. Its governing themes were the essential sinfulness of capitalism, Western cultural arrogance ("Eurocentrism"), and the oppression of the Third World peoples. By the late 1960s, liberation theology was in vogue in politically aware Protestant and Catholic seminaries. Soon the documents of the WCC rang with denunciations of colonialism, cultural imperialism, and oppression. Liberation theology was a speciality of left-wing Latin American Christians, flourishing during the Reagan years, while the Soviet Union was still actively subsidizing the social experiment in Cuba, and when Cuba (cooperating with the Sandinista regime in Nicaraugua) was lavishing propaganda and arms in support of a multitude of guerrilla movements that were then seeking to destabilize pro-American regimes throughout the area and in Africa. When Soviet subsidies to Cuba and Nicaragua were withdrawn under the presidency of Mikhael Gorbachev, anti-Western guerrilla movements began to wither and "liberation" rhetoric began to lose its popularity. Before long elections were taking place throughout the region, and yesterday's freedom fighters either shifted into civilian costume and became politicans, or skulked away into remote jungles. For political theorists and activists in liberal Christian ranks, this created a vaccum – into which, in due course, Palestinian Christians swiftly moved, offering a fiery "Palestinian theology" that answered to all of the old enthusiasms.

Thus, "Palestinian contextual theology" arrived on the scene just as the vogue of liberation theology was beginning to wane. Marxism had never been in vogue in the Churches of the East; Eastern churchmen quickly discovered, however, that Western church intellectuals were eager to hear of the history of the oppression of their communities by European empires. Every graduate of every Western university of serious standing could quickly visualize the Palestinian war against Zionism as part of the struggle against the consequences of the imperialism that followed inevitably from capitalism and from Eurocentrism – the central themes of liberation theology. From liberation theology, Palestinian contextual theology draws its fierce polemical quality and its wholehearted secular-political orientation. While they make no explicit use of Marxist philosophy or of the vocabulary that derives from the theory of dialectical materialism, "Palestinian theologians" presume the indictment of Western capitalism that the liberation theologians established. They play to the sense of guilt that was implanted in the liberal Christian's mind by the liberationists and exploit ecumenical Christianity's conviction of the relativity of its own message, and its openness to the unspoiled values of pre-industrial aboriginal cultures.

The principal spokesmen for Palestinian theology make a supreme virtue of the fact that it is "contextualized" – that it arises from the specific conditions of the local environment, and thus responds to the "self-understanding of the Palestinian people." Just as Latin American liberation theologians drew inspiration from a guerrilla uprising against the pro-American regime of Nicaragua and beatified its leader, Augusto Cesar Sandino, murdered by Nicaraguan government forces in 1934, so Palestinian theologians have magnified the event called the Intifada – a sustained popular uprising against the Israeli presence in Arab Palestine that changed forever the course of Israeli-Palestinian relation. The uprising started, apparently spontaneously, on 8 December 1987 as a protest against the death of an Arab youth at the hands of an Israeli settler. The popular uprising was marked by stone throwing, the burning of rubber tires, and destruction of property. Apparently leaderless at first and thus bereft of any political philosophy, the continuing protest was quickly adopted both by the Muslim terrorist movement called Hamas and by the Palestinian Liberation Organization of Yassir Arafat. While the slogans and philosophy of Muslim radicalism rang no responsive chord in the West, those of the PLO did. These latter drew heavily on the all-purpose insurrectionary ideology that served contemporary guerrilla revolutionaries, from the Shining Path in Latin America to left-wing terrorists such as the Black Panthers in the US and the Bader-Meinhoff gang in Europe. Key concepts were the "occupation" and "oppression" suffered by Third World people and their common cause with the marginalized poor and visible minorities that dwell in the capitalist world.

On 22 January 1988, as soon as it had become evident that the incident of 8 December 1987 had escalated into the Intifada, the leaders of most of the Christian communities in Jerusalem gathered to publish a declaration against Israel's injustice and oppression, calling upon Christians to pray, and to contribute to keeping the movement alive. According to Palestinian-Christian reckoning, this was "the first time in 1500 years that all the leaders of the Christian communities issued a common declaration. It proved to be the beginning of a series of further common declarations and the churches were drawn closer to one another due to the common concern for their peoples."[30] In short order, the scholarly wing of the Western ecumenical church announced that a "renewal of theology" had been brought about by the Intifada. Conferences and seminars on "Palestinian Liberation Theology" sprang up. A First International Symposium on Palestinian Liberation Theology was held at the Tantur Ecumenical Institute for Theological Studies in Jerusalem, 10-17 March 1990, where discussion was focused on Naim Ateek's new book, *Justice and Only Justice: A Palestinian Theology of Liberation* (1989). Here, according to a historian, Harald Suermann, "started a process whereby Palestinian Christians of all historical traditions came to exchange their theological experiences, which were contextualized in view of a singular effort towards national liberation."[31]

On the obverse side of Palestinian contextual theology, there is the *affirmation* of the Palestinian liberation movement – a movement that its theologically inspired historians trace to "Jesus, the revolutionary, the founder of the *Intifada*." Rev. Dr Geries Khoury, a Greek Catholic priest who heads the the Al-Liqa' Centre for Religious Studies in the Holy Land, which has its offices in Bethlehem, writes under the inspiration of the *intifada* experience: "Christ Man rose against the rulers of his time because of their social injustice and against the hypocritical believers who stick to the shells of religion and neglect its core such as the scribes and Pharisees ... Heaven's uprising has been completed through redemptions so that man can live freely ... We call upon the church whom we love to be active and present with all her sons everywhere particularly here in Palestine and at this glorious time; the time of the intifada during which we make our history, the history of our salvation, as we only want to liberate ourselves, get our independence and restore our dignity taken away from us through injustice and wickedness."[32]

On its reverse side, Palestinian contextual theology displays its *repudiation* of the doctrine of God's election of the Jews – the keystone of

Christian theory of history since the mid-second century, when the Church formally denounced as heresy the doctrines of Marcion, which proposed the rejection of all Jewish Scripture. As the Palestinian theologians see it, the West's capitulation to the process that culminated in the creation of the State of Israel in 1948 could only have happened because bemused European and American politicians, responding dimly to the nonsense they were taught in their Sunday Schools, imagined that they were doing the Will of God. Palestinian theologians unanimously reject the thought that anyone anywhere had ever been under a religious duty to bless the people of Israel by assisting the Restoration of the Jews to their alleged homeland. Following Geries Khoury's outline of these matters we find that anyone who ever believed that the events of 2 November 1917, 29 November 1947, and 14 May 1948 were "God's interference in History" was simply a victim of a "manipulation of the Bible by the Jews."[33] Palestinian theologians make no apology for reading the God of Israel out of all discussion about the rights and wrongs of the conflict in the Middle East. Proceeding from the present unhappy political reality – the "alienation" of the Palestinians "from their own homeland, the land of their forefathers, the Philistines"[34] – the Palestinian theologians simply insist that the God of Israel does not belong in the Christian religion. If the God of Israel cannot be read out of the Bible, then so much the worse for the Bible!

In this spirit, Dr Mitri Raheb, pastor of the Lutheran Evangelical Church in Bethlehem, describes "a process of alienation between me and the Bible" which began when he was a youth: "Joshua and David, with whom I was quite familiar, became suddenly politicized ... [The Bible] was no longer concerned with my salvation and that of the world, but with my land, which God had promised to Israel and in which I had no longer a right to live. The God, whom I knew since my childhood as love, had suddenly become a God who expropriates land, leads holy wars and destroys people. I started now to have doubts about this God."[35] Openly embracing the doctrine of Marcion, Palestinian theologians say: "Before the creation of the State, the Old Testament was considered to be an essential part of Christian Scripture, pointing and witnessing to Jesus. Since the creation of the State, some Jewish and Christian interpreters have read the Old Testament largely as a Zionist text to such an extent that it has become almost repugnant to Palestinian Christians. As a result, the Old Testament has generally fallen into disuse among both clergy and laity, and the Church has been unable to come to terms with its ambiguities, questions, and paradoxes – especially with its direct application to the twentieth-century events in Palestine. The fundamental question for many Christians, voiced or not, is: How can the Old Testament be the Word of God in light of the Palestinian Christians' experience with its use to support Zionism?"[36]

Similarly, Munib Younan, who in 1998 became bishop of the Evangelical Lutheran Church of Amman (a jurisdiction that includes Jerusalem and Bethlehem), has written: "The OT is conceived by Palestinian Christians as a support for Zionism. It is conceived as a book that breeds injustices, especially to Palestinians. Certain texts, especially the Exodus stories, create frustrating conflicts for them."[37] Between our first meeting in November 1995 and our second in May 1998, Dr Raheb's attitude on this matter had mellowed. Now he was reluctant to dwell on the matter of the alienation that young Palestinians feel on reading about Israel in the Old Testament. Now, he affirmed, "I am one of those calling for a revived use of the Old Testament. The problem is not in the Old Testament *per se*. It is *not* better *not* to read it. The problem is with the people who politicized this book." Indeed, Raheb had recently taken on the responsibility of teaching the Old Testament class in the school run by his denomination in Bethlehem – but, he cautioned, with a sophisticated appreciation for the different historical contexts in which the word "Israel" appears in sacred text and in the daily newspaper. This degree of sophistication, he conceded, was probably not within everyone's reach; and so it was probably true that in many Palestinian churches the Old Testament was largely passed over in teaching, preaching, and liturgy.[38] Other Palestinian theologians have not mellowed in recent years but, if anything, have become more adamant. Bishop Younan said in May 1998: "The Bible is a contextual book. The Israel of today is not in any sense the Israel spoken of in the Old Testament."[39] Bishop Younan's own denomination has purged references to Israel and Zion from the Arab version of its official prayer book. The Anglican denomination in the Middle East had not followed suit, as of 1998.[40]

In 1992 Andreas Meier undertook to explain "Palestinian contextual theology" to an audience of German Protestants: "Palestinian theology practises solidarity with and takes the side of its own people as the victims of structural violence and political injustice, following the universal principle of justice ... Thus it sees itself as a Palestinian variation of the ecumenical theology of liberation found in the Asian, African and Latin American contexts, which combine love for one's enemies with resistance ... Palestinian theology opposes the direct claim laid by the Jewish State of Israel to the biblical concept of election and the promise of land given to God's people Israel in order to legitimize its territorial policy. At the same time it rejects analogous theological arguments put forward by some Christian representatives of Jewish-Christian dialogue in Germany."[41] (The last remark probably alludes to a pro-Zionist order, the Sisterhood of Mary, headquartered in Darmstadt, to which I refer on page 183.)

Palestinian theologians are aware that outsiders may judge that they are taking liberties with the received tradition of the Church. To this they have an answer: "Although the general Christian theology assists us to understand properly the Christian doctrine, it cannot answer all queries that occupy the hearts of believers in every time and space ... The role of contextualized theology ... [is] to find in this tradition something to assist the believers in understanding, formulating and living their faith at a particular historical period."[42] Bishop Younan puts the matter more succinctly: that "ortho-praxis (right acting) is ultimately more important than ortho-doxy (right doctrine.)"[43]

Still, outsiders might wish to question the method by which these theologians decide what to exclude and what to include from Scripture. Again the "contextual" theologians have an answer – a "hermeneutic key": "When confronted with a difficult passage in the Bible or with a perplexing contemporary event, one needs to ask such simple questions as: Is the way I am hearing this, the way I have come to know God in Christ? Does this fit the picture I have of God that Jesus has revealed to me? Does it match the character of God which I have come to know through Christ? If it does, then that passage is valid and authoritative." This hermeneutic key enables Canon Ateek to conclude that "Jesus attached in his preaching no importance to the land. His major proclamation concerned the announcement of the God's kingdom and this kingdom was not attached to a land but to a believing heart."[44]

The Old Testament has become virtually forbidden literature in much of the Palestinian-Christian world. Formulae and texts from the Psalms, for example, that exalt the God of Israel have been purged from liturgical books. According to one Palestinian Christian: "In the mass-books used by Palestinian Christians, the Bible has been mutilated. All the passages considered unacceptable to Muslims have been eliminated from the Arab version. Entire generations of Palestinian Christians have grown up ignoring God's alliance with Israel and the Jewishness of Jesus, of the Madonna, of the Apostles. To them, they were all Arabs!"[45] Thus Marcion has won his long-postponed victory – not only in the the the local Christian communities of the Middle East, where the prevailing anti-Israeli spirit makes it seem politically astute to deny the God of Israel, but in ecumenical Christian circles, where political correctness has made the intellectuals and bureaucrats increasingly sensitive to the mindset of the oppressed Palestinians, and increasingly insensitive to the demands of dogmatic theology and historical truth.

Palestinian theologians do not hesitate to say, in the name of "solidarity," that their reading of theology, church history, and dogma is binding upon all Palestinian Christians. Nor should any feel that they are being deprived of liberty of thought on these theological matters without reward; for the all-important reward for solidarity will be the political unity of the Palestinian-Arab people. In the words of Geries Khoury: "The Christian community in our country ... is part of a wider and more universal movement which is the search of the whole Arab world for a mode for its existence and role in the civilization of the present age.[46] ... Under occupation there is no difference between Orthodox or Catholic, Armenian or Syrian, Coptic and Maronite, or Lutheran and Anglican, for we are one nation, the Palestinian people, despite our different denominations. Our destiny is one, our pain is one, and our hope is one Jesus Christ, the Son of God. So if the Lord is one, baptism is one and our socio-political circumstances are one, what could prevent us from unifying the local church?"[47]

Geries Khoury and other principal spokesmen of Palestinian theology are bluntly contemptuous of Christians who speak of the possibility of a peaceful reconciliation with the Jews. Former US president Jimmy Carter, who accomplished the Camp David accords (October 1978) between Egypt and Israel while still in office and has ever since been pursuing with unflagging commitment the possibility of a negotiated peace on all fronts of the Middle East, is a conspicuous object of their contempt. When Christians like Carter imagine themselves to be "evenhanded," says Geries Khoury, they make the fundamental mistake of accepting that the Zionist side has anything redeeming about it. Zionism is a purely evil construct, an unprincipled embodiment of brutal force: "Today brings us back to twenty centuries ago. Herod is nowadays represented by the rulers of Israel who are behaving as he did and the newly born babies will never stop calling for justice, truth and peace in the manner of the babe of the grotto." Alluding to the book *Love Your Enemies*, by Canadian Mennonite theologian William Klassen, Khoury told me in November 1995, that "Palestinian theology is different one hundred percent from your practical Canadian theology; here Sharon comes with machine-guns."[48]

THE NEW SITUATION CREATED FOR CHRISTIANS BY THE OSLO ACCORDS

Between 1965 and 1989, 650 Israelis were killed by PLO terrorists (compared with 4,464 killed in wars in that period). Violence against

Jews and outsiders was as nothing, however, compared to that exerted by the PLO against Arab Palestinians during that same period: "The lowest possible estimate of Palestinians who have died by the hand of fellow Arabs in civil disturbances is 35,000, and the true figure may be much higher."[49] This record of criminal brutality did not deter the WCC from championing the cause of the PLO throughout the 1970s and 1980s as the legitimate voice of the Palestinian people. Accordingly, the official bodies of the Churches of the West were unanimous in welcoming the new situation created by the Oslo Accords of 1993, following which Christians of the region would be governed not by outsiders and not by Israelis but by their fellow Palestinians, by the PLO.

It is very difficult to get at all the truth about life for Christians under the Palestinian Authority. The official Palestinian press speaks of the unqualified enthusiasm for the new situation, which extends to the whole Christian community. Arab Christian spokesmen insist that relations beween Christian and Muslim Palestinians have never been better. But there is a compelling body of evidence indicating that Christians are now facing many more obstacles to the free exercise of their faith than they ever endured under direct Israeli rule.[50] Designated spokesmen for the various Christian communities all insist that they have no concern for the future of Christianity in a Muslim state. One would expect, therefore, a growth in the numbers of Christians living in the area – or at very least an end to their emigration. Instead, the rate of emigration has risen and is now double that of Muslim Palestinians. Palestinian church leaders and activists whom I interviewed in May 1998 spoke of large numbers of Palestinian Christians from abroad who returned in the early months of self-rule, but they also conceded that most had left again. Their disappointment, all insisted, had nothing to do with concern about the prospects for their religion (or their irreligion) but rather reflected the lack of economic opportunity.

Returning Christians might well be discouraged by the economic situation. Since the Arafat regime has taken responsibility for the Palestinian people, unemployment rates have risen to over fifty percent, and living standards have declined to one-third of pre-Intifada levels.[51] Per capita annual income in 1997 was $1,578, about twice the figure for Egypt but in the same bracket, roughly, with Jordan, Algeria, and Tunisia. In a part of the world where the poverty level is set at $650 per capita per annum (less than two dollars per day), 19.1 percent of the Palestinian population is living in poverty.[52] In European and American government circles, in the offices of the boards of major industries and banks, and among policy makers in the international agencies, there is agreement about the primary cause: in the words of an official

European Union report on the European contributions to the Palestinian Authority, "the PA is wasting EU monies without any supervision." Although over two billion dollars were transfered from Europe to the PA in the four years prior to the end of 1997, the Palestinian economy had shrunk by one-third in the same period, and the number of unemployed had doubled from twenty percent to forty percent.[53] Large portions of the funds earmarked for housing for the poor were applied instead to luxury housing for the leaders of the PLO. In mid-1997, the PA's own auditors reported that forty percent of the Authority's budget had been stolen or misappropriated. Notwithstanding, in December 1998 forty countries pledged an additional US $3 billion in aid to the PA.[54]

Spokesmen for the Palestinian churches do not deny that there is unhappiness among those who live under the PA. They attribute it, however, not to the performance of their new governors but to the economic consequence of Israel's periodic closing of its borders against Palestinian workers (following terrorist incidents, or on other occasions of heightened security concern), and in general to the spiritual oppression following from the knowledge that Israel has not withdrawn finally and for all from the disputed areas. "I do not demonize Israel," says Zoughbi Zoughbi of the Palestine Conflict Resolution Centre, "but as a Christian who lives here and works in the churches, we see a systematic strategy of Israel, to evacuate the people of the land, Arabs and Christians." He speaks of Israel and "right-wing Christians throughout the world" trying to "destroy our national identity. Their motive is to magnify conflicts. Through 'yellow media' they try to create a culture of conflict."[55]

With one voice, spokesmen for the Christian communities deny that fear of Islam has anything to do with the situation. Bernard Sabella says categorically: "Persecution does not exist in Arab countries."[56] Jack Khasmo, writer and spokesman for the Syrian Orthodox community, says: "There is more understanding of the Christians under the PA than under Israel, because we are Arabs. Relations between Christians and Muslims is far better than between Christians and Jews ... Arafat is interested in keeping Christianity alive, but Israel is not."[57] Ghassan Khatib, publisher of the *Palestine Report*, goes so far as to insist that, under the PA, there is "a bias *in favour* of the Christian communities." But he describes this as "a positive discrimination – a wise policy. Arafat wants a strong Christian community for political reasons. Arafat understands public opinion in the West, and wants to demonstrate that Christians and Muslims can work together."[58]

A common retort to a North American interviewer's questions about the propects of life under a Muslim majority is that the West, at a loss for an ultimate enemy since the collapse of communism, has made Islam (as Bishop Younan puts it) "the second demon after Communism." Western Christians are reminded that "we Christians and Muslims have lived together here for 1,400 years. We know how to live together."[59] Some insist that, in the future as in the past, the secret of Christian survival and prosperity will be to recognize that the majority culture is a Muslim culture. Yet the same people will deny that the communities they belong to think of themselves as minorities. "We were Arabs before Islam was here," says Zougbhi Zoughbi. "We have been victims of the Israeli nation. We realize that we belong to Islamic culture. We have no fear of being swallowed up. As Christians, we are to be the salt in the society in which we find ourselves."[60] Joudeh Majaj, director of the YMCA in East Jerusalem, stresses that we must put the present situation in the longest historical context; and when we do, he says, we will conclude that "there is not an Islamic culture, but rather an Arabic culture. The culture does not come from the religion, but from the long history of the Arab culture." On this interpretation, all the various religions participate in this common Arabic culture: "Islam and Christianity merged together to produce the Arab scientific, cultural golden age," and, with some ups and downs, it remains true that "there is no existence of Muslims without Christians, because the Christians *plus* the Muslims make up the essence of the Palestinian."[61]

Yet to be reckoned against all this is indisputable evidence that Christians who find themselves under the aegis of the PA are voting with their feet against the regime; many, safely out the door, have declared that they left out of concern for the future of Christians under a Palestinian-Muslim majority that is increasingly under the influence of what has come to be called "fundamentalist Islam."[62] The rate of Christian emigration from the PA is at least twice that of the Muslims and is much higher now than it was when Israel ruled. This contrasts with the steady, though modest, growth of Arab Christian numbers living in Israel itself (primarily in Jerusalem and Galilee.) In the early 1990s Israeli, European, and American media began to report on the increasing exodus of Palestinian Christians from Judaea and Samaria, largely provoked, it was said, by fears of increasing Muslim hostilities.[63] After the Palestinian Christians came under the regime of the PA (following implementation of the Oslo accords), the theme took on greater interest.[64] Reporters who have conducted interviews on this matter tell us that Arab Christians will speak to them only anonymously, out of fear of retribution. Christian Arabs told Israeli journalist Judith Sudilovsky that, although they increasingly identified themselves with the "Palestinian people," they were experiencing ever-mounting distrust: "In a society that is becoming more Islamic and looks toward Saudi Arabia and Syria as role models, many Christians feel like outsiders. They are more likely to identify with Europe and the West – and in some ways even with the liberal community of Israel ... [They say:] 'To the Israelis we are Palestinians and to the Palestinians we are Christians, Crusaders.'"[65]

Official spokesmen for the Christian groups uniformly put a brave face on the new situation and insist that talk of Christian-Muslim animosity is being planted by the enemies of the Arabs. "Christians and Moslems in Jerusalem have no animosity toward each other," says Ibrahim Kandalaft, Palestinian Authority deputy minister responsible for Christian Religious Affairs (the PA counterpart of the Israeli director for Christian Communities) and a member of the Greek Orthodox church. "On the contrary, we believe we are one nation with the same destiny and the same aspirations." If there are disputes, they "are on an individual basis, not on a wide scale." Sudilovsky quotes as typical the judgment of one young Palestinian Christian that it is "provocative" to ask questions about Christian-Moslem relations. "We are trying to distance ourselves from these labels," he says. "The West comes and reinforces these ideas of Christian and Moslem, and that the Christians are oppressed by the Moslems, but this is not true."

It has to be kept in mind that the ecclesiastical leaders mix with the political and social élite of the other camp, while the daily life of the laity is lived out with the Muslim masses. Salim Munayer, a Baptist and the academic dean at Bethlehem Bible College, has one foot in and one foot out of this eccleciastical establishment. Out loud, he joins the concensus that the Palestinian Christians will fare better under the PA than under the Israelis, but he also believes that "the traditional churches are using the PA for inter-church contests"; their concern to be politically correct on the matter of the prospects for Christian life in Palestine is causing them to minimize the matter of Muslim harassment of Christians. "They do not share the evangelicals' concern for religious freedom," he warns, and this has caused them to look the other way when new believers of Muslim background face their trials at the hands of the upholders of *shar'ia*, or Muslim law.[66]

Outside investigators report that the positive note taken for publication by Church leaders is not echoed by the anonymous laity. Speaking of radical Muslim journals and pamphlets, one Christian layperson says: "We read what they write and it is threatening. They don't understand about 'the other' living in this country." In my own conversations with Palestinian Christians who were *not* designated spokespersons for their Church communities, I was told of abandonment of the ordinary Christians by the political opportunists who are the leaders of their congregations. According to Sudilovsky: "Privately, Arab Christians will say what they dare not say publicly: that most Christians would rather live under Israeli authority than risk living under another Moslem regime." Yossi Klein Halevi quotes one of the few remaining Christian merchants in the Christian Quarter: "Our leaders are liars: They tell the newspapers that everything is OK. But when Christians go to the market, they're afraid to wear their crosses."[67]

In a booklet of fifty-six pages, the Palestinian human rights organization called LAW/The Palestinian Society for Protection of Human Rights and the Environment, an affiliate of the International Federation for Human Rights and of the International Commission of Jurists, reports that it has found "no evidence of persecution of Christians as a part of a policy on the part of the Palestinian Authority, although some degree of tension between the Christian and Moslem communities does exist."[68] LAW blames the enemies of the PA and of the peace process for disseminating the canard of Muslim persecution of Christian Palestinians – mentioning, specifically in this category, the current Israeli government; the International Christian Embassy Jerusalem; the Municipality of Ariel (which has permitted the activities of the Christian evangelist David Ortiz in their own midst and in the surrounding Arab-speaking villages, and which is alleged to receive funds from Christian Zionist organizations in the United States to subsidize its municipal budget); the Christian Coalition; the Christian Broadcasting Network; Jerry Falwell; the pro-Israeli majorities in the two US Houses of Congress (which heard some of this evidence in the course of their deliberation on the International Religious Freedom Act, introduced to Congress in March 1998 and passed into law on 10 October 1998);[69] the US State Department (which had recently declared that Palestinian Christians *do* qualify for admission as refugees from systematic religious persecution); and the United Jewish Appeal, "which in fact receives the bulk of its funding from Evangelical organizations."

Nevertheless, "incidents exist," the report concedes. There *is* occasional vandalism of Christian properties, including churches and cemeteries, and there have been anti-Christian demonstrations and even riots. The report also concedes that several Arab Palestinians who converted from Islam have been consigned to Palestinian prisons for long periods, although the stated charges have never included conversion but rather insulting clergy and selling land to Jews (which is punishable by death, under a law passed in 1997) or selling to Christians (who, according to a *fatwa*, or binding theological declaration, from Sheik Sabri, are equally included in the terms of the bill).[70] The authors of the report ask us to keep in mind at all times that conversion to Christianity has ruinous effects on Palestinian solidarity. This is particularly true when the conversion is to Pentecostal Christianity: "Moslem converts to Pentecostal Christianity at the least lose their nationalist ideology, and at the most embrace the concept that the Holy land is for Jews only and that Arabs do not belong. Conversion to a faith with Zionist teachings is thus viewed with extreme suspicion by the local population as being antithetical to their decades-long struggle to free their land from foreign occupation and colonization ... [In any case, all those who have come forward with claims of persecution] had different and troubling stories of their behavior within their communities ... This is not to say that there were not violations of human rights involved in the arrests and interrogations of the above ... But from their stories, and *given their background* [emphasis added], a credible case cannot be made that the various security services sought them out and persecuted them specifically for their faith." Then comes this strange reassurance: "Indeed, the PA has recently engaged in mass arrests of Moslem activists, in which hundreds have been detained for long periods without charge by various security services ... It is more correct to say that conversion to Christianity, already frowned upon by Shari'a law, and prolonged and close relation with illegal settlers, plays a role in how these converts were treated and the line of questioning put to them while under interrogation. More importantly, their conversions, the subsequent change in belief-structure, and resulting relations with Israeli settlers affected negatively their relations within their communitites."[71]

Such compulsive sociology-speak is typical of position papers that emanate from Palestinian agencies and Palestinian churches on this theme. Never examined throughout the report is the assumption that social consideration is paramount in religion. The notion that people are drawn to a religious truth because it seems to them to be true – because it is about matters more important to them than the arguments about family, tribe, and nation – is never raised.[72] The beginning and end of the matter for LAW is that the political solidarity of the Palestinian people cannot afford the consequences that follow when people freely decide to choose Whom to worship.

It can be assumed that many acts of Muslim outrage against Christians are never reported to the police. The Christians fear that if they turn to the Israeli authorities they will be labelled by the Muslims as collaborators. At the same time, some say that Israeli police do not deal in full seriousness with issues that arise between Muslim and Christian Palestinians, preferring (reports Sudilovsky) "to keep the embers of dispute among the Palestinians burning, as part of a divide-and-rule policy." Yossi Klein Halevi speaks of official Israeli-church relations falling to a low estate under the government of Binyamin

Netanyatu (1996–99), because of the dominant role in that government of Shas, the political party that represents the Sephardis and harbours many anti-Christian zealots. In 1997 the three ministries that had dealings with the churches – Religious Affairs, Labour, and the Interior (which adjudicates requests for visas) – were all held by Shas. In the government of Ehud Barak, formed in July 1999, the first two of the three were again held by Shas. It is not without significance, presumably, that the Director for Christian Communities in the Ministry for Religious Affairs during the Netanyahu years was an expert on Islam with, by his own confession, little background in Church history.[73] Similarly, Halevi writes, relations of the churches with the Municipality of Jerusalem suffered when the many friendly and informal contacts established over the twenty-eight-year administration of Mayor Teddy Kolleck were thrown aside in November 1994 by the new administration of Mayor Ehud Olmert, whose advisor on Christian Affairs, Shmuel Evyatar, is seen as being close to right-wing Orthodox groups. Whether or not any of this is true, there has certainly been a decline of goodwill between Israeli officialdom and the Christian communities since the latter rushed to declare their support of the Intifida in January 1988, going on thereafter to issue "a series of some dozen collective anti-Israeli proclamations."[74] My own impression of the attitude of those Israelis responsible in some official way for relations with the Christian communities is that their primary concern is to keep the Christians who live in Israel aware of the superiority of their care and feeding under Israel, for the sake of good relations with Western governments and the tourist trade.

As the Oslo process came into effect, it became clear that the PA intended to take a much larger part in the lives and affairs of the Christian communities than Israeli authorities ever had. Shortly into the new regime, Ibrahim Kandalaft, PA deputy minister of Christian Affairs, announced that every church appointment "should have the approval of the courts that are under the authority of the PA ... This is the way it is in Jordan when the church nominates a priest or judge, and the Jordanian authorities must approve this."[75] PA president Yassir Arafat took possession of the Greek monastery near the Church of the Nativity in Bethelehem, making it his official residence during his visits to the city, and has since then simply ignored the protests of the Church authority.[76] For the time being at least, this iron-fisted approach to the Churches of the East seems to coexist with a velvet-glove approach towards the Churches of the West. Arafat has issued a number of friendly signals to those local churches that account for the bulk of tourism from the West but has nonetheless felt obliged, from time to time, to yield to Muslim pressures to crack down on missionary activities.

Palestinian spokesmen all insist that the PA's benign attitude towards the churches and towards Christianity is reflected in the placement of Christians in positions of authority in the new regime. Some go so far as to insist that Arafat's closest advisers are "mostly all Christians" and cite the examples of Emile Jajou'i (on the executive of the PLO); cabinet officers Hanan Ashwari, Ministry for Higher Education, and Nabil Qassis, Minister of State and responsible for the Bethlehem 2000 celebrations; Ramzi Khoury, Director General of the President's Office; Nabil Abu Rudeineh, media adviser and spokesman; Jirius Attrash, General Director, Bethlehem Office; and Sami Mussalam, General Director, Jericho Office.[77] The *PASSIA Diary* indicates with an asterisk which Members of the Palestinian Legislative Council are Christian. The present basic law provides that seven of the eight-eight seats in the National Assembly are to be set aside for the Christians, who constitute no more than three percent of the population. (An additional seat is set aside for the Samaritans.) The mayors of Bethlehem and Ramallah are Christians, as are the mayors of several smaller villages. Palestinian spokesmen acknowledge that this disproportionate presence of Christians at the top reflects the generally higher educational attainments of the Christians, their possession of European languages, and their larger contact with the outside world. These Christians are "the cream of Palestinian society," says Ghassan Khatib, publisher of the *Palestine Report*.[78] Given that the Muslim community has scarcely begun to catch up on this great relative advantage, they say, Christians can be assured of remaining for the forseeable future in positions of responsibility, able to watch out for the welfare of the Christian communities. At the same time, these Palestinian observers concede that Christians are not among the key policy advisers, and none has an independent basis of popular support of any significance.[79] "Usually, Christians do not run for public office," admits Sami Mussallam.[80] Yet, they say, the best proof of the secure situation of the Christians is that so many Palestinian Muslims have chastised Arafat for his policy of "favoring Christians."[81]

PALESTINIAN NATIONALISM AND *JIHAD*

Readers of Western newspapers are aware that Islamic loyalty is growing dramatically throughout the areas now under Palestinian authority. Hamas is a powerful force among the masses and has made itself the real opposition party. As this was written, the student bodies of all the Palestinian universities were controlled by Islamist fundamentalist groups.[82] It is difficult under the circumstances to take seriously the assurance that violence against people who convert from

Islam to Christianity is "not likely." Yet Palestinian academics, confident that Palestinian society is moving towards secularism in mind and in policy, assure us that the essential live-and-let-live spirit of the Muslim majority will persevere over what the West calls Muslim fundamentalism. As we wait for that day, we have to consider that nothing like the American notion of the separation of church and state has yet been found anywhere in the context of the Middle East (with the qualified exception of Turkey).

One constant feature of the history of the Middle East in modern times is that no matter how many wars they have fought amongst themselves, and no matter how much Arab blood they have shed in civil strife, the Arab and Muslim regimes of the region remain united on one theme only: that the Zionist state is the source of all unhappiness in the region. In a book whose entire thrust is to dispel our fears about radical Islam, John Esposito exposes the fixation of Arab politicians upon Zionism: "For Arab leaders, Palestine provided a no-lose cause (not threatening class, political, or religious interests) that each could exploit domestically and internationally as rulers competed in the force of their denunciations. Military leaders and monarchs, the educated and the uneducated, the landed and the peasants, the secular and the Islamically oriented – all could identify with the plight of the Palestinians. The struggle against Israel symbolized the battle against imperialism, provided a common cause and sense of unity, and distracted from the failures of regimes and of Arab nationalism/socialism."[83]

Islamic states and international Islamic organizations have never reversed their public declarations regarding the duty to wage *jihad*, "holy war," against Israel – such as that emanating from the Third Islamic Summit Conference on Palestine and Jerusalem, January 1981, when thirty-eight Muslim heads of state and Yassir Arafat representing the PLO proclaimed from Taifa, Saudi Arabia : "The liberation of Palestine and [the] putting an end to Zionist penetration, political, economic, military and propaganda, into Moslem States is one of the duties of the Moslem world. We must fight a Holy War (*Jihad*) against the Zionist enemy, who covets not only Palestine but the whole Arab region, including its holy places."[84] Neither, for that matter, has the PLO ceased to use the term *jihad*, with all its implications, in speech-making. Only a week after signing the Oslo Accords in 1997, Arafat proclaimed to a rally in Dehaishe: "We know only one word: *Jihad, Jihad, Jihad*."[85] On 3 August 1999 Arafat told a crowd in Ramallah that his people would "continue with our struggle, our *jihad* ... and once again enter the city of Jerusalem as the Moslems did for the first time."[86] Yassir Arafat always calls for *jihad* against Zionism when given the opportunity to address the faithful in a mosque. When confronted with a reporter's knowledge of such an incident – as, for example, on his visit to South Africa in May 1994 – Arafat's spokesmen explain that *jihad*, in this context, really means a peaceful struggle for the minds and the hearts.[87]

Western Christians have not taken up the chorus of *jihad* – at least, not in those words. Western Christian anti-Zionists labour mightily to persuade us that, in any case, *jihad* is not a relevant issue in these matters: it is, they say, something that exists only in the margins or on the dark underside of the Islamic world. At least until the Palestinian Authority was established and the PLO came to power, Western Christian anti-Zionists habitually drew our attention to the repeated promise by the PLO to create a "secular state" – the first in the Muslim-Arab world. Now they remind us that many Christians are in leadership positions in the Palestinian movement and "Palestinian nationalism" has become the benign succesor to *jihad*.

Outshouting the PLO propagandists in the contest for the attention of Muslim Arabs everywhere are the Muslim theologians, who tell us that among Muslims it is understood that the keystone to the arch of all their belonging is the Nation of Islam. One "moderate" Islamist who has held prestigious positions in several American universities, and who has been at the centre of interreligious dialogues and trialogues, speaks of the irrelevance of the model of "nationalism" in the Muslim setting: "In modern times [the evil of tribalism] has risen again among Muslims in the aftermath of colonialism under the name '*qawmiyah*' or nationalism. Fortunately, *qawmiyah* has not penetrated to the Muslim masses, who remain aware of but one identity – Islamic – from the Atlantic to the Pacific. *Qawmiyah* was adopted by a Westernized upper crust of Muslim society which had been trained by the colonialists to hold the reins of power after their departure and to perpetuate the fragmentation of the world-*ummah* into mutually conflicting factions ... *Qawmiyah* is the committed enemy of the universal brotherhood of Islam, of world-unity under the aegis of Islam. Undoubtedly, the oppposition of *qawmiyah* to the world-*ummah* will be the 'battle of the century.'"[88]

It is in this light that we have to see the dilemma of the Palestinian national leadership. In the first days of the PA's jurisdiction in Bethlehem – the only place presently within their jurisdiction that has a substantial body of Christians, and that is also of much interest to Christian visitors from abroad – Arafat has made a considerable public display of goodwill towards the Christian community. An extraordinary opportunity for this was provided by international media coverage of the first Christmas Eve service in Bethlehem under PA rule, at which Arafat declared: "We pronounce this holy land, this holy city, the city of the Palestinian Jesus, a liberated city forever, forever, forever! ... Tomorrow my brother Elias [Elias Freij, then mayor of Bethlehem, a Christian] will celebrate together and for the first time the birth of our Lord Jesus Christ under the Palestinian flag ... And tomorrow we shall meet and pray in Jerusalem at the Al Aksa Mosque and the Church of the Holy Sepulchre."[89] Earlier, Mrs Arafat (who converted from Christianity to Islam on marrying the Palestinian leader, but who is still viewed as a "Christian" with great influence on the leadership) had entered the Church of the Nativity and, according to the *New York Times*, "descended with her child to the crypt revered as the site of Jesus' birth; there, crossing herself and getting on her knees, she placed Zahwa on the star marking the traditional place where Jesus lay, and stayed a while in prayer."

Western newspaper correspondents and editors are evidently not as well aware as most Western churchgoers that Muslims take a dim view of fellow Muslims who refer to "Our Lord, Jesus Christ"; and that Muslims would certainly never permit Elias Freij or any other non-Muslim to participate in the prayers at the Al-Aqsa Mosque or any other mosque. None paused to note the anomoly that only a few months earlier Arafat had been photographed "bowing to Allah while on Hajj [pilgrimage] to Mecca."[90] Since December 1995, in response to the overwhelming growth of Muslim absolutism among the masses of Palestinian Arabs, Yassir Arafat has been going more and more out of his way to display his Muslim belonging. Simultaneously, the Palestine National Council has brought the Palestine entity in line with Muslim states everywhere by the passage of laws that establish the Muslim character of the "nation," and that countenance the application of the death penalty by Muslim citizens against other citizens who convert to Christianity. Since the end of 1997 the Western media have shown no further interest in this story. Given the WCC's record of complacency in the face of increasing persecution of Christians in Muslim countries, there is no reason for surprise that that body has pretended not to notice these actions of the PA. Were the MECC to speak out, then perhaps the WCC and the Western media would bring this matter to the world's attention. Under the circumstances, the PA has had little need to defend its position.

According to the "Basic Law" passed by the Palestinian Legislative Council on the matter of religion: "Palestinians are equal before the law, they have the same rights and obligations, their liberty and freedom to worship and practise their religious beliefs are protected. The Palestinian people are also governed by Shari'a law, as the Shari'a law is the law of Islam and is adhered to with regard to issues pertaining to religious matters."[91] For stories on this matter of the PA's entrenchment of Muslim law we have to go well outside the mainstream press and the mainline churches. Pat Robertson's Christian Broadcasting Network has given air time to interviews with people from Israel with stories to tell of Muslim persecution and run a video released by the ministry team of Jay and Meridel Rawlings entitled "Between a Rock and a Hard Place," which deals with PA persecution of converts to Christianity. Featured in the video is an on-camera interview with Ziad Abu Ziad, a Palestinian legistlative council member and legal advisor to PA chairman Yassir Arafat, who says: "Muslims are not allowed, according to the Islamic religion, to convert their religion or to become non-believers ... A Muslim who will convert his religion and publicizes that and he says that he has quit the Islamic religion, he will be treated according to the Islamic law. And the Islamic law is that he should be warned and asked to make up his mind and come back to Islam, but if he insists, then the rule for that is killing."[92]

Still, the PA's Ministry of Information complains that the Western press's reiteration of anonymous complaints of persecution against Christians is "guided by an agenda ... to inflict the utmost damage on the reputation and credibility of the PA." To those who aver that there is a contradiction imbedded in the authority's Basic Law on Religion, the PA office explains: "According to *shari'a* Law, applicable throughout the Muslim world, any Muslim who declares changing his religion or declares becoming a non-believer is committing a major sin punishable by capital punishment. In practice, this has never happened in the Palestinian territories, nor is it like to happen at all. Having said that, the PNA cannot take a different position on this matter. The norms and traditions will take care of such situations should they occur. The PNA will apply the land of the land, and will protect citizens accordingly."[93] This double-barrelled proposition – that a Muslim who leaves Islam deserves death while nonetheless this is "not likely to happen" – was found by LAW to be "not overly reassuring"; however, they did not argue with it.

All of this contradicts what the outside world has always understood to be the PLO's commitment to a "Secular state of Palestine." This consideration does not move spokesmen for the PA. Dr. Sami Musallam, director of the Office of the President of the PA in Jericho, who describes himself as Greek Orthodox, denies categorically that the PLO had ever promised to create a secular state, and he challenged his interviewer to find any document that makes such a declaration.[94] We are now told that the "impression" that the PLO had ever been committed to a secular state or anything like the notion of separation of church and state is "a myth perpetuated by the Islamists who want to delegitimize us." The PA is committed, says Musallam, not to a secular state but to a democratic state, in which there will be equality of the sexes, freedom of expression and political association, and freedom of religion. The PA recognizes that Palestinian society is preponderantly Muslim, and that among the Muslims *shar'ia* is law. Among other complications, it appears that the PA Basic Law is at odds with *shar'ia* on the matter of the rights and responsibilities of women – one reason why Muslim countries have always refused to ratify the UN Declaration on Human Rights. To most outsiders it remains a question how the PA's laws about the free exercise of religion can be squared with the Muslim law that forbids conversion – that is, forbids a born Muslim to change his or her beliefs as a result of peacefully conducted persuasion. This does not seem to be a problem to the official Palestinian mind. When pressed about the state's responsibility in the event that a Muslim converts to Christianity and is then put to death by a citizen carrying out his Muslim duty, PA officials admit that they would have no choice but to turn their official back.[95] This anomaly seems not to disturb the Christian anti-Zionists.

On the Middle Eastern scene, "complete religious freedom" is an alien species. The expectation that the common national identity of the Palestinian people will always count for more than differences of religious allegiance between Christians and Muslims cannot be supported by reference to the history of the Middle East. Despite all the wishful thinking and all the double-talk, it is clear that "Palestine" is not yet an exception to the generalization that "every Arab state is a despotism, whose constitution specifies that Islam is the state religion."[96]

4 The Palestinians

> The assassination of Arab brethren like Goliath, by Jewish sheep-
> herders like David, is the sort of shameful ignominy that we must
> yet set aright in the domain of the occupied Palestinian home-
> land.
>
> Anwar Sadat[1]

Prior to the question "Who are the Palestinians?" is the question
"What is Palestine?"

The eleventh edition (1911) of the *Encyclopaedia Britannica*, the
last we have before the Balfour Declaration, defines "Palestine" as
follows: "PALESTINE: ... conventionally used as a name for the territory which, in the Old Testament, is claimed as the inheritance of the
pre-exilic Jews ... We may describe Palestine as the strip of land
extending along the eastern shore of the Mediterranean Sea ... East-
ward there is no such definite border. The river Jordan, it is true,
marks a delimitation between western and eastern Palestine; but it is
practically impossible to say where the latter ends and the Arabian
desert begins." In the record of the deliberations of the British,
French, and Americans leading to the Balfour Declaration, it is taken
for granted that what is being proposed is a homeland for the Jews
in some part of what has *always been defined as* that part of the world
where the Jews once had their inheritance. There was no other
useful way of defining the area.

For well-intentioned Westerners, one source of confusion is that not
more than a half-century ago, when the future of the Mandate of
Palestine was before the United Nations, the term "Palestinian" generally meant "Jewish resident of Palestine." Organizations that in those
days promoted the Zionist solution of a Jewish state had such names as
the Pro-Palestine Federation and the American Christian Palestine
Committee. (Students who are new to the history of modern Israel
experience something of a jolt when they first encounter this inversion

of terminology in the documents.) In any case, that usage (as I shall argue) was no more accurate from a historical point of view than the current usage. This matter illustrates a hazard that seems to be peculiar to late twentieth century political rhetoric: namely, that in the absence of general respect for historical knowledge, the key concepts in political discussion are handed down from journalists, who derive them immediately from contemporary political rhetoric and ultimately from Sociology 100.

Of course, anyone who has any respect for the history of the Middle East knows that at the time of the Balfour Declaration in November 1917 Jews were a minority in Palestine as a whole, constituting probably about 60,000 out of 700,000 people.[2] In light of this, the Balfour Declaration clearly says that in making a Jewish state, all parties would have to deal as justly as possible with the claims of those other communities. None of the other communities, however, was ever identified as "the Palestinians" – certainly never by themselves. They were Arabs, along with some small pockets of other races.

Palestine had never been a province of the Ottoman Empire. Indeed, "from the end of the Jewish state in antiquity to the beginning of British rule, the area now designated by the name Palestine was not a country and had no frontiers, only administrative boundaries; it was a group of provincial subdivisions, by no means always the same, within a large entity."[3] All over the political front during the 1920s, 1930s, and 1940s, there were organizations like the Palestine League, Pro-Palestine Federation, Christian Council for Palestine, American Christian Palestine Committee, and so on, all of them lobbies on behalf of the Jews – on behalf of Zionism. The various opposing lobbies, like the Arab Congress, upheld "Arab rights in Palestine."

The name Palestine is not an invention of the Arabs, nor of the Jews. It is an invention of the ancient Romans. In the second century of the Common Era, following the Bar Kokhba revolt, the names "Judaea" and "Samaria" were abolished by the Romans, and the name Palestina was applied. The intention was to insult the Jews and their history by memorializing the already long-vanished Philistines. It was important to obliterate memory of the Jewish nation from this place where their sovereign kingdom had once been, and where they had lived continuously as part of the subsequent empires of the Assyrians, Babylonians, Persians, Ptolemies, Seleucids, and Romans – lest their resistance to Rome's tyranny become an inspiration for other subject peoples.[4]

This insult and this policy are perpetuated and given yet another twist by the capture of the name Palestine by the Arab populations of that part of the world today and by their anti-Zionist supporters else-where. These newly minted "Palestinians" have, of course, no more historical connection to the Philistines than do the Jews. Nowadays, the term "Palestinian nation" serves to give colour to a claim to *aboriginal* habitation of the vicinity – as the term "Arab" obviously does not. Yet there never was an Arab province, let alone an Arab state, called Palestine. The very name Palestine fell into disuse among the Arabs, only to be revived by the British. At that point it was appropriated (unwisely as we now see) by the Zionists. They believed that it would strengthen their proprietary claims to the land to employ the local term preferred by the British. Secular Zionists had another motive: a name that affirmed contemporary geographical associations would distinguish *their* vision of the past and the future of the Jewish people from that of religiously inclined Zionists, to whom the record of the past and the hope of the future was better conveyed by the term *Eretz Israel*. (Incidentally, for a while during the 1920s and 1930s the more zealous secularists took to calling themselves "Canaanites"; but that vogue passed.)

Prior to 1967, Arab leaders never talked of a Palestinian nation.[5] In the Arab Covenant of 1919, proposed by the Arab Congress in Jerusalem in 1919, we read: "The Arab lands are a complete and indivisible whole, and the divisions of whatever nature to which they have been subjected are not approved or recognized by the Arab nation."[6] Syria's late dictator, Hafez al-Assad, despite his window-dressing support of liberated "Palestine," once declared: "Palestine is not only a part of our Arab homeland, but a basic part of southern Syria."[7] Through the 1970s and 1980s, King Hussein of Jordan bobbed and weaved between two definitions of Palestine. When the PLO was relatively strong and he was relatively weak, the late king acknowledged that to the PLO belonged the leadership of "the Palestinian people." But when he was relatively strong and the PLO relatively weak, he took an entirely different view: "The truth is," he said publicly in 1981 and repeated in so many words throughout the 1980s (but *not* throughout the 1990s), "that Jordan is Palestine, and Palestine is Jordan."[8]

Sometime after Israel's War of Independence, Arab rhetoric took a 180-degree turn. Now the local Arab-speaking people became "the Palestinian people," the aboriginal inhabitants, the rightful owners of the land "since time immemorial." This concept first appears with full clarity in the Palestinian National Covenant of 1964, which rejects the legitimacy of the concept "Jewish people/nation" and calls for Israel's destruction. Henceforward Arab politicians everywhere nodded agreement as Yassir Arafat explained that the "Palestinian people" were in

place before the Jews arrived; that they are the authchthonous population of the region, the descendants of the Canaanites, the Philistines
and the Jebusites. It is not enough for Yassir Arafat to claim that "Palestine," prior to the mischievous Mandate, was "Arab land"; he is convinced, and wants the world convinced with him, that this land was the
home of a civilization higher than any that has ever been seen anywhere else. This he described before the Assembly of the United
Nations in 1983:

It pains our people greatly to witness the propagation of the myth that its
homeland was a desert until it was made to bloom by the toil of foreign settlers, that it was a land without a people, and that the settler entity caused no
harm to any human being. No, such lies must be exposed from this rostrum
for the world must know that Palestine was the cradle of the most ancient cultures and civilizations. Its Arab people were engaged in farming and building,
spreading culture throughout the land for thousands of years, setting an
example in the practice of religious tolerance and freedom of worship, acting
as faithful guardians of the holy places of all religions ... Religious brotherhood ... was the hall-mark of our Holy City before it succumbed to catastrophe.
Our people continued to pursue this enlightened policy until the establishment of the state of Israel and their dispersion. This did not deter our people
from pursuing their humanitarian role on Palestinian soil. Nor will they
permit their land to become a launching pad for aggression or a racist camp
for the destruction of civilization, culture, progress and peace. Our people
cannot but maintain the heritage of their ancestors in resisting the invaders,
in assuming the privileged task of defending their native land, their Arab
nationhood, their culture and civilization, and in safeguarding the cradle of
the monotheistic religions.[9]

Travellers' accounts of the land belonging to the period described
by Arafat give a different picture. Alphonse Lamartine (1790–1869)
described what he found in Jerusalem in 1835: " We were seated the
whole of the day before one of the principal gates. We walked round
the walls; no one passed in or out ... We saw, indeed, no living object,
heard no living sound; we found the same void, the same silence as we
should have found before the entombed gates of Pompeii or Hercula-
neum ... [It is] the tomb of a whole people."[10] At that time, Jerusalem
had a population of about fourteen thousand.
    Indispensible and (one would think) irrefutable testimony to the
situation in Palestine at the time of the Mandate is found in the work
of Walter Lowdermilk, assistant chief of the US Soil Conservation
Service and author of several seminal scholarly studies on global
natural resources.[11] Over the course of twenty years he conducted vast

field research on all the inhabited continents to find the lines of causal connection between the use of land and the prosperity of nations. He noted: "An Arab legend tells us that once upon a time an angel, carrying a sack of stones, flew over Palestine; suddenly the sack burst and all the stones were strewn about upon the hills." But having searched the archaeological record and surveyed the conditions in the land as he found it in the mid-1930s, he was able to conclude: "The true story reads differently. Once upon a time the hills of Palestine were covered with rich red earth and protected by forests, smaller vegetation and terraces. Then the trees were cut down, the terraces were neglected, the fertile soil was washed away by rain and finally only the stones were left on the fields ... Desert Arabs poured into the land and to the very gates of Jerusalem, stealing and plundering on the roads throughout the country. The country became a desert land with no one to till the soil ... The decay of Palestine reached its darkest stage in the four hundred years of Turkish rule, from 1517 to 1918."[12]

THE PAN-ARAB CLAIM TO PALESTINE

Getting history wrong is an essential part of being a nation.

Ernest Renan

Most people will detect a logical problem in combining the claim that Palestinians make to authchthonous standing in the region with their equally fierce claim to Arab ancestry. Quite apart from anything else, none of the oldest pre-Israelite inhabitants seems to have been Semitic at all. Certainly they were not Arabs. Yet when the polemical occasion requires it, the same Palestinians do become "the Arab people" whose nation is "the Arab nation, extending from the Atlantic to the Red Sea and Beyond," as Arafat declaims (on Mondays, Wednesdays and Fridays.)

The Arabs entered the area with the Moslem conquests in the seventh century. Arab rule – to be distinguished from rule by other subsequent Moslem conquerors who eventually used the Arabic language – was extremely brief, virtually coinciding with the years of the regime of the first Muslim conquerors, the Umayyads (660s to 750). Thereafter the area fell to a succession of conquerors: European Christian Crusaders, Kurds under Saladin, and Ottoman Turks. Jews and Christians still worked the land because the Arabs, being Bedouins, had only contempt for agricultural life. Soon, "the word Arab reverts to its earlier meaning of Bedouin or nomad, becoming in effect a social rather than an ethnic term."[13]

If it is historically insupportable to speak of "many centuries of Arab rule," it is perfectly correct to speak of many centuries of *Muslim* rule. Bernard Lewis makes the point that our Western notion of belonging to a nation should not be carried into our reading of Middle Eastern history: "The majority belonged to the Umat-al-Islam, the community or nation of Islam. Its members thought of themselves primarily as Muslims. When further clarification was necessary, it might be territorial – Egyptians, Syrian, Iraqi – or social – townsman, peasant, nomad. It is to this last that the term Arab belongs. Arab nationality, identity, in the sense promulgated today – as 'a group of people with a common homeland, language, character and political aspirations' – derives from the West, and came into the world less than a century ago."[14]

Speaking before ideologically secure audiences, PLO statesmen, until recently at least, would admit, and indeed brag, about the frailty of the "Palestinian-identity" argument. Thus Zaheir Muhsin, a member of the PLO Executive Council, said in March of 1977: "Yes, the existence of a separate Palestinian identity serves only tactical purposes. The founding of a Palestinian state is a *new* tool in the continuing battle against Israel."[15]

THE MUSLIM CLAIM TO JERUSALEM

> The Muslims say to Britain, to France, and to all the infidel nations that Jerusalem is Arab. We shall not respect anyone else's wishes regarding her. The only relevant party is the Islamic nation, which will not allow infidel nations to interfere.
> Sheik Ikrama Sabri, Mufti of Jerusalem, 11 July 1997[16]

From at least 1870 onward, we have creditable census reports, and these show a Jewish majority in the whole city of Jerusalem.[17] In 1870 Jews were also a majority in the Old City (that is, the walled city where all local life had been confined until the late nineteenth century.) All the evidence suggests that Jews always were a majority there, except during those brief periods when Roman emperors or Christian kings forbade their presence on pain of death. (Even then, some historians believe, the number of Jews illicitly present may have been greater than the number of people who were legally present.) At least one-half of the Muslims resident in the city in 1948 had arrived there after 1920. In 1948 Jews were expelled from every part of Jerusalem that came under Jordanian rule, in order that Jordan might continue the policy of a Jew-free kingdom that dated back to the creation of Transjordan in 1922.

The fact that so few Muslim Arabs were interested in living in Jerusalem until the years of the mandate reflects the relative weakness of the theological motive among Muslims of the time – which contrasts strongly with present Muslim interest in the "Holy City." Somewhere in recent times, Muslims began speaking of Jerusalem as Al Quds (the Holy Place) and as "the third holiest place in Islam." Yet Jerusalem is neither named nor alluded to in the Qur'an. In AD 691, when the Ummayid dynasty, based in Damascus (660s to 750), was in possession of the region, but not of Mecca or Medina, Abd el Melek Ibn Merwan proposed that the Temple Mount was the site of Mohammed's mystical night-time journey to Al Aqsa – "the furthest mosque" (*il masjad al aksa*). An indentation on the rock was identified as the print left by Muhammed's horse Barak (who had a woman's head and a peacock's tail) as horse and rider ascended into the heavens. None of this is in the Qur'an. The whole reference, in Sura 17:1–2, is as follows: "Glory to (God) / Who did take His Servant [Muhammad], / for a journey by night / From the Sacred Mosque [at Mecca] / To the Farthest Mosque, / Whose precincts We did / Bless, / – in order that We / Might show him some / Of Our signs; for He / Is the One who heareth / And seeth (all things)." There was, of course, no mosque at the site in Muhammad's time, only a Byzantine church that was later replaced by the present Al Aqsa mosque. In modern times, this holy association has been magnified to match the political requirements: when Muslims speak to Western Christians, they insist that historical associations make Jerusalem (Al Quds) equal in spiritual importance to Christians, Jews, and Muslims; when speaking to Muslim audiences, Muslims state that Al Quds is pre-eminently and pre-emptively sacred to Islam. Yet no Muslim ruler ever regarded Jerusalem as his political capital, let alone his cultural or religious capital. The only spots in the region ever to have served (briefly) as the capital of a Muslim regime were Ramle – the only town in Palestine that dates from those years of Arab rule – and Amman, during the Jordanian years.[18]

THE CHURCH AND "THE PALESTINIANS"

Many Christians who regard themselves as realists and also as people of goodwill ask: What does it matter if the case for the Palestinian people lacks historical substance? Would it not be better if we all simply nodded agreeably as the "Palestinians" recited their national history, the story of their descent from the Canaanites, the Jebusites, and the Philistines and then get on with the work of Reconciliation?

In recent years, Christian liberals have found support for this thinking in an unlikely place: among those Israeli politicians who were the authors of the policy of seeking peace through negotiation with the Palestine Liberation Organization – the process that brought about the 1993 Oslo Accords. Shimon Peres, the Israeli politician who invested more than any other in this process, suggested in a book written in 1993 what we might call a Gordian-knot approach to the embarrassment of dealing with the Palestinians' arguments about their history. After reviewing the story more or less along the lines that we have just followed, he concludes: "Until the 1948 War of Independence, the Palestinian people did not exist as a separate entity, either in their own consciousness or in the minds of other people, including the Arab nations ... Only during the ideological struggle against the State of Israel and the Zionist movement did the ideologues of the Palestinian camp begin to speak about a specific historical Palestinian connection to this controversial land, a connection that is independent of any pan-Arab context. At that time, the Palestinians began to be described as the descendents of the ancient Jebusites, and some even suggested that the Palestinian people existed 'from time immemorial.'" But then Peres sweeps away this *mere history*: "These facts do not question the legitimacy of Palestinian national consciousness. The modern democratic outlook recognizes the validity of forming a new national association, termed 'people building' in the professional literature, based on the consciousness of independence by any group that establishes such a national association ... The Palestinians became a people when they decided to do so and when they began to act as a national collective. Questions of how they began to act as a national collective and what factors led to this awakening are of interest to historians and sociologists, but the speculations make no difference in determining strategy. Strategy depends upon present reality."[19]

Perhaps such contempt for historical fact makes sense to a man who could say in May 1994: "Today we have ended the Arab-Israeli conflict. Utopia is coming."[20] Historians and others who take history seriously have reason for concern regarding the recent thinking of Christian organizations that patronize the fantasy-histories of alleged "aboriginal" people and others who claim to be victims of "Eurocentrism," "linear thinking," and other putative vices of the Western mind. It used to be better understood than it is today that Christian faith depends upon the historical validity of certain entirely specific events, which appear in historical documents that have been subject to critical examination for some nineteen hundred years, and that capture, Christians claim, the largest meanings in human history. This realization is at the heart of the entirely unique preoccupation with the determination of historical fact that characterizes Western civilization. But respect for historical fact is not widespread in an age when historical thinking is generally despised, and historical content has been almost entirely driven from the curriculum of schools.

5 The Church and Islam

PROSPECTS FOR THE CHRISTIANS OF THE
HOLY LAND UNDER ISLAMIC MAJORITY

In chapter 3 I noted that leaders of the Christian communities in Israel and those living under the Palestinian Authority offer to the public an optimistic vision of their future under Islam. Indeed, some go so far as to state that the character of Islam has no relevance to this situation: "The bonds which the Arabs have in Palestine and the historical right which they have therein is everlasting, genuine, and indisputable ... Palestine is a gift from heaven; it is deep in the heart of every Muslim and every Christian; those people who make half the total population of the world today. The conflict is not only between Muslim and Jews, it is also between the Muslims and Christians on the one side and the Zionists on the other."[1] Taking up this notion, the MECC and the WCC promote Muslim-Christian dialogue as the key to a happy future.

The problem is that there is a gigantic element of denial in the MECC's recollection of past Muslim-Christian relations, and this denial colours thinking about prospects for peace based upon Muslim-Christian dialogue today. To make this point, we must take a brief look into the history books.

Islam was founded by the prophet Muhammad (c. 570–632) who received the text of the Holy Qur'an in a series of visions imparted directly to him by Allah somewhere around the year AD 610. At the time that Muhammad received this text, the Christian people (with whom he was slightly acquainted) had been living for somewhat less than six hundred years with what they believed to be God's final revelation to mankind, while the Jews (with whom he was very well acquainted) had been living (by their own admission) without any new prophecy from God since the closing of the era described in the books of their canon (that is, for about nine hundred years). The Holy Qur'an, which Muhammad now proclaimed, completes the message regarding the purposes of God that is imperfectly conveyed in the holy books of the Jews (what the Jews called Tanach, and what the Christians call the Old Testament) and in the holy book of the Christians (including the New Testament.)

At the time of Muhammad's revelation, there were several thriving communities of Jews in the Arabian peninsula. The principal source of the theological and historical speculations that appear in the Qur'an is the Hebrew scriptures, which in various oral forms (because he was illiterate) Muhammad absorbed in the years of his spiritual quests. One historian of Israel, Abram Sachar, writes: "The Arabs wondered at the facility with which the Jews could read and write, and their respect for the queer people of the book was almost a fear ... 'the awe which book-learning evokes in those who are absolutely without it.'"[2] But however awesome Jewish Scripture may have seemed to him, Muhammed was not intimidated by it. Indeed, the inspired Qur'an declares that the whole of the Jewish Scripture from Genesis 15 forward is full of lies. The Qur'an offers a counter-history, wherein God's promises devolve upon Ishmael, not upon Isaac. In Sura 2:125 we read: "Remember We made the House [the Ka'ba, in Mecca] / A place of assembly for men / And a place of safety; / And ye take the Station / Of Abraham as a place / Of prayer; and We covenanted / With Abraham and Isma'il, / that they should sanctify / My House for those who / Compass it round, or use it / As a retreat, or bow, or / Prostrate themselves (therein in prayer.)" A widely respected edition of the Qur'an offers this explanation of the text: "Abraham and Isma'il together built the House of God in Mecca (long before the Temple of Jerusalem was built.) They purified it and laid the foundations of the universal religion, which is summed up in the word Islam, or complete submission to the Will of God. Abraham and Isma'il were thus true Muslims ... Historically the Temple at Mecca must have been a far more ancient place of worship than the Temple at Jerusalem. Arab tradition connects various places in and around Mecca with the name of Abraham and identifies the well of Zam-zam with the well in the story of the child Isma'il [Genesis 21: 14–21]. Arab tradition also refers the story of the Sacrifice to Isma'il and not to Isaac, therein differing from the Jewish tradition in Gen. xxii 1–19."[3]

Islam completely supersedes Judaism. Islam teaches that the destiny of the faithful has been unlinked forever from the destiny of the Jews. Its scripture, the Qu'ran, is authentic *because* in it the Jewish Scripture is rejected. Islam cannot tolerate the notion that the promises made to the Jews continue in force in any sense whatever after the revelation to Muhammed. In contrast, *Christianity never rejects Jewish scripture.* Precisely as it criticizes, even denounces, Judaism for rejecting Jesus as the fulfilment of scripture, it affirms the letter and claims the spirit of that scripture. Whether Jews should rejoice in that knowledge is another matter. But certainly they should understand that Judaism's quarrel with Christianity is conducted on altogether different ground than its quarrel with Islam.

The Christians, too, declined to accept Muhammed's own estimate of himself and his message; but this was less of an obstacle for Muhammad's self-understanding. Christianity was a universal religion, like his own. By definition, there could not be two valid universal religions: so Muhammad simply reinterpretated the stories upon which Christian doctrines stand and incorporated them into Islam.

Muhammad's expectation that the Jewish people would turn to his message was reflected in his initial decision to require his followers to pray towards Jerusalem. He expected, in plain terms, that Judaism would simply close down – that the Jews would accept the Qur'an. Instead, they jeered at him (as he later recounted in the *Qur'an*). Whereupon, the Prophet denounced the Jews for infidelity. This indictment stands today at the heart of the Muslim-Jewish relationship. In Sura 5:41–3 of the Qur'an we read: "[The Jews are] men who listen to any lie ... It is not God's will to purify their hearts. For them there is disgrace in this world, and in the hereafter a heavy punishment ... For they are not really people of Faith." Many other sections of the Qur'an develop the Prophet's diatribe against the Jews. (Among these, the scholars of this subject direct us especially to Sura 17 ("The Children of Israel," and to Sura 2.)

In his widely recognized commentary on the Qur'an, A. Yusuf Ali sums up the contrast between Christian and Islamic teaching on Judaism: "[The Christian Church] recognized the Old Testament in its present form (in one or another of its varying versions) as Scripture. It was the merit of Islam that it pointed out that as scripture it was of no value, although it recognized Moses as an inspired apostle and his original Law as having validity in her period until it was superseded. In its criticism of the Jewish position it [Islam] said in effect: 'You have lost your original Law; even what you have now as its substitute you do not honestly follow; is it not better, now that an inspired teacher [Muhammad] is living among you, that you should follow him rather than quibble over uncertain texts?'"[4]

In his first years as a conqueror on behalf of Islam, Muhammad dealt fiercely with the large community of Jews then living in Arabia and liquidated those who did not convert or flee. The Jews of Arabia "irritated him by their refusal to recognize him as a prophet, by ridicule and by argument; and of course their economic supremacy [in Medina and elsewhere in the Arabian peninsula] ... was a standing irritant."[5] The best-remembered chapter in this early story was the fate of the Jewish-Arab tribe called the Banu Qurayza who were allied with Muhammad's pagan adversaries (the Quraish) in fortified places that stood on his path to Medina, and then back to Mecca. Unable to defeat these allies at first, and thus unable to take Mecca, Muhammad entered into the *Khudaibiya* (or *al-Hudaybiyah*) agreement, a ten-year peace pact. Before the end of two years, however, having gained in military strength, he broke the truce unilaterally and without notice, captured the Quraish stronghold, and slaughtered virtually the whole population.[6] This deed is commemorated by Muhammad in Sura 23:26–7 of the Qur'an: "And those of the People / Of the Book who aided / Them [the Unbelievers] – God did take them / Down from their strongholds / And cast terror into / Their hearts (so that) / Some ye slew and some / Ye made prisoners. / And He made you heirs / Of their lands, their houses, / And their goods, / And of a land which / Ye had not frequented / (Before). And God has / Power over all things."[7]

Yassir Arafat reverts to these events when he speaks to audiences of the faithful about the Oslo Accords: "When the prophet Muhammad made the Khudaibiya agreeement, he agreed to remove his title 'messenger of Allah' from the agreement. Then, Omar bin Khatib and the others referred to this agreement as the 'inferior peace agreement.' Of course, I do not compare myself to the prophet, but I do say that we must learn from his steps and those of Salah a-Din. The peace agreement which we signed is an 'inferior peace'. The conditions [behind it] are the intifada, which lasted for seven years." Asked whether he has any doubts as to the wisdom of signing the Oslo Accords, Arafat replies (to Muslim audiences): "I suggest that we maintain quiet. We respect agreements the way that the prophet Muhammad and Salah a-Din respected the agreements which they signed ... Allah's messenger Mohammad accepted the al-Khudaibiya peace treaty and Salah a-Din accepted the peace agreement with Richard the Lion-Hearted."[8] (The second of Arafat's historical references is to Salah a-Din (Saladin), who entered into a ceasefire with the Christian armies, then – inspired by the prophet's example in the matter of the Jewish and pagan tribes – unilaterally declared a *jihad* against the Crusaders and captured Jerusalem on 2 October 1187.)

Arafat's theological-historical excursus should be studied in the light of the "Plan of Phases," officially adopted by the PLO in 1974, under which the PLO undertakes to "establish a national, independent, and fighting government over every part of the soil of Palestine to be freed" (Article 2); then, "after its establishment, the national Palestinian government will fight for the unity of the countries of confrontation, to complete the liberation of all the Palestinian land and as a step in the direction of overall Arab unity" (Article 8.) Routinely, when speaking of the Oslo agreement of 1993, Arafat reminds Arab audiences of this Plan of Phases.[9]

As Muslims conquered the various communities of the Middle East, they made a fundamental distinction between Jews, Christians, and Zoroastrians (on the one hand) – "the People of the Book" (*ahl al-khatib*) – and the people adhering to all the other religions. The latter were obliged to convert or be slaughtered. The Jews, beginning with the remnant that had survived the massacres conducted by Muhammad throughout the Arab peninsula, became *dhimii* (protected people). The major objects of conquest during these years (seventh to eleventh centuries) were the provinces of the Byzantine (Greek Orthodox) Empire. The Byzantine masters had administered a system based upon segregation of the various religious communities, with steep divisions of privilege and opportunities. In this empire, Jews had been a severely persecuted minority, while the people belonging to the Oriental churches, as we saw in Chapter 3, had lived under great restrictions. Those Orthodox Christians who converted to Islam assisted the new masters in transposing the elaborate legal framework left by the Byzantines (notably, the Theodosian Code of of 438 and the Justinian Code of 534) into a new key: the Muslims now stood where Orthodox Christianity and the Greeks had stood, while Orthodox and Oriental Christians and Jews now shared a common lot, outside the bounds of the *dar al-Islam,* the world that obeys Allah.

There is a powerful irony in this story: "In the territories that came under its rule, Islam was able to use, for the destruction of the Eastern Christendom, the remarkable system of oppression which the Byzantine Church had elaborated and perfected for use against the Synagogue. In imposing its anti-Jewish legislation, the Church Fathers – unconscious agents of history – having arrived at the height of their power, were simultaneously laying the ground for the destruction of Eastern Christianity."[10] Yet, painful to report, the several subject communities did not learn compassion from their shared humiliation.

Instead, the best of their surviving energies now went into competing against each other with the new master for the sake of relative marginal improvements in the contracts that the masters negotiated with the leaders of the various *dhimmi* communities. The bitter divisions over matters of theology and all kinds of ancient unfinished business kept the communities apart from one another; their differences became more, not less, important to them as props to their sense of superiority. (This key to human psychology served well all the succeeding Muslim masters of the Middle East, North Africa, and the Balkans, and continues its dark work in the Balkans, long after the Muslim masters themselves are gone.)

Not only among Muslims but among Western secularists, portions of the Jewish public, and, with differences of emphasis, Orthodox and Oriental Christians there is a tendancy to portray this period as a golden age of religious toleration. Each of the parties has a different motive for minimizing the oppressive side of the story. The politics of intergroup relations in the region cannot be understood apart from this fact.

Muslim scholar Mahud Awan summarizes this history of religious toleration and explains its significance for our present perspective on Israel: "The history of Islam presents us with no such phenomena as those of Judaism and Christianity. There is nothing comparable to the history of Judaism, where a diametrical reversal has taken place: namely, from being the most persecuted and tyrannized-over minority in Europe, to becoming the perpetrators of genocide against the Palestinians ... the innocent Palestinians whose crime in Jewish eyes is that of having lived in Palestine for millennia before and after the Hebrews had established themselves in the territory for a comparatively brief period of its long history. The irony is double when we consider that religiously and culturally, the Palestinians are an integral part of the *ummah* which alone in the whole of human history, acknowledged Judaism as divine religion, its Torah as the law of God, and welcomed and protected the Jews wherever Islam was dominant."[11]

Muslim motives for presenting their history in the best possible light are obvious. And in truth, there are many features of the story that do relative credit to Islam. Muslim leaders learned rather early that having a variety of subject peoples, each with ancient grudges against the other, presented possibilities for displacing hostilities that would otherwise react upon the regime. Typically, caliphs and sultans did what they could to keep the separate scholarly and cultic traditions of their minorities in place, recognizing that those traditions gave them access to wisdom, that wisdom gave access to knowledge, and that knowledge was a great source of strength for the regime. Accordingly,

Muslim princes governed through well-educated Jews and well-educated Christians, and even, for a while, Zoroastrians. The fact that their Muslim subjects often complained about the prominence of non-Muslims in high circles has often been taken as proof that Christians and Jews fared very well indeed under Islamic rule. But this rosy view overlooks the harsher reality.

Historian Michael Field has said that "modern Arabs ... are much more conscious of their history than Westerners are of theirs,"[12] a thought that is frequently found in the current literature. The generalization should be handled with caution, however. It is true that, while the subject called "history" has virtually disappeared from the primary and secondary school curriculum in the West, and course offerings in history are disappearing from the undergraduate catalogues in North American universities, Muslim students are immersed in instruction about their past. But instruction about the past is not necessarily history. Islam's intolerance of critical examination of its sacred texts and traditions has delivered its intellectual institutions from the burden of history, as the concept has been understood in the West. Arab politicians, preachers, and commentators do not wait upon academic historians before delivering their grandiose assertions about their past.

Indeed, the Arabs' descriptions of their glorious past look suspiciously like a mirror image of the Western intellectuals' descriptions of their own inglorious past. Even while the habit of critical enquiry begat moral relativism among our intellectuals, begetting in turn the current attitude of contempt for the European historical record (an attitude that college graduates ignorantly parrot), Islamic scholars have maintained a pristine uncritical attitude towards Islamic texts in all arenas of public discussion. They are assisted in this by the readiness of Western scholars to join in on denigrations of the imperialistic record of the Christian West.

As early as the eighteenth century, the century of the European Enlightenment, Muslims found that intellectuals in the West were attracted to the Muslims' portrayal of the golden age of religious tolerance under Muslim empires. Instructive contrast could always be made to the bloody history of religious wars in Europe – the Inquisition, the hanging of witches, the expulsion of Jews and Moors from Spain, pogroms, et cetera. Today well-read Christians are at least as well informed about this dark side of their history as are the secularists, and all Church bodies have gone to the greatest possible lengths to lay before the world the whole story and to repent of the record. Secular intellectuals have a larger agenda: intent on demolishing respect for the Christian heritage, they gleefully collaborate with

Muslims in pretending that such dark episodes as the Inquisition and the expulsion of the Jews and Moors from Spain are the whole truth about the Christian centuries. Western intellectuals are drawn to historians of the Middle East like Edward Said who specialize in the sins of the imperialists. In those circles, "racism" and "orientalism" are blamed for the low self-esteem of the Arabs. Appreciation for the history of Muslim tolerance towards the Christians and Jews is the proper antidote. Thus, those who serve the post-Christian agenda nod appreciatively while Muslims present their cleaned-up picture of the golden age of Islamic toleration and cultural achievement. This allows all involved to put all the blame for the present unhappiness of the Muslim Arabs upon dead white European males.

In the United States, a particularly vicious application of these insights is to be found in the Nation of Islam, the black Muslim movement whose members are taught that their rightful heritage is Islam, which, everywhere in the world today and always in the past, has been exempt from the sin of racism, in contrast to Christianity, "the White Man's religion," the religion of slaves. Not coincidentally, black Muslims openly sell the *Protocols of the Elders of Zion* in New York subways. The teachings of the Nation of Islam have been publicly endorsed as authentic Islam by certain authorities in Libya and elsewhere, but they have been disowned by Muslim authorities generally.[13] For my purpose, the issue is not the theological authenticity of this teaching but rather its contribution to a popular and politically powerful perception of Islam as the constant foe of racism, a source of progressive attitudes for people oppressed by Christianity. Many non-Muslim black intellectuals and academics in the United States have echoed these themes in their retelling of black history. In Europe, something parallel to the influence of the black Muslim movement exists in movements of fundamentalist Islam among the underclass of *émigré* workers. But less well known in North American is a vogue for Islam that has recently come over French intellectuals. There have been several conversions of prominent Marxists, neo-Marxists, ex-existentialists, and even ex-Christians (notably Roger Garaudy).[14] It would be impossible to overestimate the propaganda advantage that has come to the Muslim side from these conversions among the European intelligentsia.

It is puzzling but true that many Jews are likewise disposed to remember the years of Islamic empire as a golden period. The thinking of secular Jews is, *pari passu*, in line with that of the post-Christians and perhaps needs no separate treatment. Yet there is a longer historical root that has to be considered. In the Byzantine Empire, Jews were at the very bottom of the pyramid of power and privilege; then, when the Muslim regime replaced the Byzantines, their Christian masters were kicked down into the cellar with them. Now there was an opportunity for the Jews to negotiate modest improvements in their contractual situtation. While remaining in the category of subordinated people, the Jews enjoyed relatively greater opportunities for freedom of movement and social improvement than before. When the Crusaders came in the eleventh century and the work of liquidating the Jews was resumed in earnest, the Muslim period came to be remembered as relative paradise; so that when the Crusaders were in turn routed and Muslim conquerors reappeared in the thirteenth century and afterward, the Jews of the Middle East quickly persuaded themselves that rule by Christians was the worst of the possiblilities that history afforded them. Even to this day, there is a tendency among Jews to minimize the oppressive reality of the Muslim period, in the more-or-less wilful effort to remind contemporary Christians of the crimes that Christian Europe has perpetrated against the Jews.

In the West, where historical research remains a domain for lively enquiry, and where standards of proof required for historical facts and historical generalizations are well developed, there has been abundant review of the Christian centuries, and lessons about Christian failings have been engrossed in all the textbooks. In their official statements, all the Church bodies of the West (including the Roman Catholic church) have amply recalled and expressed contrition for their sins. In too many instances, this has led much further: to an unworthy, unscholarly tendency to get in line with Third World thinking by endorsing uncritically the claims of Muslim historians. Needless to say, there is no reciprocity from the other side, where the political advantage of Western cultural self-loathing is always appreciated.

If this were merely an exercise in cultural condescension, or an expression of intercultural courtesy, there might be nothing to complain of. But in fact there are great hazards in this tendency towards selective amnesia. In the present world, where at last neither Christians nor Jews are at risk of domination by the other, Christians and Jews have no need to go on endlessly reminding each other of the crimes that marked the era of Christian domination, nor to go on pretending to see symptoms of the continuing will-to-persecute in the other's behaviour. Nowhere in the world today are Jewish communities living under persecution by entire Christian communities. To make this statement, it is not necessary to deny the continuing presence of (on the one hand) an anti-Semitic spirit among some Christians, most ominously in the vicinity of the former Soviet empire but also in North America, or (on the other) fear and loathing of Christians on the part of some Jews. In contrast, there *is* ongoing and increasing persecution against both Jews and Christians in many parts of the world by the same third party – namely, Islam.

Palestinian contextual theologians are largely responsible for the pro-Palestinian anti-Zionist rhetoric in the ecumenical Church, being assisted in this by the minimal familiarity of Church people (not excluding the clergy) with the history of the early Church, and, specifically, with the history of the struggles over the heresies known as Gnosticisim and Marcionism. The readiness of neo-Marcionite Christians to enter into dialogue with secular anti-Zionists and Muslims and against Zionism is thus no mystery.

Only in present-day Israel are there to be found Christians who are subjects of a legal system organized and enforced by Jews. And here the extremely bitter politics of the Arab-Israeli conflict presents the temptation to poison the relationship between Jews and Christians with distorted and selective reports of persecution of Christians by Jews. Minimizing the reality of Muslim oppression of Christians and Jews in the past *and the present* while exaggerating or dwelling obsessively upon the wickedness of the Christian empire of the past gives an enormous propaganda advantage to present-day Arab politicians, who see no need to concede any flaws in the history of Muslim empires. Indeed, all Arab politicians recognize the urgency of improving their Muslim credentials, as they seek to maintain the allegiance of Arab populations that are increasingly enthralled by Muslim absolutism.

Muslims today join hands with anti-Christian and anti-Zionist historians and ideologues in an effort to get us to understand that Christians and Jews were "protected" communities under Muslim empire. They never pause to ask, "Protected against whom?" And, of course, the answer to that is protected from Islam. The protection that the Muslims extended to the Jews and the Christians was (like that dispensed by the mafia) from Muslims, not from some third party – as all others were converted or liquidated.

The governing reality in this history is the *dhimma* – the pact, or contract, under which conquered People of the Book (Christians, Jews, and Zoroastrians) acknowledged the inferiority of their religion and accepted to live under the command of their communities' leaders, who in turn agreed to supervise the people's adherence to specified limitations on their lives and to report on their compliance to the Muslim masters. *Dhimmi* people (that is, all Christians and Jews) paid a heavy tax (*jizyah*) from which Muslims were exempt. They were forbidden to own land, which greatly limited the economic prospects of the masses. Their clothing was restricted to certain types and styles, and on it they wore distinguishing badges – a symbol of a monkey for the Jews, a symbol of a pig for the Christians – so that they lived without dignity. Since they were not allowed to bear witness against a Muslim, they were constantly vulnerable to fraud and extortion. They could not build new churches or repair old ones without express permission of the Muslim ruler.

The key to all this is that the *dhimma* was an unequal contract, subject to revision by the master party whenever a new idea occurred for wringing profit from the *dhimmi*'s situation, and subject to rescinding altogether when an excuse occurred for accusing the *dhimmi* community of bad behaviour or treason. All of these restrictions became reasons for the weak (or the cunning) to convert to Islam. That, of course, was part of the purpose. What is really remarkable is not that Christians and Jews converted (while Zorastrians virtually disappeared) but that a substantial minority still had not done so by the nineteenth century,[15] when the intrusion of European powers into the area provided them for the first time with a measure of real protection.

Secularists and most Christians who have been raised in a modern limited state seem to find it difficult to understand that their notion of religious exercise as a fundamental right (along with freedom of speech, freedom of association, and other "First Amendment" rights) has nothing whatever in common with the rules that govern Muslims. In Islam, the possibility of not being a Muslim is *permitted* to certain *communities* – historically, mainly Christians and Jews – that Allah explicitly exempted from the necessity of conversion. Conversion by force is the only option for others. For those born Muslim, conversion *away from* Islam is punishable by death. There are no exceptions or extenuating circumstances. In the words of Jacques Ellul: "For the conquering Islam of today, those who do not claim to be Muslims do not have any human rights recognized as such. In an Islamic society, the non-Muslims would return to their former *dhimmi* status, which is why the idea of solving the Middle East conflicts by the creation of a federation including Israel within a group of Muslim people or states, or in a 'Judeo-Islamic' state, is a fantasy and an illusion. From the Muslim point of view, such a thing would be unthinkable."[16]

HISTORICAL ROOTS OF MUSLIM HOSTILITY TO THE JEWISH STATE

The modern state of Israel is one of the Jews' brief success stories, but this must be the last.

Ahmad Shafaat[17]

Islam calls upon and orders Muslims to own all means of power and superiority.

Abd Rahman Abbad[18]

Whoever has occupied part of Palestine or Jerusalem faces *jihad* until Judgement Day. Our destiny is *jihad.*

> Sheikh Muhammed Hussein, preaching at the
> Al Aqsa mosque, May 1998[19]

Muslim-Jewish dialogue is still non-existent. It has absolutely nothing to show for itself; no precedent, not even a hypothetical agenda. The creation of the state of Israel and the continuous hostility this has engendered between Jewry and the Muslim World prevented any dialogue from taking place.

> Isma'il Raji al-Faruqi, Chairman, Islamic Studies
> Group, American Academy of Religion[20]

In the arsenal of anti-Zionist propaganda, nothing is so potent as the identification of Zionism with imperialism. To keep Westerners persuaded about the illegitimacy of Zionism and therefore doubtful about the permanence of Israel's right to be in the world at all, Arab and Muslim spokesmen harp constantly on the great dislocation that Israel's creation has caused. One Western scholar of the present-day Arab world has recently written (with a straight face): "Had it not been for what happened in Palestine, the post-Second World War years might have been the beginning of a period of happiness and prosperity for the Arabs."[21] This is music to the ears of all Arabs, as it excuses them from responsibility for their failure to experience the "happiness" that is the general lot of mankind everywhere else on earth.

From time to time, it is necessary for those of us who live in such giant nations as the United States, Canada, Australia, and Britain – Britain *is* a giant, by comparison with Israel, which is about the size of Wales – to remind ourselves of how small Israel is, and, more pointedly, how small a portion of that neighbourhood – which is otherwise a Muslim Arab neighbourhood – she possesses. Today there are twenty-one separate states, as well as the PLO, in the Arab League, a total population of over three hundred million – that is, about fifty times the population of Israel. The Arab states take up some five million square miles, which accounts for about one-tenth of the landmass of the world, even though they are no more than about one-twentieth of the population of the world. Arab lands amount to some 650 times the landmass occupied by Israel (eight thousand square miles), which has about one-one thousandth of the world population. To help us visualize this disparity, we could think of the entire landmass of the US, including Hawaii and Alaska, along with about three-quarters of that of Canada, compared to the approximate landmass and the approximate population of Maryland alone.

Why does the miniscule presence of a non-Arab, non-Muslim entity cause such derangement of life in that part of the world? Why is it that the issue of Israel and her relationship with her neighbours is such an obsession at the UN?

Israel's offence follows not from any of the properties that Western-ers (Christian or secular) imagine they can measure (size, population, wealth); nor does it follow from any of the categories of moral evalua-tion that they use when reckoning the rights and wrongs behind other current political issues. *Israel's offence follows from the nature of Islam.* It is because Israel is the only non-Muslim sovereign state in the heart of the Muslim world that Muslims cannot be at peace with it. Israel has accomplished what is theologically impossible and impermissible. She has taken a portion of the Muslim world into the world of anti-Islam. The Qur'an states that, for their refusal to heed the prophet, "humili-ation and wretchedness were stamped upon them [the Jews] and they were visited with wrath from Allah" (Sura 2:61; compare with Sura 3:112.). Muslims understand this as an eternal judgment on the Jews. The creation of the State of Israel is an intolerable reversal of this judg-ment, an assault on the credibility of Islam that cannot be permitted to stand.

A Muslim contributor to a conference of the Life and Peace Insti-tute of Uppsala (which "seeks to contribute to justice, peace and rec-onciliation through research, seminars and publications") explained the "Muslim perspective" of Israel to his mainly Christian audience in 1992: "[With the Balfour Declaration,] Britain granted Islamic land, which did not belong to Britain, to people who did not live on the land, and had no relation to it except a religious connection ... In the year 1967, Israel invaded and declared war on neighbouring Arab countries, and occupied all of Palestine. The West Bank, Gaza, the Sinai Desert, and the Syrian Golan Heights, and all Islamic holy places and shrines fell under Israeli military authority, most notably the Al-Aqsa Mosque, the 1st Qibla for Muslims."[22] The *Qibla* is the fixed point in the mosque that indicates the direction in which to pray, which in every mosque in the world today is towards Mecca. This remark bears out the Islamic view that Muhammad's *original* intention to pray towards Jerusalem, later corrected, is now to be understood as fixing the exclusiveness of Islam's claim to *this* Holy site *no less than* its claim to Mecca and Medina. In Islam, nothing, once possessed, is ever given up to the other side. When, in June 1967, the combined Arab forces failed to save the "Holy Places of Islam" from Israeli armies, "the responsibility for liberating the Mosque, as well as the Islamic land was transferred from their hands to the Islamic nations. Nothing will delay its liberation when a leader such as Saladin appears to call for struggle and gather Arab countries ... We lived on this land since the beginning of its existence. We have never left it ... The occupation of Palestine left a deep wound in every Muslim's heart ... In Islam, peace is the foundation upon which relations are built, according to God's word. All believers should participate and share in peace ... But Islam calls upon and orders Muslims to own all means of power and superiority as the Quranic verse says: 'You have to prepare power by all means so as to frighten your enemy.'"[23]

The Balfour Declaration of 2 November 1917 put the Muslim world on notice that the major nations of the world intended to help the Jewish people put off all traces of their past state of dhimmitude. The same powers that pledged to the Jews that they would have a homeland in Palestine also made pledges to certain Arab rulers, which the latter took to mean that all of the Ottoman Empire would become an Arab regime – something that no responsible British or French figure, not even the egregious Lawrence of Arabia, had ever said. With their selective recollection of these events, Arab nationalists and their friends among the popular historians of the West have insisted that to the extent that the resultant situation has fallen short of the pan-Arab dream, there has been a betrayal of the promises to Abdullah, Faisal, and "the Arab people."

A depressing history of efforts by subject (non-Arab) populations to achieve nationhood by separation from Arab majorities marks the subsequent seventy years or so. The Kurds have been struggling since the 1920s for national independence against Turks, Iraqis, and Iranians. The French formed Lebanon with a central core of Christians surrounded by Muslims, wherein the Muslims were, at first, a minority. When the Muslims became a majority, they began to retract the guarantees made to the Christians, and in recent decades they have resorted to terrorism to reduce the will of the Christians to continue. The presence of Israeli forces on both sides of the border has probably prevented the liquidation of the Christians – at least, of the smaller Christian sects. Iraq came into being under British auspices, a state comprising Arab Sunni Muslims in the centre, Arab Shiite Muslims in the south (Basra), and Kurds and Assyrians in the north (Mosul). Promises to protect the Assyrians (sometimes called, the Chaldeans, adherents of a very early pre-Chalcedonian Christian branch originally called "Nestorian") were abandoned without apology, with the result that the Iraqi regime simply liquidated them during the 1930s, while the world's attention was on other matters. In northeastern Syria, attempts by one million Christians to create an ethnic enclave were resisted by the French during the years of their mandate there so that, upon independence (1947), the Syrian government was free to disperse the Christian minority throughout the country. The Copts of Egypt, who claim to be descendants of the original Egyptian people and thus non-Arab, and who were a Christian nation for many centuries before the arrival of the Muslim-Arab conquerors, declared in 1912 their intention to form a state in upper Egypt but were crushed by the Arab government, supported by Britain. Today they live under an Arab regime, nominally Muslim, and increasingly incapable (to the dubious extent that it is willing) of protecting them against the terrorism of Muslim absolutists.[24]

In similar machiavellian spirit, Great Britain, after the Second World War, turned a deaf ear to the fears of African Christians, as well as African animists, in the south of the Sudan region and dealt them into the Muslim Arab state of Sudan, where they have faced increasing persecution, culminating in recent years in a deliberate war of genocide – likewise little noted by the world.

As in the days of the original Arab conquests, these non-Muslim, mostly non-Arab, people have been faced with the choice between forced conversion to Islam or communal death by a thousand cuts, almost totally ignored by the Western press. While American and European news services maintain large camera crews at the ready to catch (and, on slow days, provoke) the next rock-throwing incident in the West Bank or Gaza, or in the vicinity of the Temple Mount, no camera crews are permitted to disturb the anti-Christian atrocities of any of the Arab regimes under which Christians suffer daily. Politicians and journalists who talk about "comprehensive settlement in the Middle East" rarely bring into this ambit the national aspirations of the Kurds, Assyrians, Coptics, the Dinkas of southern Sudan, or the many others suffering under Arab majorities. So far as one could infer from the mountain of documents pouring out from the WCC, only the "Palestinians" have suffered the indignity of being denied "a land of their own."

With the restraining hand of the Ottomans and then the British and French removed, Arab majorities returned to the unfinished business of the past. Anti-Jewish and anti-Christian mob violence occurred everywhere in the newly liberated Arab Middle East. The Jews were the most vulnerable. The creation of the State of Israel, followed by Israel's successful War of Independence, resulted in the relocation to the new homeland of virtually all of the roughly 800,000 Jews who had been resident in Arab lands. In this way, the Jewish *dhimmi* ceased to exist. This exodus of the Jews from lands where they had been been underprivileged minorities, marked by the effects of centuries of dhimmitude, left the local Christian populations with no others to share their minority status. Some of these Christians were Arabs, but most were not. In the latter category are the six million Copts in Egypt (about six percent of the whole population), the seven million black Africans in Sudan, the Armenians, Lebanese Maronites, and others.

Taking this longer historical perspective, we see Zionism in quite a different light than that shed by the college history textbooks – not as part of the legacy of "imperialism" but as a uniquely successful effort to establish national self-government by a non-Arab, non-Muslim people in the heartland of the historical Middle Eastern empires. And that is why, forgetting all else, the Muslim Arabs of the region have for fifty years remained unreconciled to its bad example. The Jews succeeded because they were not dependent only on those of their people who had been shaped by the experience of centuries of submission to the succession of authoritarian regimes that governed in this area; instead, they had the moral, political, and financial resources necessary to attract millions of their people from the furthest recesses of the world – people who had been untouched by the mentality of dhimmitude. For the other minorities of the region – the Kurds, Assyrians, Copts, African Sudanese – the Jews offer the only model of successful nationalist liberation.

In this light we can see why the Christian communities of Palestine work so hard at stressing their common Arab heritage with the Muslim majority. They are struggling to save themselves from ending up in the same camp with the Copts, Armenians, Assyrians, Kurds, Black Sudanese. Some spokesmen for the Christian communities in Israel do not blush to say, "We are Arabs first, then Christians." Those who do not go quite that far still dwell upon "a common culture, a common history, a common language ... a common land ... a common heritage."[25] Beginning in the late nineteenth century, Christian Arabs participated in nationalist movements, first against the Ottoman (Turkish) Empire, then against European-controlled "Mandates." During the Mandate period (that is, the 1920s and subsequently), these better-educated, more-adaptable, bilingual or multilingual Christians took advantage of the demand for teachers, civil servants, and so on. They flourished in the professions, in banking, and in commerce. In fact, Christians played a disproportionately large role in Arab nationalist movements because of their much greater educational and economic accomplishments and their greater familiarity with the European situation (all of this owing to the European missionary presence). When independence came to the Arab states, at a time when most

Muslims were illiterate or at best partially literate, unskilled, working the fields of powerful, unsympathetic Turkish or Arab landlords, Christians were well placed to give leadership in the political movements that carried the banners not only of local nationalism (that is, as Egyptian, Syrian, Iraqi, Lebanese) but also of the sometimes parallel, sometimes contrary, movement of pan-Arab nationalism. But these very same circumstances equally assured that the Christians of the Middle East were better able to avail themselves of the opportunity to go to the West in search of new life as immigrants. Then followed a push-pull effect: as the numbers of Christians declined (because of emigration), the remaining Christians felt their greater vulnerability at home; and this led more to contemplate emigration, so as to be reunited with those who have preceded them to the West. Thus, while Christians in the Middle East were becoming more prominent in the various nationalist and liberationist movements in the region, the constituences from which they came were shrinking. This phenonomenon is important for our understanding of the PLO and the PFLP, in both of which Christian Arabs have been disproportionately prominent.

The closing-down of the Jewish *dhimmi* communities in the Middle East, beginning in 1948, left the local Christian populations with no others to share their minority status. This alone might explain the energy that Christian minorities put into asserting their anti-Zionism. But the anti-Zionism of Middle East Christians is not merely a matter of political opportunism. It draws on a deep well of Judaeophobia which goes back before the Muslims were on the scene – back to the days when Jews and Oriental Christians both lived in submission under Byzantine Christians. And it draws on theology: the *supersessionism* that remains a vital part of the self-understanding of both the Orthodox and Oriental churches

The very concept of the Restoration of the Jews to Israel seems to be alien to the mind of the Oriental churches. Archbishop Philip Saliba, metropolitan of the Antiochan Orthodox Christian archdiocese of North America, speaks for the Eastern churches: "The obvious biblical truth is that the current nation of Israel has nothing to do with God's true Israel. In rejecting Christ the messiah, the modern nation keeps the conditions of neither the old nor the new covenant ... Political Zionists are not heirs of any of God's promises ... In this gross misunderstanding of the word of God – in this modern and novel so-called 'biblical interpretation' – murder, torture, rape, and persecution are justified by professing Christians. Injustice is glorified, and racism is perpetrated. It is astonishing but true that today, in the United States of America where we pledge that we believe in 'liberty and justice for all,' some people actually encourage Israel to seize the homes of Arabs and even kill the Palestinians and their children – and then cheer when they do so. Is this the spirit of Christ?"[26] Christian Zionism, in turn, owes everything to the heresy of "restorationism": the idea that Israel "must return physically to the land it occupied for some of its history is notably modern – which even most proponents of the view admit. Only in the twentieth century has the idea that Israel is destined to return to the holy land been held by more than a handful of people, and until recently, by none but a minute segment of independent protestants."[27]

Bishop Saliba reviews the history of Israel and finds that, indeed, "Israel was eventually given the land under the old covenant, and the several peoples there were driven out because of their sin." (How then, one must wonder, did they get to become the aboriginal ancestors of "the Palestinians"?) But later, Israel "was driven out because of their sin." In the old covenant there was no "unconditional promise to the land ... God has revealed that the old covenant is over! ... Can the Jew be saved through Jesus Christ? Absolutely. Virtually the entire first wave of converts in the New Testament were Jews. But to find salvation, the Jew does not need to be back in the land ... God is no longer in the real estate business."[28] From this point, the metropolitan elaborates the full-blooded supersessionist doctrine, using the heading "The Promises of God are for the Church."

Thus, the historical argument (that the Palestinians are the autochthonous people of the land) combines with the theological argument (classical supersessionism) to make an airtight case against the legitimacy of the State of Israel: Israel is an ungodly interloper, and her defenders are the enemies of God – precisely the Muslim argument, improved by the addition of Christian theological vocabulary.

Church leaders and theologians in the East reject Restorationism in anger. And, as always, anger leads to denial, in this instance denial of the historical record of support for the creation of the State of Israel in the Christian West, which was never confined to "a minute segment of independent protestants" but broadly maintained inside the Churches of the West up to the day of the creation of the State of Israel. The Eastern Churches have a great deal invested in this fiction – that Christian Zionism is an aberrant "fundamentalist" creed kept alive by pamphleteers, confined to the garbage dumps on the edges of the respectable Church world, where all kinds of septic theological debris can be found lying around. At the same time, this characterization has great appeal to the theological establishment of the mainline churches. Not coincidentally, the core of pro-Zionism within the Churches of the West has been eroded in recent decades, precisely as the Roman Catholic church has drawn closer to the Churches of the East, and as the World Council of Churches has actually brought these Church bodies of the East within its ranks.

In their patronizing of the worldview of the churches of the Middle East, the Churches of the West are putting at risk all the work that has been done towards reconciliation with the Jewish people. Wittingly or not, the Churches of the West have permitted the Judaeophobia that still grips the spirits of the Christians of the East to infect their own declarations on "the Middle East situation." Leaders of the Western Churches are told that the Palestinians are "the living stones" that constitute the real presence of Christ in the Holy Land, in contrast to the dead stone edifices to which the tourists come, and which their Muslim neighbours (understandably) resent as souvenirs of the Crusades. They are told that, unless they avoid all appearance of pro-Zionism in their public utterances, unless they keep the heat on Israel at every moment of the "peace process," they will be seen as acessories to the crimes of the oppressors of the living Church – persecuting the very descendants of the first Christians. Thus we hear more and more from bishops and moderators and Christian leaders just back from in-depth two-week tours of the Holy Land of the "wickedness" of the Zionists, of their "sinful oppression" of Christians and Muslims alike, of Israelis having the heart of conquerors and the spirit of Herod.

Yet the reality is that, even as a political strategy, the "living stones option" is not working. However constantly and however harshly the Churches of the West denounce the Israeli occupiers for their sins, the local political stock of the various Christian communities and throughout the Middle East keeps going down. Nothing can shake the Muslims' conviction that the West is the enemy of Islam, that local Christians, the spawn of the Crusaders, are obstacles to the peace that will come – when, again, "Muslims own all means of power and superiority." The reality, as Bat Ye'or has shown, is that "Arab anti-Zionism is fundamentally anti-Christian. It is part of the same ideology which justified a millennium of war against Christians of the lands conquered by jihad. The delegitimation of the State of Israel constitutes a delegitimation of the West itself" – certainly not because the West likes or supports Israel but because the two Peoples of the Book are indissolubly linked in the *jihad* dogma and in the concept of dhimmitude. Thus, Western anti-Zionism has resulted in the strengthening of Islamic and anti-Western radicalism.[29]

ISLAMIC *JIHAD*

In the arguments that we hear in support of recognition of Palestinian nationhood there is much that is historically unsound, much dubious racial theorizing, much that is invented or wilfully denied, much that is borrowed from the history of the Jews and of Zionism and inverted. But there is another way to make the case against the Jews' possession of the land of Israel that is much harder to refute, because it does not rest on the facts of history – in fact, has no interest in them. That is the case that rests on Muslim theology.

A wonderful clarification of all the cloudy argumentation follows when we get onto the ground of Muslim theology. The claim to *Muslim* ownership of Palestine follows powerfully and irresistibly from the central Muslim doctrine of *jihad*, under which everthing we need to know about human affairs follows from the division of the world into two irreconcilable camps: the *dar-al-Harb* (the territory of War), and the *dar-al-Islam*, the territory that has been taken irreversibly out of the *dar-al-Harb* and is now submitted eternally to Allah.[30] In the *dar-al-Islam*, Islam rules everything. In the *dar-al-Harb*, Islam rules nothing (which does not contradict the other reality, that *Allah* rules over everything). Islam forbids that there should ever be peace for Muslims so long as any part of Allah's world withholds *submission* (which is what "Islam" means). Reconciliation between dar-al-Islam and any part of dar-al-Harb is not envisioned for a moment. A state of truce is permitted, so long as it is modelled on the truce that the Prophet made with the infidels from time to time in his lifetime – the classic instance of which is the Treaty of *Khudaibiya* (see page 106).

If, when we read PLO documents, we try the exercise of transposing the secular rhetoric into the key of *Islam*, a marvellous clarity comes into everything – into the historical presumptions, into the moral assumptions, into the ideological assumptions, into the tactical and strategic assumptions. For example, we read in the PLO covenant: "Article 1: Palestine is the homeland of the Arab Palestinian people; it is an indivisible part of the Arab homeland, and the Palestinian people are an integral part of the Arab nation ... Article 13: Arab unity and the liberation of Palestine are two complementary objectives, the attainment of either of which facilitates the attainment of the other. This Arab unity leads to the liberation of Palestine; the liberation of Palestine leads to Arab unity." The logical difficulties that follow from trying to think of the same people making these claims as "Arabs" and "Arab Palestinians" and "Palestinians" all at the same time vanish instantly when we see that what is being talked about is the *dar-al-Islam*. This helps to make sense of Article 9: "Armed struggle is the only way to liberate Palestine. Thus it is the overall strategy, not merely a tactical phase ... Therefore the aim of the Palestinian revolution is to liquidate this entity [Israel] in all its aspects, political, military, social, trade unions and culture, and to liberate Palestine completely."[31]

On rare occasions we are given a look into this reality. Speaking to the faithful, in settings believed to be secure, Yassir Arafat will proclaim (as he did during a visit to a mosque in South Africa six days after signing the first Oslo Accord) that Muslims must rise up as *mujaheddin* (Islamic warriors) and join the *jihad* for Jerusalem's liberation – that the Oslo Accord is a *solha donia* (despicable truce), which should be understood in the light of the peace treaty that Mohammed made with the Quraish tribe.[32] Some time after the signing of the Oslo Accords, Arafat told a gathering of Arab diplomats: "I have no use for Jews. We now need all the help we can get from you in our battle for a united Palestine under total Arab-Muslim domination."[33]

In the logic of *jihad*, the State of Israel is simply illegal; countenancing it in any way is immoral and blasphemous. What *can* happen is truce. And truce can be called "Peace"; for that, the example comes from Muhammad himself. But it can never be considered permanent. These facts give the so-called Israeli-Arab conflict its cosmic importance.

What can we say, then, of decisions recently taken by Egypt, Jordan, Mauritania on 29 October 1999) and even (tentatively, and with escape clauses) the PLO, to "recognize" Israel? There are governments, like those in Egypt and Jordan, that imagine that they have "fundamentalist" forces at bay and can enter into diplomatic arrangements under which a state of affairs less than the Muslim ideal is chosen as the alternative to constant conflict and dislocation and derangement of daily life; in other words, they might choose to act as other nations do. But we should never lose sight of the fact that in doing so they are making themselves enemies of Islam. Where the ruler of such a nation is himself a serious Muslim and states or imagines that such an effort is undertaken in the spirit of Islam (as the late Anwar Sadat believed – or told Jimmy Carter that he believed before, during, and after the Camp David peace negotiations in 1975), he will find that others who claim to know the heart of Islam better than he does will make him a target forever of Muslim correction and, in doing so, will have the applause of all the Muslim theological academies and the Muslim masses.

These are the political realities about Islam that have to be kept in mind by Western statesmen, educators, and political commentators: First, Islam is the fastest growing religion in the world. Where Islam is already a major religious force, it daily becomes greater; in parts of the world where it has hitherto had no significant presence, it is taking hold and spreading rapidly. For example, it is estimated that in the UK in recent years five hundred churches have been turned into mosques. In the United States, there are now more Muslims than Episcopalians.[34] Muslims are becoming aggressive in asserting rights under the constitutional arrangements that are already in place in European countries, in Britain, in Canada and other former Dominions, and in the US – rights that are nowhere conceded to non-Muslims where Muslims rule. In some places, they have already gone beyond that to demand official public recognition and accomodation for the religious practices that are peculiar to Islam, and that were never envisaged when the relevant constitutional charters (the Bill of Rights in the US, the Charter of Rights and Freedoms in Canada, and the various statutes that make up the Religious Settlement in the UK) came into existence: in other other words, they are demanding to be dealt into the religious establishment.

Second, Islam is an intensifying presence where it already exists. Western commentators with extensive experience of the Middle East report that more and more people are becoming religiously serious. They are voluntarily increasing their attendance at mosques, praying with greater regularity, reading the Qur'an more regularly, reading religious tracts and books, attaching themselves to Islamic associations, and changing their habits of dress to express openly their intention to live by the faith. More and more politicians are declaring their fidelity to Islam, and their readiness to support Muslim activities.

Third, Islam is *essentially* hostile to democracy. There is nothing in the original message of the prophet that supports a democratic theory. Neither is there anything to be found in the history of the Muslim world since then that suggests a tendency towards democracy, such as developed in European history. Western commentators are constantly trying to persuade us that Muslim "fundamentalists" (to use the media's unfortunate term) who talk of a revival of Islamic purity *really* want democracy. Yet the Muslim purists have only contempt for *dimugratiyya* (democracy). It is a foreign notion: according to a slogan employed by the Algerian Muslim radical leaders, "One does not vote for God. One obeys him."[35] A.M. Rosenthal of the *New York Times* sums up the result of Middle Eastern political development in our time: "Since World War II, the Arab world has failed to produce a single government that shares power with its people, a single government that holds itself accountable to its people, a single government based on genuine parliamentary process, religious freedom and democratic restraints ... The failure of democracy to take root in the Mideast enabled Arab leaders to slaughter and smother their people while convincing the survivors that their real enemy was Israel and the West. And it is the reason why no matter how much land Israelis surrender for peace, the next day they will wake up still surrounded by regimes that survive by hate and the sword."[36] The situation in contemporary Arab Palestine is summed up in a recent monograph published by an American university press and written by a Palestinian scholar who teaches at Bir Zeit University: "From a theoretical and doctrinal point of view, Palestinian Islamists dismiss the concept of democracy as a Western concept that has no place in a Muslim society."[37]

At virtually every session, the UN Commission on Human Rights denounces violations of human rights in Israel. It has never denounced China or Saudi Arabia.[38] Western newspapers that report the UN judgments on Israel never include the information that in the vanguard of the nations that have whipped together the majorities for such votes are Muslim states that have *officially stated* that the United Nations documents under which Israel is being condemned do not apply to their own citizens. In this category are the Universal Declaration of Human Rights (1948), the International Covenant on Civil and Political Rights (1966), the UN Declaration on the Elimination of all Forms of Intolerance and Discrimination Based on Religion and Belief (1981), and others. Muslim governments and Muslim theologians take the position that such declarations cannot bind their populations, since the only legal authority in this world is *shari'a*, God's revealed law. Furthermore, *shari'a* is in clear contradiction of these documents, which (whatever their original authors may have thought) reflect Western values, not universal ones. During deliberations leading to the several revisions of the UN Declaration of Human Rights, Muslim states publicly exempted themselves from any applications that could be interpreted as conflicting with *shari'a*. In doing so, they were acknowledging the Islamic Declaration of 1980, which states: "The Sharia is the supreme law of the Muslim community and must be enforced in its entirety on all aspects of life. Each and every Muslim country must explicitly make Sharia the criterion by which to judge – and the chief source of legislation in the country."[39] Of immediate interest, for my purposes, is the affirmation by Muslim states of their right and obligation to impose the death penalty for conversion from Islam.[40] Speaking for all Muslim states, the Republic of Mauritania responded to criticism found in a UN Human Rights Report of executions imposed for the crime of conversion: "Apostasy from this religion is regarded as high treason ... (Islam) does not tolerate any alternatives or changes in this respect, because they would be incompatible with its sacred character of divinely revealed religion, based on eternal principles. No one can change what this religion prescribes, since its sacred law embraces moral principles, in which our society believes."[41]

Leaders of militant Islam recognize that Christianity is the most formidable opponent in the way of the full triumph of Islam that they anticipate. It is their intention to discredit Christianity, to prevent its missionary efforts by legal force and by intimidation, and ultimately to return Christians already in place in their midst to the *dhimmi* status of the past. Muslim fundamentalists in Algeria have publicly declared their intention to "liquidate Jews, Christians, and unbelievers."[42] In this spirit, we are to understand the slogan often seen on walls in Gaza and the West Bank, and in Muslim-Arab sections of Jerusalem and Bethlehem: "After Saturday, comes Sunday!" – or, more explicitly, "On Saturday we will kill the Jews; on Sunday, we will kill the Christians."[43] The recent history of Iran makes clear that Christians have no hope for authentic tolerance in regimes that come under the sway of militant Islam. The Baha'i community, to which previous Iranian regimes had accorded gestures of protection and respect as proofs of their own toleration and the tolerant spirit of Islam, has been virtually liquidated. Those Jews unable to flee Iran live in a mileu of intolerable harassment, as do the few Christians. Converts to Christianity are summarily executed, and the whole of the indigenous Christian population knows that Iran's leaders are listening sympathetically to reiterated calls from the press and politicians for their elimination.[44]

The example of Iran inspires Muslims elsewhere to harass and persecute Jewish and Christian communities, as a preliminary to Iranian-style revolution – notably in Sudan, Pakistan, and Indonesia. Sudan has advanced furthest along this route. Here a militant Islamic Arab-dominated regime established by a military coup in 1989 is sleeplessly engaged in the work of liquidating its Christian and other non-Muslim populations, mainly Black Africans, concentrated in the south. Despite a death toll estimated as high as three million, as the consequence of the regime's policy of deliberate starvation of the non-Muslim population, little attention has been given the story by the Western press. In 1996 the United Nations issued a Human Rights Report on Sudan, prepared by a delegation led by Dr Gaspar Biro, and including Geraldine Ferraro (who had been the vice-presidential candidate of the Democratic party in 1984). In denouncing the report, the attorney-general of Sudan, Abdulaziz Shiddo, declared Biro to be an "enemy of Islam," guilty of "blasphemy" and comparable to Salman Rushdie – that is, worthy of assassination.[45]

Meanwhile, the Middle East Council of Churches reported on the visit of "an ecumenical team" to Sudan in 1993 and found much to say in favour of Sudan's attitude:

The conviction expressed by some church leaders in the Sudan is that the policy of the central government is oriented towards the Islamic and Arabic portion of the whole society. This was said to be felt by Sudanese Christians through restrictive measures taken by the government in the fields of education and humanitarian service. If this is truly happening, then a possible explanation was expressed that Muslim decision makers are reacting to the process of evangelization that they believe was undertaken by the Christian schools during the colonial period ... Therefore the WCC team felt Muslims should be helped to discover that, through interreligious ecumenical dialogue, Christians would like to move from a past of religious misunderstanding and cultural confrontation into a future of mutual respect and cooperation in the fields of ethics, justice, and peace. Through dialogue, Christians could also be liberated from the misinterpretation that Islam is the religion of violence, or that after communism Islam is the enemy of modern civilization. It is expected that the same process would liberate Muslims from the traumas of the Crusades and the fear of the so-called "western" culture."[46]

The principal policy recommendation that members of the MECC brought home with them was that there needed to be greater study of Islam in Christian schools.[47]

In Turkey, the only Middle Eastern state that is formally secular but that has an overwhelming Muslim majority, a struggle is under way to contain the political effects of militant Islam. But this necessitates some appeasement of anti-Christian attitudes among the masses, with the result that persecution continues, to the point where the once numerous Christian communities of Turkey are now virtually extinct.[48] In regimes that have, in one fashion or another, declared themselves formally Islamic but still committed to religious tolerance (for instance, Egypt), official concern for religious minorities has to be measured. Thus, the Sadat and Mubarek regimes in Egypt have alternated gestures of protection towards the Copts with gestures of harassment.[49] Under these pressures, the Coptic community of Egypt is steadily withering away. Donald Wagner, the leader of Evangelicals for Middle East Understanding (see chapter 7) has this advice for the Copts: "They will need to reconcile with their Muslim sisters and brothers and at the same time provide the spiritual and economic reasons for keeping numbers of Christians from emigrating."[50] In Lebanon, where we find the only politically important concentration of Christians in the Arab world, there has been an increasing flow of immigrants since at least the beginning of the twentieth century. Once officially considered to be one-half of the population (on which consideration a precarious balance of governmental authority was entrenched in the Lebanese consitition), they are now reduced to about twenty-five percent. Moslem terrorism is determined to reduced this number to zero.

In chapter 3 I described and illustrated the surprisingly anodyne attitude that official Church circles profess towards the issue of the future prospects for Christians in the Holy Land. Recently, however, there have been signals of a possible change of direction. In January 1998, there came from an assembly of the MECC held in Nicosia, Cyprus, a pastoral letter on the challenges facing Christians in the Middle East. Here we read: "Today, Christians face many problems which keep them from effective participation in public life, something which in turn gives rise to feelings of fear and anxiety. But despite these problems, which test the presence of Christians and their faith, we urge our sons ... to deal with the present situation in a spirit of objectivity and wisdom and free from exaggeration and scare-mongering. But this does not mean that we should make light of the gravity of the situation and the need to deal with it." Observers noted that the letter "appeared at pains to avoid details of the problems facing Middle East Christians or blame anyone for them," but they also agreed that it was something new for the MECC to be even hinting at the existence of a problem between Christians and Muslims. "The number of Christians is dwindling everwhere in the Arab world," said Tarek Mitri, a Lebanese who deals with interreligious relations at the World Council of Churches. "Everyone has been whispering about the decline in the numbers, but now it is being openly discussed."[51]

THE QUR'ANIC VIEW OF CHRISTIANITY

All those with a stake in minimizing the need for Christians to fear life under a Muslim majority place great stress on the importance of distinguishing between Muslim "fundamentalism" (which everyone deplores) and what is various called "mainstream Islam" or the Islam of the man in the street, etc. But Muslim hostility to Christianity is not a passing phenomenon, not an *epiphenomenon* attributable to certain correctable features of the current social and ecomonic scene. It is rooted in theological absolutes that cannot be removed from the Qur'an. This hostility should therefore be recognized as a permanent reality, not susceptible to modification through dialogue and sympathetic study of Islam's history and theology.

The beginning of wisdom on this matter is to recognize that the term "fundamentalist Islam" is a complete misnomer, theologically speaking. It is a term borrowed from the specific history of the Protestant church in the West, which has been wilfully smuggled into the Islamic setting by Western commentators to achieve an impression of parity between the pretensions of the two religious traditions. The essential inappropriateness of this usage can be seen only in the light of the history of the term "fundamentalism" in our tradition. And that can only be seen in the light of the history of Protestant liberal theology of the last two centuries.

Building upon the work in "textual criticism" that had developed over many generations since the Renaissance in secular scholarship, and building upon current archaeology, studies in comparative linguistics, and paleography, nineteenth-century academic theologians, Church historians, and scholars of religion applied the criteria of the secular sciences to the sacred texts in the most rigorous manner. This resulted in what is called the liberal critique of the authority of Scripture and dogma. Ever since, Protestant and Catholic seminaries alike have been obliged to present the teachings of their denominations in tandem with academic research. Concerned that their clergy-candidates should be as well armed with current learning as secular professionals, some mainstream Protestant denominations have farmed out virtually the entire work of academic certification to university schools of religion, in which almost nothing of a dogmatic character is taught. "Fundamentalism" was a movement of reaction against this situation, emerging at a fairly precise moment (on the eve of the First World War) and leading to lively contests about the authority of the Word, of dogmas, and of creed, heard in every corner of the Protestant church and (belatedly, and with some modifications of vocabulary and some differences of emphasis) within the Roman Catholic church since at least the years of Vatican II. It is not possible to be a preacher or a teacher in any corner of the Church today without, on a daily basis, confronting and giving answers to the questions that come out of that debate.

A noted Muslim scholar, Muhammed Abd al Rauf, sharing insights with Christian and Jewish academics in a recent forum of the three faiths, explained that "Islam rejects the Christian claim that the texts of scripture are integral records of the message Jesus had conveyed. In this however, as well as in other criticism, Islam is not alone. Countless biblical scholars and theologians have said the same thing. Even among 'the Apostolic Fathers,' and certainly in the Nicene, ante- and post-Nicene Fathers, countless others have maintained more or less exactly what Islam said."[52] Nothing in the recorded responses of the participating Christian scholars suggests that any of them dissented from this judgment on the sacred texts of Christian and Jews.

Muslim scholars welcome the insights of Wellhausen, Ritschl, Harnack, and the succeeding champions of "scientific" study of Scriptures but remind us that the Prophet Muhammad long ago saw everything that they saw: "In the former Divine Books [i.e., Hebrew and Christian Scripture] man mixed his words with God's, but in the Qur'an we find only the words of God – and in their pristine purity. This is admitted even by the opponents of Islam ... The former Divine Books were sent down in languages which died long ago. No nation or community now speaks these languages, and there are only a few people who claim to understand them ... The language of the Qur'an, on the other hand, is a living language ... On account of man's interpolation, many things have been inserted in those books [the Bible] which are against reality, revolting to reason and an affront to every instinct of justice ... obscene, indecent, and highly immoral. The Qur'an is free of all such rubbish."[53]

It is not easy for an educated Christian, one who believes the Creed and believes that he knows the reasons for his confidence in the reliability of the Christian and Hebrew Scriptures – who knows that the documents upon which his faith is based have for at least two centuries been going through the fire of textual criticism, historical criticism, archaeological discovery, the challenges of comparative religion, and several generations of philosophical fashions – to sit quietly while being told that the need for critical examination of the Qur'an cannot arise: "From the beginning to the end, the Book is full of Wisdom and truth. It contains the best of philosophy and the choicest of law for human civilization ... At last the most perfect code of guidance was imparted to mankind through Muhammed (blessings of Allah and peace be upon him) and all previous codes were automatically abrogated ... This is why it is incumbent on each and every human being to have faith in Muhammed (blessings of Allah and peace be upon him) and follow him alone."[54] In contrast to the Qur'an, wherein "we find only the words of God – and in their pristine purity", the "corruption and pollution of the Books [i.e., Jewish and Christian Scripture] has been so large and so evident that even the Jews and the Christians themselves admit that they do not possess their original texts, and have only their translations, which have been altered over many centuries and are still being changed ... God's words and those of man are mixed together in these books, and we have no means of knowing which portions are from God and which from man." In this spirit, apologists for Islam in the West present their religion as the beneficiary of the legacy of nineteenth-century Christian academic theology. They rejoiced in former times to hear of the discovery of the Documentary Hypothesis by Jewish scholars and of Form Criticism by Christian scholars; they applaud today each dispatch from the Jesus Seminar of California announcing the exposure of yet another "inauthentic" saying of Jesus.

Of course Islam has been unchanged by textual criticism – for the good and sufficient reason that it has never permitted textual criticism.[55]

All the serious apologists for Islam in the West know that the way to the heart of Christian theologians is to hold out the hand of fellowship in the battle against the "fundamentalists." And he knows that nothing embarrasses the liberal Christian theologian more than the persistence, in the dark, unlit periphery of the Church, of faith in the predictive force of biblical prophecy. Therefore, having gained the moral upper hand on the Christian theologians by appealing to the textbooks on biblical criticism that most clergy will dimly recall from their days in seminary, the Muslim apologist draws his Christian dialogue partners into partnership against the Christian Zionists by demonstrating how the Christian Zionist case follows from discredited texts and discredited theorizing. Thus, a Muslim theologian expects nods of approval when he explains that "traditional Christian interpretation, still held officially by many Churches and shared by many of their members, sees most of the messianic prophecies as literal words of God giving exact details of future events." This interpretation, the Muslim apologist explains, was encouraged in the early Church by the belief that "various messianic predictions in the Old Testament were fulfilled by events in the life and work of Jesus." But while these instances of alleged fulfilment of the Old Testament prophecies by Jesus "might in earlier times have helped increase faith in Jesus ... for the modern readers of the Gospels they are generally an embarrassment, and serve only to point out the error of treating Scriptural passages as if they were written with some future person's life and work in mind."[56] Such an apologist knows he has the approval of the whole tenured cohort of Old Testament professors in all the university departments of Religion when he pronounces: "[A] careful study of the history of messianic tradition reveals that it was never really a concern of the prophets to foretell the future ... The prophets are primarily concerned with revealing certain conceptions of God ... Why should it ever matter, for example, where the restorer of David's kingdom should be born?"[57] Hopefully, however, the Old Testament professors would draw the line at what follows: "These needs were fulfilled ... through Islam, with Christianity playing a preparatory and helping role ... The Church ended up with a pantheon of three consciously professed gods and one idol buried in its subconscious. As a result of this, and of the mythological interpretations of the death of Christ, the concept of God sank far below the highest level that it had reached in the Jewish tradition."[58]

With respect to the matters that concern us in this book, it should be sufficient for the Muslim apologist to have the approbation of the liberal Christian world at least to the words "where the restorer of David's kingdom should be born." It would be a bonus to have the assent of the audience through to the end of the whole passage. But that can wait. The Muslim apologist believes, with good reason, that he has destroyed the case for Christian Zionism when he has discredited the prophetic possibilities of Old Testament Scripture; and he knows that for most liberal Christians that consummation was wrought long ago, following as it does from the denigration of the "literal reading" of biblical texts. Liberal Christians of the West, who so freely disparage their own "fundamentalists," and whose hearts are so devoted to the exercise of comparative religion, openly abet this triumphalism by sitting patiently while Muslim theologians wield the slogans of biblical criticism against the Christian faith and parade the perfection of Islam. Thus the MECC, happy to be of one mind with its Muslim brothers on so vital a matter, denounces "Western Fundamentalist Christian Zionism," while the WCC nods approval. All smile benignly while the Muslims talk of their perfectly inspired texts. (What harm is there in a little courtesy?) They connive in the tactic of equating Muslim absolutism, untouched by the scientific enquiries of the the last two centuries, with Western fundamentalism. But the Western fundamentalists are not the establishment within their religious house, as the Muslim absolutists are within theirs. Instead, facing the contempt of all the institutions that hand out all the certificates that are required for success in the secular world, they seek to present one side of a debate that Islam has never permitted to begin.

What should a responsible and fair-minded Christian think about the invitation to hold a dialogue with Islam?

Cardinal Francis Arinze, president of the Pontifical Council for Inter-religious Dialogue, addressing the subject of "Christian-Muslim Relations in the 21st Century" at the Center for Muslim-Christian Understanding at Georgetown University, Washington, DC, 5 June 1997, spoke of positive signs but also of "obstacles." As for the latter, he notes that there are different approaches to human rights and especially to religious freedom in the two religions: "Christians see human beings as having been created in God's image and likeness.

They are brothers and sisters of Christ, the Son of God made man. The Muslim vision is different. The human person is the servant of God ... Christians see man as created with certain inalienable rights. Prominent among these is the right to religious freedom ... Again, the Muslim view is somewhat different. Indeed, some predominantly Muslim countries have their reservations regarding the United Nations 1948 Universal Declaration of Human Rights, which they see as an expression of Western culture." Related to this is the failure of Muslims to allow reciprocity of religious rights: "A religion should not ask for religious freedom for its followers in one country while denying the same right to other believers in a country where it is the religion of the majority. That is what reciprocity is all about."[59]

In the final analysis, the prospect for profitable dialogue with Islam must depend on what is common in their respective visions of the person of God. The judgment of Pope John Paul II on this matter is as follows: "Whoever knows the Old and New Testaments, and then reads the Koran, clearly sees the *process by which it completely reduces Divine Revelation.* It is impossible not to note the movement away from what God said about Himself, first in the Old Testament through the Prophets, and then finally in the New Testament through His Son. In Islam all the richness of God's self-revelation, which constitutues the heritage of the Old and New Testaments, has definitely been set aside. Some of the most beautiful names in the human language are given to the God of the Koran, but he is ultimately a God outside of the world, a God who is *only majesty, never Emmanual, God-with-us. Islam is not a religion of Redemption.*"[60]

6 Roman Catholic Attitudes in Transition

Modern Zionism is not the true heir of Biblical Israel, but a secular state ... Therefore the Holy Land and its sacred sites belong to Christianity, the True Israel.

Osservatore Romano, 14 May 1948[1]

When the flag of the State of Israel was raised, all of the Vatican's doctrines of the outcast, miserable Jews collapsed. We returned to our land, and it became clear that the Eternal One of Israel will not lie.

Tzvi Yehuda Ha Cohen Kook[2]

The Old Covenant has never been revoked by God.

Pope John Paul II, November 17, 1980[3]

HISTORICAL ATTITUDES OF THE ROMAN CATHOLIC CHURCH TOWARDS THE JEWISH QUESTION

Robert Drinan, an American Jesuit priest who served as a US Congressman from Massachusetts (1970–80), was an advocate of the closest possible relationship between the US and Israel. He argues in his book, *Honor the Promise: America's Commitment to Israel* (1977), that America's commitment to Israel should be valued above Israel's strategic value, above its economic value – even above its value as an embodiment of America's own political and moral values. It should be valued for Israel's own exceptional sake, because it is the embodiment of the promise of Restoration that God declared in Scripture He intended to accomplish for the Jews, and the most compelling proof possible that the God whom Christians worship will fulfill His promise to them. Drinan quotes the Zionist theologian Rabbi Abraham Joshua Heschel: "To the eyes of the heart, it is clear that returning to the land is an event in accord with the hidden Presence in Jewish history. It is a verification of a biblical promise. It has saved so many lives, it has called for so much dedication and sacrifice, it has revived hope." For his own part, Drinan says: "It is disappointing to have to note that there exist very few reflections from a Christian viewpoint about the tumultuous events that led to the re-establishment of a Jewish state."[4] But this is simply not true. In fact, a mountain of theological reflection on the forthcoming Restoration of the Jews dates from the earliest Puritan times, and literary outpourings on the theological meaning of Israel's Restoration and her ensuing adventures continue to this day. These products, however, are not to be found on the lists of major publishing houses. Well before Drinan's own time, Puritan theology, from which Restorationism and Christian Zionism both derive, had been displaced from the centre of the American culture; this legacy was now in the keeping of the residual heirs of that tradition – the despised "fundamentalists."

Drinan quotes with approval Monsignor John M. Oesterreicher, who said that Israel's success "is not altogether due to the cunning of her statesmen, the superior strategy of her generals, the bravery of her soldiers, and the steadfastness of her citizens. Rather was it the 'outstretched arm' (Exodus 6:6) of the Lord which once more rescued His people ... Today's Israel is new proof that God stands by His covenant; that the last word lies, not with the inventor of the 'final solution,' but with Him."[5]

This Christian Zionist viewpoint is rare among Roman Catholic clergy, as it has never been taught in the seminaries. Yet there is reason to think that it has become much less exceptional in Roman Catholic ranks in recent years. Both official and lay Roman Catholic attitudes towards Israel are changing, moving in directions that Christian Zionists find more congenial, although still short of what Christian Zionists desire to see. At the official level, recent statements and actions of the Church, beginning in the pontificate of Paul VI (1963–78) and continuing through the pontificate of Pope John Paul II, have redefined the theoretical and practical relationship between the Jewish and Christian communities in ways that have fostered improved Catholic-Jewish relationships in the present. The Roman Catholic church has recently entered into full diplomatic relations with Israel, and her representatives are daily striving alongside representatives of the State of Israel to find resolutions for the practical points of irritation between the State of Israel and the Roman Catholic church in the Holy Land. As for the laity, many Roman Catholics are now appearing in the ranks of Christian Zionist organizations such as the Friends of Israel and the International Christian Embassy Jerusalem.

In the past, End Times speculation was positively discouraged and had little place in Roman Catholic preaching. But in the post-Vatican II reality, Roman Catholic lay people depend more upon their own reading for perspectives on current issues; and they tune into the religious programming on television. Thus, while Roman Catholic theologians are now struggling (for their sins) with Form-Criticism, the "Documentary Hypothesis," and "the problem of the Historical Jesus," the laity are becoming acquainted with popular Protestant End Times literature.

Before we can discuss these developments, we must put in place the story of the early dealings between Roman Catholicsm and Zionism.

Surveying the literature on the origins of Zionism, Drinan finds "scarcely any mention of Christian interest or involvement in this then revolutionary concept. About the only reference to contact made by Herzl with Christians is the interview which the founder of Zionism had with Pope Pius x in 1903."[6] These remarks betray unfamiliarity with the long history of Protestant Restorationism and suggest, as well, that Fr Drinan has not penetrated very far into Herzl's diaries, which have many lengthy passages documenting his relationship with William Hechler and other early Christian Zionists. However, he certainly hits the mark with respect to the barren relationship between Zionism and the Roman Catholic branch of Christianity. Simply stated, Roman Catholicism has always been tone-deaf to Zionism – until very recent times.

When Theodor Herzl set about to achieve that interview (alluded to by Drinan) with Pope Pius x (1903–1914) in January 1904,[7] he pretended to himself and others in his circle that a solid understanding with that religious dignitary would be enough to bring the full weight of most of the Christian world into the political equation on the side of the Zionist solution to the Jewish question. This, as anyone familiar with the religious situation in Europe could have told him, was quite unrealistic. And we have reason to think that he knew as much. As a citizen of Austria, it is true, he had been raised to think of Christianity and Roman Catholicism as the same phenomenon. But in the previous decade he had invested much effort in bringing on board certain Protestant princes, including the kaiser of Germany and the prime minister and foreign minister of Great Britain. His first steps in this direction had been taken under the guidance of a Protestant preacher, William Hechler, who had succeded in making him aware of the Restorationist tradition in evangelical Protestantism, and who had demonstrated in rather dramatic ways its political possibilities. As we can see today, this Restorationist tradition was of inestimable value in bringing on side the two great Anglo-Saxon powers, Great Britain and the United States. In 1904, however, it was far from clear that the

American-British connection was going to be the determining element in the achievement of the Zionist dream. Herzl was ready to give up in a moment all the work that had gone into this courtship of Protestant princes, if that was to be the price for solid endorsement of his work by the pope.

To begin with, a man of Herzl's élitist temperament and aristocratic philosophy was instinctively drawn to hierarchical organizations. The more hierarchical the better. Herzl thought instinctively in Great Power terms – that is, from the top downwards. He talked often of the Congress of Berlin (1878), where Disraeli, Bismarck, and Cavour set their feet under the same table and disposed of Russian and Turkish assets. In like manner, Herzl, plenipotentiary of the Jews of the world, and the pope, the Vicar of Christ, would consititute a kind of congress of Judaeo-Christian civilization. He would not hesitate to propose to His Holiness that he, Theodor Herzl, could work out the conversion of the entire Jewish race to Roman Catholicism, as part of the deal by which they should acquire their homeland.[8] Herzl was aware of Christian interests in the holy places, and he expected that, after a certain amount of theological rumination, the pope would get around to his concerns for the Roman Catholic presence in the Holy Land. In response, Herzl would direct him to the passage in *Der Judenstaat* (1896) where he states what would be the official Zionist position on the matter down to the day when the holy places in fact came into Israeli custody in June of 1967: "The sanctuaries of Christendom would be safeguarded by assigning to them an extra-territorial status such as is well known to the law of nations. We should form a guard of honour about these sanctuaries, answering for the fulfilment of this duty with our existence. This guard of honour would be the great symbol of the solution of the Jewish Question after eighteen centuries of Jewish suffering."[9]

Herzl's summit conference with the pope did not go well. The fundamental problem seemed to be that the Roman Catholic church did not have Herzl's confidence that the conversion of the Jews could be easily arranged – and this not because of any fault of the Church. In the exploratory session (22 January 1904) with the Vatican's secretary of state, Cardinal Merry del Val, he was told: "I do not quite see how we can take any initiative in this matter. As long as the Jews deny the Divinity of Christ, we certainly cannot make a declaration in their favor ... How then can we, without abandoning our highest principles, agree to their being given possession of the Holy Land again? "Inwardly appalled, Herzl calmly replied: "We are asking only for the profane earth; the Holy Places are to be extraterritorialized." But the cardinal was not mollified: "The history of Israel is our own heritage, it is our foundation. But in order for us to come out for the Jewish people in the way you desire, they would first have to be converted."[10]

The interview with the Pope was no more successful. According to Herzl's diary, the pope's response to the Zionist proposal was that "We cannot prevent the Hebrews from going to Jerusalem, but we could never sanction it ... The Jews have not recognized our Lord, therefore we cannot recognize the Jewish people." Herzl tried again, saying that "our point of departure had been solely the distress of the Jews and that we desired to avoid the religious issues." But the pope would have none of it: "The Jewish religion was the foundation of our own; but it was superseded by the teachings of Christ, and we cannot concede it any further validity. The Jews, who ought to have been the first to acknowledge Jesus Christ, have not done so to this day ... We pray for the Jews, that their minds be enlightened ... And so, if you come to Palestine and settle your people there, we shall have churches and priests ready to baptize all of you."[11]

When the Allied governments were laying the groundwork for what would become the Balfour Declaration, they set up a meeting between Nahum Sokolow of the World Zionist Organization and Pope Benedict xv (1914–1922) for 10 May 1917. This was a much more congenial and apparently profitable encounter than that between Herzl and Pius x in 1904. In fact, Sokolow reports back on "a most satisfactory attitude on the part of the Vatican towards Zionism." The pope exclaimed: "The revival of Israel through the people of Israel. Have I understood the purpose of Zionism correctly? What a turnabout of fate! 1,900 years ago Rome destroyed your homeland, and today, when you seek to rebuild it, you have chosen a path which leads via Rome! ... Yes, this is the will of divine Providence; this is what the Almighty desires." As for the holy places, the pope said: "I have no doubt that we shall be able to reach a satisfactory understanding ... Yes, I do hope that we shall be good neighbours."[12] No doubt the different attitudes of the two popes owed at least something to the different political settings. In 1904 Zionism had no sponsors among the Powers, prepared to take the necessary actions to dislodge Syria-Palestine from the grip of the Turks. In 1917 the Allied powers (including Italy) believed that they would soon be able to dispose of Turkey's empire as they saw fit; and, as the pope well knew, a "homeland for the Jews" was in their plans.

As the Jewish community (the *Yishuv*) began to develop under British rule in Palestine, some features of the institutional, social, and political life of the state-to-come began to appear. The Vatican was anxious about the prospect of leaving the Christian population of the area locked up in a Jewish state. During 1921–22, Chaim Weizmann of the World Zionist Organization met with Cardinal Gasparri, the Vatican secretary of state, in an effort to allay Vatican fears." *C'est votre université que je crains!*" ("What I am afraid of is your university!") Cardinal Gasparri told Weizmann.[13] The next formal encounter recorded between official Zionism and the Vatican did not take place until April 1945 (by which time all of Italy had been in and then out of the clutches of the Nazi-Fascist regime), when Moshe Shertok (later Sharett) of the Jewish Agency was greeted in private audience by Pope Pius XII (1939–58). Perhaps it was that the pope's English was not up to the occasion; but it is more likely that the pope, like most people, had not yet absorbed the reality of the Holocaust and the desperate situation of the homeless Jewish survivers: in any case, Shertok's effort to learn the mind of the Vatican with respect to the Jewish homeland (in his own words) "went nowhere."[14] Nonetheless, the Israeli scholar Pinchas Lapide[15] reckons this same Pope Pius XII was a Christian pro-Zionist. In his early days as a nuncio, Eugenio Pacceli played a key part in carrying off the friendly visit between Nahum Sokolow and Pope Benedict XV in 1917. In his years as Cardinal and Secretary of State for the Vatican (1929–39), Pacceli promoted a friendly attitude towards Zionists and Jewish Agency figures. While the Latin Patriarch in Jerusalem was conveying to the Vatican consistently hostile reports on the behaviour of the Jewish Agency during the Mandate years, both Popes of the period (Pius XI, 1922–39, and Pius XII) were well disposed to Zionism as the solution to the Jewish question; both were confident that, until such time as the Roman Catholic church should succeed in making itself the acknowledged custodian of the holy places, the Church could deal at least as effectively with a Jewish state as with the British government or any other imaginable successor (as, for example, a UN trusteeship, or the United States).

Still, the path towards Restoration of the Jews did not lead *via* Rome, as Pope Benedict XV had foretold. Indeed, many of the roadblocks that appeared along the way were owing to the Vatican's reiteration of its concerns about the future of the holy places in a Jewish commonwealth. Then came the revelation of the truth about the Holocaust, which brought world opinion around abruptly in favour of a Jewish state. Responding to the overwhelming popular support in the democracies for the Zionist solution – a compound of humanitarian concern for hundreds of thousands of Jews, alarm at the prospect of having to lower immigration barriers in their own countries, and the transient mood of religious or quasi-religious interest in the restoration of the Jews to their land – the Vatican effectively stood aside in 1947–48. No effort was made to dissuade the statesmen representing Catholic nations from joining in the transitory pro-Zionist parade. This circumstance made it easier for the Government of the United States to coax Latin American nations (which at that time made up nearly one-half of the nations seated in the General Assembly) into support of the partition of Palestine in November 1947.

Summarizing the attitude of the Vatican in those early days, Drinan observes: "The negative view of Israel revealed by the Holy Father to Herzl had not improved by the day of Israel's birth on May 14, 1948. On that occasion, *L'Osservatore Romano*, the semi-official daily of the Vatican, declared editorially that 'Modern Israel is not the heir to biblical Israel. The Holy Land and its sacred sites belong only to Christianity: the true Israel' ... Catholics simply are not in a position to understand the centrality of the state of Israel for modern Judaism."[16]

Attitudes of Catholic laity were probably accurately reflected in the family magazine *Sign*, and in the *Catholic World*, which throughout 1948 complained that politicians were too much led about by "the Jewish vote." On the eve of the declaration of the state, the *Sign* observed that "American backing for the Zionist cause comes chiefly from politicians and from kindly hearted people with a laudable sympathy for the sufferings of their [*sic*] Jewish people but a meager knowledge of history and geography." The *Catholic World* struck a sardonic note: "Will the Zionists themselves be as generous about finding a homeland for all other wanderers as they were about finding a home for themselves?"[17] The general attitude of Roman Catholic intellectuals at the time is efficiently documented by referring to such journals as the Jesuit magazine, *America*, and to the liberal-Catholic journal, *Commonweal*. Editorials in *America* reluctantly accepted partition in November, 1947; but an article signed by C.G. Paulding on 10 October 1947 expressed fear that partition could not work, and would lead to endless Arab-Jewish bloodshed. Therefore, the US "had better ask the British to change their minds and stay in Palestine, and leave the Jews without a state." A year later, *Commonweal* sustained the pope's declared wish that the Jerusalem must be internationalized: the pope, after all, was "not concerned with the sovereignty of Israel, nor of any other state"; as for the Jews and their designs upon Jerusalem, it should be recalled that "for most of the Jews, Jerusalem is symbolic, not sacramental."[18]

During these months, the Vatican insisted that it was a stakeholder in all deliberations about the Holy Land. Representatives of the hierarchy in the US lobbied constantly with responsible State Department persons on the point that only the internationalization of the whole city of Jerusalem could preserve and protect the holy places. On 17 June 1947 the Near East Welfare Association (a branch of the Sacred Oriental Congregation, headed by Monsignor McMahon) advised the UN assistant secretary general in charge of Trusteeship Affairs that "it is manifestly false to assert [as certain Zionist spokesmen had recently done] that 'Christianity is not an indigenous force in Palestine.' It is also false to charge that 'as an organized religion, Christianity is the creation of Rome and always represented in the east the introduction of a foreign civilization' ... There is now living in Palestine a sizable minority of 51,000 Roman Catholics."[19] But the UN rejected the Church's bid to be involved.

What strikes one now more than it would have done at the time is the virtual identification of the "Christian presence" with the Roman Catholic community. In fact, then as now, Roman Catholics were a minority in a diverse Christian population of the former Mandate – the largest constituency being Greek Orthodox, with whom, in those days, Roman Catholic relations were not good. Walter Eytan, director-general of Israel's foreign ministry, wrote on 8 June 1948: "The Catholic Church is opposed to the custody of the Holy Places being vested in the Jews, the Protestants, the Greek Orthodox and the Moslems – in this order; i.e., the Moslems, although not exactly desirable, would be in the eyes of the church the least objectionable custodian."[20] By the 1980s, Roman Catholic and Protestant spokesmen had changed their tune: they would now carefully emphasize *total Christian* numbers and would concede the longer historical tenure of Orthodox and Oriental Orthodox churches. By then, habits of cooperation among all the Christian communities were considerably advanced, owing to the creation and ultimate expansion of the World Council of Churches, the conscious adoption of the "ecumenical" worldview by the Roman Catholic church following Vatican II, and by the adoption within ecumenical Christianity of a self-consciously "anti-imperialist", political philosophy with a Third World bias. Along the way, the attention of the Roman Catholic church came to focus on possibilities of limiting Israeli sovereignty in ways that would best secure freedom of action for itself in the Holy Land, while maximizing possibilities of collaboration towards goals shared with the Arab population.

Cardinal Spellman, the most powerful figure in the American Roman Catholic community in the immediate post-war years, sought to persuade the Truman government to withold its support for the admission of Israel to the UN until Israel got in line on the matter of the "internationalization" of the city of Jerusalem. "It is common knowledge," he complained to the President, "that the rejection [of the recent motion to deny Israel's admission to the UN] was due in no small degree to the attitude and influence of the United States' Delegation" – as though implying that Truman himself could yet disown the vote of the delegation, and win back the good graces of the Catholic community. "The traditions and interests of millions of Christians of the United States and of the entire world, who look to Palestine also as their Holy land, must be articulated ... by your representatives, if the United States is not to be regarded by the whole Christian community as having failed them by default." It was clear to the Cardinal that Israel's victory in the late war with the Arabs was making the Israelis cocky:

[T]he issue is becoming somewhat befogged at the moment by the attitude of many Israeli officials, as reported in American and Palestinian press, who assume the attitude that the christians [sic] of the world are unappreciative of Israeli benevolence and condescension in even permitting any vague form of internationalization to be discussed. Is there any wonder that this occasions a rising indignation of christians ...? We did not favor or oppose the establishment of a Jewish state, provided our century old Christian interests would be preserved; provided our christian clergy and faithful would be unmolested; provided we might have free access from all the world to the cradle of our Christian heritage ... Yet, recent authentic reports received from Jerusalem show an adverse Israelitic [sic] attitude, based on alleged provisions of security, which denied Christians – several of whom were Americans – access to the scene of the Last Supper, in the Jewish, "New City," during Holy Week, in April of the current year, while Jews were permitted to visit the Tomb of David in the same area.[21]

When President Weizmann of Israel made it clear that he was eager to appease Catholic consternation over the matter of the holy places, President Truman worked out a meeting between Weizmann and Cardinal Spellman at the latter's Madison Avenue residence, to take place during Weizmann's visit to the US in June 1949. Weizmann turned on his world-class charm, so that afterward the press could be told that "our aims in the Jerusalem matter though not identical are nevertheless reconcilable." This, as it turned out, was to be the high point in diplomacy between the Church of Rome and the State of Israel for many years to come. From the Roman Catholic perspective (as the cardinal's biographer puts it), "the rest of the story is one of humiliation for the United Nations." In September 1949, the Reverend Raphael Quinn, secretary to the Roman Catholic Custodian of Holy Places, accused "elements of the Israelis" of "responsibility for the ruin of a number of shrines." And Catholic spokesmen continuously insisted that Israel's claim to jurisdiction anywhere in Jerusalem was "illegal." Charles Malik, a Maronite Christian and the delegate from Lebanon at the UN General Assembly (and later its president), read out to the assembly a statement from Cardinal Spellman condemning "the effrontery of a member of the United Nations, the State of Israel, which has, without right and in defiance of these resolutions and votes, tried to make the 'new city' of Jerusalem its capital." Likewise, about the same time, Monsignor McMahon, speaking for the pope, ruled out any compromise along the lines of internationalization of the holy places *within* a Jewish capital (the solution proposed by Weizmann), by declaring that "the Catholic body throughout the world, as is evidenced by the repeated statements of their leader, Pope Pius XII, will not be contented with a mere internationalization of the Holy Places."

"And so it went with some monotony in 1954, and in 1956 ..." sighs Robert Gannon[22] And – had he not been in a hurry to finish his biography of the cardinal – he might have written, "for another forty years."

As I noted in chapter 2, the issue of the status of Jerusalem took on new life after the events of June 1967. The Roman Catholic church agreed with the WCC that Jerusalem did not belong to Israel; but its own declarations emphasized historical claims of its own that did not commend themselves to the Protestants. Among the few prominent Roman Catholic pro-Zionist voices in those years was Monsignor John M. Oesterreicher, director of the Institute of Judaeo-Christian Studies at Seton Hall University, New Jersey. He responded to complaints in the Church about the holy places with the argument that, "while Christians and Moslems in Israel enjoy freedom of worship, this right was denied Jews under Jordanian administration. They were not even allowed to pray at the Western Wall though access to it and to other sites was confirmed by article VIII of the 1949 Armistice Agreement between Jordan and Israel. This treatment of the Jews, as well as restrictions imposed on Israeli Moslems and Christians, violated the Agreement, but no Christian bishop cried out against it. Where was the Christian protest against the destruction of all Jerusalem's synagogues while Jordan ruled? Where the denunciation of the use of Jewish tombstones to construct footpaths in an Arab Legion camp?"[23] Addressing King Hussein of Jordan's outcry against "Jerusalem in Captivity," Oesterreicher wrote in 1974: "The Jerusalem of today is not a city 'in captivity,' as the King likes to think. It is free, as it has never been before ... No, I cannot agree with the King that Jordan or the Arab world is the city's 'rightful owner.' Biblically speaking, Jerusalem is God's city, as the land is God's land. Men are but tenants. The glory of the Israelis is to have been good stewards, to have been worthy of His trust ... The people whom God made His own out of sheer love, have gathered in Zion; the divided city is One again! and 'what God has joined together, man must not separate' (Matt. 19:6)."[24]

Another atypically pro-Zionist voice in those days was that of the eminent Roman Catholic theologian Jacques Maritain: "It is a strange paradox to see that the Israelis are being denied their right to the one and only territory to which, considering the entire history of humanity as a whole, it is an absolute certainty that one people has incontestable claim: for the people of Israel is the one and only people in the world to which one land, the land of Canaan, has been given by the true God, the unique and transcendental God, the Creator of the universe and of the human species. And what God has given once, he has given for all eternity."[25]

Relations between Israel and the Roman Catholic church throughout the post-war period were clouded by the Jews' belief that the Vatican had failed to rally the conscience of Europe, as it might have done, to prevent Hitler's policy of elimination of the Jews. This is a complex story, happily outside the limits of this book. But the recollection of those years has embittered the attitude of many Jews towards the Roman Catholic church. Particularly painful is the fact that, where Christians *did* respond charitably to the desperate situation of local Jews, there were often long-range side-effects that embittered Christian-Jewish understanding. For example: many children had been saved by being taken into monasteries and Church facilities. Immediately after the war, the Chief Rabbi of Israel, Isaac Herzog, interviewed the pope but failed to win his support for the effort to recover those children for Judaism. Chaim Herzog (the rabbi's son and eventually the president of Israel) recalls: "My father asked the Pope [Pius XII] to issue instructions to churches, monasteries, and other institutions to allow these children to return to their families or to the Jewish community. He refused. It is almost unfathomable that he did refuse and totally unfathomable why. Perhaps he was unwilling to relinquish his hold on these new Catholic converts. Perhaps it was for the same unknown reason that the Church gave so much help to fleeing Nazi war criminals."[26]

A number of meetings between senior leaders of the Roman Catholic church and the State of Israel occured during the state's early years, including one on 28 March 1953 between Pope Pius XII and Foreign Minister Moshe Sharett, which was the first meeting between an Israeli minister and a pope; and one between Prime Minister Golda Meir and Pope Paul VI in January 1973.[27] In January 1964 Pope Paul VI made a pilgrimage to "the Holy Land," most of it spent in Jordanian jurisdiction. Eleven hours on 5 January were spent in Israel. The pope was amiably received in public, but (according to Golda Meir) a meeting with Prime Minister Eshkol and the cabinet was rocky.[28] A little over three years later, all of the holy places that Pope Paul VI had visited were under Israeli jurisdiction.

In the beginning, the attitudes of American Catholic laity towards the State of Israel were no different from those of the clergy – and not because the latter were whipping the former into submission. American Catholics simply lacked enthusiasm for Zionism. There is an interesting political dimension to this story. Jews – alongside Italians, Poles, Irish, and other sons and grandsons of immigrants, and also alongside Blacks – were part of the Roosevelt or New Deal coalition. (During the 1970s and 1980s, a majority of the Italians, Poles, Irish, and others followed the logic of economic self-interest into the Republican party; only blacks and Jews remained faithful to the Democratic party by the 1990s.) In the early years of the campaign for the creation of a Jewish state, Jews anticipated that, in the spirit of the coalition, Irish, Poles, blacks, and others should be united and active in support of the issue that was closest to the hearts of all Jews. That expectation was not fulfilled. The news of the Holocaust, of course, had a chastening effect on most Catholics: compassion for the suffering Jews of Europe, mixed with alarm at the prospect of having to accommodate perhaps a hundred thousand Jews as immigrants, disposed most Catholics to support partition and the creation of an Israeli state. Organized labour (whose ranks were still largely Catholic) gave official support to Israel at the beginning and, for the most part, throughout the years to follow. But the Catholic hierarchy did not. And so far as the pollsters could find, few Catholic laity could be counted as constant friends of Israel.

Part of the problem was the vein of historical Catholic anti-Semitism that had surfaced in the years of the celebrity of Father Coughlin, and that did not dry up after Coughlin had been retired by his superiors from public life in the latter 1930s. During the 1950s, Catholic politicians often made reference to the fact that so many Jewish intellectuals of the 1930s had been Communists or friends of communism. This knowledge prevented many Catholics from embracing Zionism –

another product of Jewish intellectuals. Simultaneously, it occured to Irish, Polish, and Italian Catholics that American Jewish politicians were not wholeheartedly engaged in the struggle against domestic communism: Jewish organizations did not speak out in support of Senator Joseph McCarthy, at a time when there was widespread support for him among Roman Catholic clerical and political leaders – notably, in New York State, which had the largest contingent of both Irish and Jewish voters, and in Massachussets. In a milder way, these attitudes foreshadow the bitterness that overcame relations between Jews and blacks in the 1970s and 1980s, when many leaders in the black community embraced anti-Zionism, while others switched to Islam.

NEW DIRECTIONS IN ROMAN CATHOLIC TEACHING ON THE JEWS AND ISRAEL

The attitude of the Roman Catholic church towards the whole issue of the creation of a State of Israel was controlled by the fact that the Church still taught, as late as the 1960s, the doctrine called "supersession" (or "replacement") – that is, that the Church is heir to *all* of the promises that God made to Abraham. In spite of this official teaching, it seems that at least some of the popes and some of the Vatican theologians of our period were not immune from the spell of "Restorationism," especially after the events of 1948 and 1967. I have already noted the judgment of the Israeli scholar Pinchas Lapide, that Pope Pius XII was (quietly) well disposed to Zionism. Here and there in the 1940s and 1950s, prominent theologians had expressed their conviction that the survival of the Jews and their Restoration to the promised land called for a re-examination of the doctrine of supersession. This thinking was reinforced by the effort to understand the meaning of the Holocaust. Perhaps the creation of the State of Israel had been, after all, the only way to set right the history of persecution of the Jews, for which the Catholic church now recognized some degree of responsibility. Although this reality was not acknowledged in a formal way at the highest level until 1998 (see below), leaders of the Church were quietly involved in much soul-searching over the Church's failure to renounce the slogans that ultimately led to the liquidation of Jews. In 1963 the Vatican, under Pope John XXIII, reviewed the liturgy and eliminated language (references to "perfidious Jews," and so on) now believed to have permitted, if not encourged, anti-Semitism. At the same time, it began a study of "the question of the Jews," which culminated in the statements to be found in *Nostra Aetate*, 1965.

Nostra Aetate[29] is one of the declarations of the Second Vatican Council. It was published on 28 October 1965, and its subject is the relations between the Catholic church and non-Christians. There is no overstating the importance of the document, for it explicitly encourages Catholics to make themselves familiar with other religious traditions and expresses a respect for the many different paths to God that had never characterized Catholicism in the past. The declaration states: "Let Christians, while witnessing to their own faith and way of life, acknowledge, preserve and encourage the spiritual and moral truths found amongst non-Christians, also their social life and culture." Specific mention is made of Hinduism, Buddhism, and Islam. We are interested here in Section 4, only a few paragraphs in length, which deals with the Church and the Jews: "The Church of Christ acknowledges that, according to God's design, the beginning of her faith and her election are found already among the Patriarchs, Moses, and the prophets ... Although the Church is the new people of God, the Jews should not be presented as rejected or accursed by God, as if this follows from the Holy Scriptures ... The Church, mindful of the patrimony she shares with the Jews and moved not by political reasons but by the Gospel's spiritual love, decries hatred, persecutions, displays of anti-Semitim, directed against Jews at any time and by anyone." The developed version of this now-official Roman Catholic teaching on these matters can be found summarized in the Catechism.

The relationship of the Church with the Jewish People. When she delves into her own mystery, the Church, the People of God in the New Covenant, discovers her link with the Jewish People, "the first to hear the Word of God." The Jewish faith, unlike other non-Christian religions, is already a response to God's revelation in the Old Covenant. To the Jews "belong the sonship, the glory, the covenants, the giving of the Law, the worship, and the promises; to them belong the patriarchs, and of their race, according to the flesh, is the Christ" [citing Romans 9:4–5, and 11:29]; "for the gifts and the call of God are irrevocable" [citing *Nostra Aetate*].

And when one considers the future, God's People of the Old Covenant and the new People of God tend towards similar goals: expectation of the coming (or the return) of the Messiah. But one awaits the return of the Messiah who died and rose from the dead and is recognized as Lord and son of God; the other awaits the coming of a Messiah, whose features remain hidden till the end of time; and the latter waiting is accompanied by the drama of not knowing or of misunderstanding Jesus Christ. [paragraphs 839–40].

Jews are not collectively responsible for Jesus' death. The historical complexity of Jesus' trial is apparent in the Gospel accounts. The personal sin of the participants (Judas, the Sanhedrin, Pilate) is known to God alone. Hence we cannot lay responsibility for the trial on the Jews in Jerusalem as a whole, despite the outcry of a manipulated crowd and the global reproaches continued in the apostles' calls to conversion after Pentecost [citing Mark 15:11, Acts 2:23, 36, 3:13–14, 4:10, 5:30, 7:52, 10:39, 13:27–8, I Thess 2:14-15.] Jesus himself, in forgiving them on the cross, and Peter in following suit, both accept "the ignorance" of the Jews of Jerusalem and even of their leaders [citing Luke 23:34, Acts 3:17]. Still less can we extend responsibility to other Jews of different times and places, based merely on the crowd's cry: "His blood be on us and on our children!" a formula for ratifying a judicial sentence [citing Matthew 27:25, and Acts 5:28, 18:6]. ... We must regard as guilty all those who continue to relapse into their sins. Since our sins made the Lord Christ suffer the torment of the cross, those who plunge themselves into disorders and crimes crucify the Son of God anew in their hearts (for he is in them) and hold him up to contempt. And it can be seen that our crime in this case is greater in us than in the Jews. As for them, according to the witness of the Apostle, "None of the rulers of this age understood this; for if they had, they would not have crucified the Lord of glory" [citing Hebrews 6:6, I Corinthians 2:8]. We, however, profess to know him. And when we deny him by our deeds, we in some way seem to lay violent hands on him [Paragraphs 597–8.][30]

Nostra Aetate had made clear that the Church's relationship with the Jews cannot be like its relationship with any other body of people, or with any other faith. A plenary session of bishops meeting in 1969 explored the implications of this new position: "The Church is not born solely of scripture but also of the living tradition of the Jewish people."[31] Following the lead of *Nostra Aetate*, Catholics began to take a much greater interest in Judaism, its past and present. In seminaries, emphasis was now placed on the Jewish context of the Gospels and the life of the Church. None of this was well received in the Middle East. Muslims denounced what they saw as a spineless retreat from the united front against the Jews and brought pressure to bear upon Christian clerics to get the Vatican's decisions reversed.

It is important to grasp throughout the story that follows that Muslim objections regarding the Vatican statements have nothing to do with theological differences between Christians and Muslims. Muslim teaching on the matter of the crucifixion turns on this text in the Qur'an, Sura 4:155–8: "(They [the Jews] have incurred divine/Displeasure): in that ... they said (in boast), / 'We killed Christ Jesus / The son of Mary, / The Apostle of God" – / But they killed him not, / Nor crucified him, But so it was made / To appear to them ... / Nay, God raised him up, / Unto Himself; and God/ Is exalted in Power ..."

A. Yusuf Ali's explanation of these verses is as follows: "The end of the life of Jesus on earth is as much involved in mystery as his birth, and indeed the greater part of his private life, except the three main years of his ministry ... The Orthodox Christian Churches make it a cardinal point of their doctrine that his life was taken on the Cross, that he died and was buried, that on the third day he rose in the body with his wounds intact, and walked about and conversed, and ate with his disciples, and was afterwards taken up bodily into heaven ... The Qur'anic teaching is that Christ was not crucified nor killed by the Jews, notwithstanding certain apparent circumstances which produced that illusion in the minds of some of his enemies ... and that he was taken up to God."[32]

Muslims (reasonably, from their point of view) pictured the Vatican's theological retreat (from supersessionism) as the augury of a coming political retreat from the united front against Zionism. For Roman Catholics it was evidently no longer necessary to hate the Jews. The Coptic Catholic patriarch spoke for all Eastern churches when he said that exculpation of the Jews "would provide the Jews with a moral weapon which they would exploit for their own ends against Arab countries." These complaints raised in the Middle East contributed to the long delay between the publishing of the declaration and the publication of the "guidelines" (1975), during which time the Vatican sought to explain "that the measure was being enacted largely to stabilize the Jewish communities outside Israel, especially those in Catholic countries (e.g., France and Latin America), in an attempt to insure that they would never again be driven by some new Christian persecution to mass emigration to the Zionist state." Middle Eastern Christians were unappeased, however. There were public demonstrations against the Church's statements throughout the Middle East; notably in Aleppo (Syria) and Jerusalem. In a joint statement, several Orthodox patriarchs warned that "the freeing of the Jews of the blood of Christ is the greatest of sins ... [It] undermines the basic principles of Christianity [and is] inconsistent with Holy Scripture." Most Catholic prelates in the area got in line eventually, but several made their unhappiness known through proper channels. Comfort could still be taken from the fact that the document spoke of the Church as "the New People of God," thus (as the prelates noted) "depriving the Jews of the weapon they had used to return to Palestine – namely that they were God's chosen People." Privately the pope assured a Latin priest from Lebanon that the council "would not allow its decision to be exploited by the Israelis," and that the decision would not adversely affect "the legitimate rights of the Palestinian people." This episode was followed by dramatic papal gestures of reconciliation towards

Islam. During the year 1970, Pope Paul VI preached on the common origin of the faiths of Muslims, Christians, and Jews and called on Christians all over the world to join in the Muslim festivities on the occasion of the Feast of Al-Adha in February of that year. He told more than thirty thousand worshippers in Saint Peter's Square that Christians have closer ties with Muslims than with any other religion, citing the respect with which Jesus and the Virgin are revered in the Qur'an. As a result, papal ties with the Arab world improved in the following years, while non-recognition of Israel continued. None of this seemed, however, to have any effect on what Arab Muslims thought of Arab Christians.[33]

Although *Nostra Aetate* undoubtedly created real dialogue at last between Jews and Roman Catholics, it did not bring the Church closer to recognizing of the State of Israel. Vatican documents still made no reference to the State of Israel as the home of the Jews. Nothing in the documents reflected a lively interest in the life of the Jews in Israel today. A case can be made that the real turning point in the story of Roman Catholic attitudes towards Israel was not any of these documents or statements but what happened at the United Nations in November 1975. On that occasion, Uganda's Muslim president, Idi Amin (who is on every historian's shortlist of the most vicious dictators of the century), delivered a furious, anti-Israel, anti-Semitic diatribe at the UN, in which he maintained that "the United States of America has been colonized by the Zionists who hold all the tools of development and power" and called upon the United Nations to pursue "the extinction of Israel as a state." Following their standing ovation to this oration, the delegates passed the accompanying resolution: "That Zionism is a form of racism and racial discrimination." The Second Annual Christian-Jewish workshop, sponsored by the US Conference of Catholic Bishops, immediately sent a letter to UN secretary-general Kurt Waldheim denouncing the resolution as a "slander against Jews everywhere ... Zionism is a sacred word and concept in Judaism and as such, it merits the respect and understanding of all Christians aware of their Judaic roots and heritage." The Jesuit magazine *America* said that the resolution meant that "an essential condition for peace in the Middle East – the recognition of Israel's right to exist – has been denied."[34] Michael Pragai wisely observes: "In a sense, by passing such blatantly unfair resolutions, the United Nations had contributed to a renewed interest in the idea of the Return and in a wider understanding of its historic implications. These were stressed in many statements by clergy, Church councils, ecumenical associations and interfaith groups."[35]

POPE JOHN PAUL II AND THE JEWS

Jews throughout the world were concerned, and many, indeed, were alarmed, when, on 16 october 1978, the Roman Catholic church chose a Pole to be its head. The mere mention of "Poland" brought the Holocaust to minds for most Jews. Many years went by before most Jews came to appreciate that in Karol Wojtyla, Pope John Paul II, the Church had chosen a man well disposed to Jews – the best friend of the Jews to sit on the papal throne in many centuries.

It is only too painfully true that Poland has, in modern times, been the stage for the most virulent kind of anti-Semitic persecution. But it is also true that there were parts of Poland where Jews and Catholics had lived together more intimately than in any other part of the world, and where close appreciation of each other's religion and style of life had forged bonds of secular goodwill of a calibre unknown elsewhere. Some of the most heroic "Righteous Gentiles" appeared in such places. Of Karol Wojtyla it has been said that "since the time of the Apostle Peter, no Roman Pontiff has ever spent his childhood in such close contact with Jewish life."[36] This is as true and important to grasp as the fact that Karol Wojtyla's hometown, Wadowice, was only thirty-five miles from Oswiecim (Auschwitz). Wojtyla's closest childhood friends and classmates in his elementary and high school years were Jews. Those friendships were kept alive over the years by correspondence. Biographers tell us that during his years as pope, Karol Wojtyla's most important off-the-record friendship has been with a Jewish boyhood companion, Jerzy Kluger.[37]

In April 1986, John Paul II became the first pope ever to visit the synagogue in the old Jewish ghetto in Rome. He sat in pained silence on the *teva* (platform) while the chief rabbi of Italy, Elio Toaff, spoke of Pope Pius XII's failure to denounce Nazi atrocities against the Jews, including atrocities going on in Rome itself. "What was happening on one side of the Tiber couldn't be ignored across the river."[38] In his reply, the pope accepted the judgment that Christians had failed the Jews, "the older brothers" of the Church, and spoke of new beginnings. On 7 April 1994, a *menorah* was lit and Kaddish recited in his presence at the Vatican, in a ceremony marking the fiftieth anniversary of the Warsaw ghetto uprising, during which he received and spoke with Holocaust survivors.[39]

THE ROAD TO RECOGNITION

Despite all the generous talk in published documents about reconciliation of past misunderstanding and about promising new beginnings, the Vatican kept avoiding making the gift of recognition, waiting for a moment of maximum diplomatic advantage, while, of course, maintaining full diplomatic relations with many Arab states. It was painfully evident that the Church was more intimidated by Arabs and by Islam than by Jews and Judaism. The nadir in relations between the State of Israel and the Vatican may have come in September 1982, when, following the Israeli invasion of Lebanon and the negotiated evacuation of the PLO, Yassir Arafat, *en route* to the newest location his government-in-exile (this time Tunisia), was offered and swiftly accepted an audience with the pope. Israel's foreign minister, Yitzhak Shamir, issued a formal denunciation of the deed: "The same Church that did not say a word about the massacre of Jews for six years in Europe, and did not say much about the killing of Christians in Lebanon for seven years, is willing to meet the man who ... is bent on the destruction of Israel which would complete the work done by the Nazis of Germany. If the Pope is going to meet Arafat, it shows something about the moral standards of the Church." The Vatican responded in kind: the accusation that the Vatican had stood by silently during the years of the Holocaust is "an outrage to the truth, couched in language completely lacking in respect for the person of the Pope." Unrepentant, the pope went on a few months later to affirm in an apostolic letter, *Redemptoris Anno*, that, like the Jews, who had established Israel, the "Palestinians" too had "the natural right in justice to find once more a homeland and to be able to live in peace and tranquillity with the other peoples of the area." In December 1988, the pope received Yassir Arafat yet again – this time with the ceremony normally accompanying visits of a head of state.[40]

Even while this encouragment of the Palestinians and this promotion of PLO leader Yassir Arafat went on, the Vatican was sending out hints of Pope John Paul's willingness to work towards normalization of relations with Israel. Then, suddenly, it began to appear that the Vatican might have waited too long.

Long before the Vatican acted on the matter of recognition, its policy had become an embarrassment – or rather a scandal. In the past, the Vatican's refusal to recognize the State of Israel drew little notice, and it had plenty of company (though perhaps not the best company). Several years earlier, in 1979, Egypt had been the first Arab state to normalize diplomatic relations. (Jordan followed in 1994, and Mauritania in October 1999.) During the several months preceding the Vatican's decision for recognition, Israel had been enjoying a virtual rush of decisions for recognition from nations that had previously drawn various kinds of refreshment from belonging to the non-recognition camp. India and China, the two largest nations on earth, extended formal recognition in the same month – January 1992. Eastern European nations, which had been compelled to toe the anti-Zionist line of the Soviet Union, overthrew their Communist governments in 1989–90, and thereafter demonstrated their appreciation of the economic and other advantages that would follow from dealing with Israel as an equal. The USSR itself resumed diplomatic relations with Israel in October 1991; long before this, the Soviet Union had withdrawn as a player in Mideast politics. Now Arab states could see more clearly the advantages of improving their relations with Israel. By January 1991, it was clear that the Vatican was running out of time. It would soon find itself in a tiny minority of the most irreconcilable enemies of Israel – the lone Christian voice in a Muslim chorus.

Early in 1991, meetings took place in Jerusalem between Israeli and Vatican authorities, leading to the establishment, on 29 July 1992, of a permanent working commission to "discuss issues of reciprocal interest" and "normalizing relations" between the Holy See and the State of Israel.[41] Finally, on 30 December 1993, Israel and the Holy See signed the *Fundamental Agreement between the Holy See and the State of Israel,* which committed the two parties to mutual recognition. The occasion was taken to rehearse the commitment of both parties, the Roman Catholic church and the Jewish state, to freedom of religion. The Church reaffirmed the declarations to be found in the 1965 *Nostra Aetate* and other recent documents with respect to religious freedom, and the obligation to condemn anti-Semitism. Both the Holy See and the State of Israel committed themselves to respect the *Status Quo* in the Christian holy places and "the respective rights of the Christian communities thereunder," and to work together to encourage Christian pilgrimage to the Holy Land. A permanent commission would study "any unclear, unsettled and disputed issues, concerning property, economic and fiscal matters," and so on.[42] It was not until late 1994 that ambassadors were in place and formal letters exchanged.

Afterwards, the pope explained his decision: "It must be understood that Jews, who for 2,000 years were dispersed among the nations of the world, had decided to return to the land of their ancestors. This is their right. And this right is recognized even by those who look upon the nation of Israel with an unsympathetic eye. This right was also recognized from the outset by the Holy See, and the act of establishing diplomatic relations with Israel is simply an international affirmation of this relationship."[43] A person would not need to be specially adept at the ways of diplomacy to detect a note of reluctance. It is, all things considered, a mystifying statement. Why was the Holy See so wary of the opinion of "those who look upon the nation of Israel with an unsympathic eye?" Why was it necessary to be so chary about the meaning of the deed? Most diplomatic exchanges between Israel and the PLO in those days showed a more hearty spirit than this.

Much more significant than the mere act of recognition was that at about the same time, the Vatican dropped its long-standing complaint about Jewish control of the City of Jerusalem and settled for assurances regarding the holy places, which Israel had always been ready to give.[44] (In contrast, the Anglican archbishop of Canterbury continued to denounce Israel's "occupation" of Jerusalem; and at its decennial conference at Lambeth in August 1998, the worldwide Anglican church formally declared that Jerusalem should serve as the capital of two sovereign states, Israel and Palestine, keeping faith with the politics of its Arab congregation in Jerusalem.)[45]

MIXED SIGNALS SINCE RECOGNITION

Many Israeli and Jewish observers remain unsatisfied regarding the nature of the Vatican's new relationship with Israel. Reviewing the two volumes edited by Helga Croner from which I have drawn so many illustrations of Jewish-Christian relations, Mordechai Waxman asks, What is missing? He concludes that what is missing from virtually all Church documents is recognition of the transcendent nature of the commitment that Jews have to Israel.

Granted the inadequacies of the State of Israel, granted its precarious political position, Jews nonetheless see its existence as the beginning of a great overturn in Jewish history and as the opening to new developments in sacred history. Christians apparently cannot share this vision nor the psychology and history which have created it. Fundamentalist Protestants, who are not represented in these documents [that is, the two Croner collections], seem to have a view of the major role of Israel, but within the context of an apocalyptic theology not shared by Jews. Catholic and mainline Protestant groups, whose moderated theology and interest in dialogue are acceptable to Jews, seemingly cannot bring themselves wholeheartedly to understand the Jewish point of view. The niggling statement, "Israel has a right to exist," conveys no sense of religious and theological grandeur and recognition ... If it is, indeed, the new posture of dialogue to understand Jews as they understand themselves, then the touchstone of a fruitful relationship may well be the ability of Christian churches to see the State of Israel with the eyes of the Jews, namely, as a stage in the reaffirmation of the covenant with Abraham and his descendants.[46]

As Waxman goes on to note, the Vatican has made a point of pairing her gestures towards Israel with gestures towards the Palestinian entity. There have been papal audiences for Arafat and Vatican representatives attending ceremonies in the PA, as well as considerable contact at the UN. Vatican statements on these occasions give no hint of any perception of incompatibility between the respect owed to Israel as a sovereign state with defined borders, and the pretensions of the Palestinian nation. On 6 November 1995 the Holy See accepted an "Office of the Representative of the Palestinian Liberation Organization to the Holy See," making clear as it did so that it looked forward to recognizing the State of Palestine.[47] At the same time, Vatican-Israeli relations have been severely strained by the pope's promotion to various senior Church positions in Israel of certain Palestinian Arabs who have records of outspoken support for factions that remain publicly opposed to the Oslo process and retain their commitments to armed struggle.[48]

In March 1998 the Vatican issued a declaration: "We Remember: A Reflection on the Shoah." This fourteen-page document calls on the Catholic faithful throughout the world to meditate "on the catastrophe which befell the Jewish people, on its cause, and on the moral imperative to ensure that never again such a tragedy will happen." While firmly linking the Shoah to the pagan ideology of Nazism, the document also asks "whether the Nazi persecution of the Jews was not made easier by the anti-Jewish prejudices imbedded in some Christian minds and thoughts." It has had a mixed reception in Israel and from Jews abroad.[49] The *Jerusalem Post*[50] described a meeting of the chief rabbinate in Jerusalem (led by Ashkenazi chief rabbi Yisrael Lau, an Auschwitz survivor) with Edward Cardinal Cassidy, head of the Vatican's Commission for Religious Relations with the Jews. Cardinal Cassidy pointed out that the document asks the Jewish people "to hear us with an open heart": this, he said, was "more than a request for pardon," it was "an act of repentance, of *teshuva*" (using the Hebrew word for repentance or conversion). The feeling of the Jews in the delegation was that this was still not the "clear statement on the silence of Christianity on the eve of the Holocaust and during the war" that Rabbi Lau had called for in the past. Lau told the cardinal that "You can't speak of rectifying the past without identifying the actions of individuals," and he singled out, in this respect, Pope Pius XII.

It is no doubt true, as Pope John Paul says (in the preface to the document), that "during and after the war, Jewish communities and Jewish leaders expressed their thanks for all that had been done for them, including what Pope Pius XII did personally or through his representatives to save hundreds of thousands of Jewish lives"; yet many insist, with Rabbi Lau, that "a clear condemnation by the Vatican at that time would have had the force to stop the terrible things done during the Holocaust." This thought is echoed again and again in Jewish reaction: that the document had not been sufficiently candid regarding Pope Pius's failure to rally Christian opinion against the anti-Jewish actions of the Nazis and Fascists. More fundamentally, many agreed with Dr Efraim Zuroff, director of the Israel office of the Simon Weisenthal Center, who said: "[The Vatican document] fails to take responsibility for the doctrinal antisemitism which paved the way for Nazi antisemitism, and which enabled Catholics to participate in the Holocaust – not only in Germany, which is half-Catholic, but more especially in places like Lithuania and Croatia. The document is a total cop-out on the role of pope Pius XII ... No blame is attached to the present pope. He was a young man at the time, and is in fact sensitive and very sympathetic on Jewish matters. Christians think him very conservative on doctrinal matters – abortion and birth control – but we can say he is very progressive and liberal on dealing with Jews. But his church's statement still lacks the guts that would make it satisfactory."[51]

With reference to the theme of this chapter, we must note that the Church did not use the occasion to link the matter of the persecution of the Jews and Christian responsibility therefor with the matter of the existence and continuation of the Jewish state. To Christian Zionists, it was a lost opportunity: surely this was the right occasion to affirm and give theological support to the prophetic meaning of the Restoration of the Jews to Zion – to state once and for all that the Jewish state was the appropriate, the theologically correct, answer to the dilemma of Jewish existence. There have been statements that come tantalizing close: for example, speaking at a Theodor Herzl symposium, Vienna on 19 March 1996, the archbishop of Vienna, Christoph Schonborn, noted that Pope John Paul II had said (in Mainz, 17 November, 1980) that "the old covenant has never been revoked." This covenant, Archbishop Schonborn explains, "obligated the Jews to serve God in the Land of Israel, the Promised Land. In that sense, the return to the land of Israel is a sacred commandment that follows from the continuing covenant ... The return to the land is a sign of hope, though not yet its full realization."[52]

On 12 March 2000, the pope again highlighted his determination to put behind forever the dark chapters of Christian-Jewish relations. In the course of a mass held especially to mark a Day of Forgiveness, John Paul expressed the Church's need and its readiness to ask forgiveness of all those against whom it had sinned in the past. In particular, John Paul said, "Let us pray that, in recalling the sufferings endured by the people of Israel throughout history, Christians will acknowledge the sins committed by not a few of their number against the people of the covenant." The statement was generally well received by Jewish religious and political leaders, although many also expressed disappointment at the failure to be specific about the Holocaust. Some suggested that the best way for the pope to make that point clear would be to put a stop to the process, already begun, leading to the canonization of Pius XII, the pope who followed the path of silence at the time of the Holocaust.

POPE JOHN PAUL II VISITS ISRAEL

In the spring of the year 2000, Pope John Paul II undertook a Jublilee Year pilgrimage to all of the sites associated with the origins of the Christian faith. From February 24–26 he was in Egypt; on March 21–23 he visited Jordan; and on March 22–26 he visited Israel and the Palestine Authority. (His intention was to follow this by visits later in the year to Greece, Turkey, and Syria. Iraq refused to oblige the pope with an invitiation.) The visit to the Jewish state was, among other things, an occasion to ponder the enormous changes that had taken place in the relationship between Catholics and Jews, and between Catholics and Israel, since the only previous occasion that a pope had visited "the Holy Land." In 1964 (as we have seen), Pope Paul VI spent just eleven hours in the Jewish state; he pointedly rejected an invitation to meet with the chief rabbis and Israeli public officials and managed altogether not to utter the word "Israel". In those days (but not for long) almost all of the Christian holy places were in Jordanian control. By March 2000, the issue of recognition of Israel was resolved. At the formal state welcoming occasion at Ben Gurion Airport, the whole front rank of Israeli office holders was present to greet the pope, as were the chief rabbis. Throughout the visit, large crowds, which obviously included majorities of non-Christians, met him at the holy sites – all of which, except Bethlehem, were now in the State of Israel – and when he arrived at Hechel Schlomo to meet the two chief rabbis, and at Yad Vashem. Jewish authorities provided an opportunity for the pope to pray alone before the Western Wall, and, in emulation of pious Jewish practice, to leave in a crack of the wall a copy of the prayer he had uttered publicly just before. In it, he asked God's forgiveness for the Church for its persecutions of the Jews: "God of our fathers, you chose Abraham and his descendants to bring your name to the nations. We are deeply saddened by the behaviour of those who in the course of history have caused these children of yours to suffer, and asking your forgiveness, we wish to commit ourselves to genuine brotherhood with the people of the covenant. (Signed) Johannus Paulus II."[53]

Just a few weeks before the trip was to begin, the pope had thrown Vatican-Israeli relations off balance suddenly by meeting with Yassir Arafat once again at the Vatican to announce a "Basic Agreement between the Holy See and the Palestine Liberation Organization" (15 February 2000), which affirms their joint support for international status for Jerusalem while in effect warning Israel not "to change the unique character of Jerusalem." An official Israeli foreign ministry statement had been released on the same day: "Israel expresses its great displeasure with the declaration made today in Rome by the Holy See and the PLO, which includes the issue of Jerusalem, and other issues which are subjects of the Israeli-Palestinian negotiations on permanent status. The agreement signed by these two parties constitutes a regretful intervention in the talks between Israel and the Palestinians. There is no denying that Israel safeguards freedom of conscience and freedom of worship for all, and provides free access to the holy places of all faiths. Similarly, there is no question that the religious and cultural character of Jerusalem is being preserved, as are the rights of all the religious communities and their institutions in the city. Consequently, Israel flatly rejects the reference to Jerusalem in the aforementioned document. Jerusalem was, is, and shall remain the capital of the State of Israel, and no agreement or declaration by these or any other parties will change this fact.[54]

But now, in March, as the pope sat together with Palestinian leaders on platforms erected on Palestinian soil, careful observers could note long faces and, afterwards, some words of disappointment from PLO spokesmen. They had presumed too much from the diplomatic exchange of February. The pope did not intend to depart from the spirit of personal pilgrimage to holy sites to share in political declarations. On 22 March, at the Grotto in Bethlehem, the pope said again what he had said many times before: "The Holy See has always recognized that the Palestinian people has the natural right to a homeland." But he gave no encouragement in word or gesture to Palestinian speakers who made the claim that the pope's presence on the same platform with them in Bethlehem consititued recognition of Palestine's right to form a "state" with "Jerusalem as Palestine's eternal capital." Israeli Public Security minister Shlomo Ben-Ami summed up the official view: "We fell in love with the man. He is an extraordinary person, full of good will, a man of heart and a man of justice." Still, the prayer of many Jewish and Christian religious Zionists that this would be the occasion for a declaration of theological recognition of the State of Israel as the fulfilment of biblical prophecy was not met.

Perhaps the most important long-term consequence of the event was that it exposed on the theatre of world opinion the absolute unreadiness of Muslim authorities to be part of any accommodation over possession of holy sites. Consistently, Arafat and other Muslim and Arab authorities used their part in platform ceremonies to raise maximalist political claims to the holy sites and to Jerusalem. Even at that, according to the *Jerusalem Post,* "Muslim protesters screamed abuse at Islamic and Palestinian authority officials" for meeting at all with the Pope, screaming that 'You people have just given the keys of Jerusalem and al-Aqsa Mosque to the infidel Pope.'" The Pope was permitted by the grand mufti to visit the site of the Temple Mount but was forbidden to pray. To most in the West, this was a new concept – Pope Paul II agreeing not to pray! Efforts by the Vatican to bring the grand mufti, Sheikh Ekrima Sabri, into a public discussion of issues were rudely rejected by the sheik. At a meeting of "inter-religious dialogue" hosted by the pope at the Notre Dame Hospice, rabbis and Catholic theologians traded thoughts on the possibilities of dialogue that lie ahead. Sheik Tatzit Ramimi, head of the Religious Court system of the PA and designated by Yassir Arafat to present the Muslim side of the dialogue, rejected the theme of the conference and spent the whole of his speaking time lecturing the Jews and Christians present on the inalienable and indivisible Muslim claim to the holy city. He spoke of "the occupier" (never stooping to use the name of Israel), of his long record of genocide, about the shooting and wounding of Palestinian children. "The establishment of an independent Palestinian State with Yassir Arafat as its president and Jerusalem as it capital – this will stop the strife between religions." Then he left the meeting abruptly rather than participate in the scheduled ceremonial planting of a tree. The grand mufti used his personal meeting with the pope in his office on the Temple Mount "to issue a string of political statements" (in the words of the *Jerusalem Post*) and to assert the absolute custody of Islam over the entire Temple Mount, bluntly rejecting the notion of any Christian or Jewish interest there. Looking the pope in the eye, he requested "that you stand by justice in order to end the Israeli occupation of Jerusalem." Characteristically, the pope did not reply in kind; he stated only that "Jerusalem has always been revered by Jews, Christians and Muslims."[55]

Scholars and churchmen have always known that the Muslim claim to Jerusalem is of this absolute and exclusive character – a point that eludes journalists and diplomats. Now the entire world saw that absolute claim rudely proclaimed before the eyes and ears of the world. The pope, who knows history as well as anyone, had hoped nonetheless for some glimmer of accommodation. As had happened so many times in the past, Muslim authorities had thrown away what would seem to Westerners a golden opportunity to *appear* flexible and accommodating on a matter that everyone in the world understands to be unspeakably dangerous – religious title to the site of the ancient Jewish temple.

7 Christian Zionism and Christian Anti-Zionism

> In those days ten men from every language of the nations shall grasp the sleeve of a Jewish man, saying, "Let us go with you, for we have heard that God is with you."
>
> Zechariah 8:23

THE SHORT LIFE OF LIBERAL PROTESTANT PRO-ZIONISM (1940S AND 1950S)

Back in the 1940s, when official Zionists were struggling to win Christian support for the creation of the State of Israel, they dealt with the liberal leadership of the mainstream churches – the eminent theologians and the responsible churchmen.[1] Perhaps the most eminent of these liberal pro-Zionist friends was Reinhold Niebuhr,[2] the principal spokesman for the Christian Council for Palestine, and later for the American Christian Palestine Committee. (As noted in chapter 4, the word "Palestinian" in the lexicon of the 1940s usually meant "Zionist".) Without doubt, Niebuhr was the most widely admired scholar of the American Protestant community and, equally important, the one theologian who commanded a wide audience in the company of secular intellectuals.

Niebuhr's prominence in the Christian pro-Zionist camp does not mark him as a Christian Zionist, however – at least, not in the sense that I use the term here, which is the sense of its current meaning. To Niebuhr, the notion of predictive prophecy was all superstition. This attitude was consistent with his theology: when it came to Scriptures, in typically liberal fashion, he swept away the miracles, the raising from the dead, the literal Resurrection. Like all consistent liberals then and now, Reinhold Niebuhr simply would not stoop to hold in his hands any literature in which there might appear the claim that the Bible foretells the Restoration of Israel. You could believe this if you wanted to; but if you did, your name would never appear on the masthead or on the board of directors of anything that Reinhold Niebuhr belonged to. That went, not least, for the Christian Council for Palestine and American Christian Palestine Committee. In the circumstances of the years immediately following the Second World War, this minority of pro-Zionist liberals was able to nudge a majority of Christians into supporting the politicians who brought about the creation of a Jewish state. This would not have been predicted a mere half-dozen years earlier, when the mainstream churches were generally hostile to Zionism. Nor, I believe, would it be possible today. The Zionists' opportunity to win the hearts of mainstream Protestants was brief, created by extraordinary and unrepeatable circumstances: the uncovering of the Holocaust; the intolerable situation of Europe's surviving "displaced" Jews; and the realization that Jews not admitted to Palestine would have to be admitted in vast numbers to the Western democracies. Thus, at the time of the creation of the World Council of Churches (a few weeks following the creation of the State of Israel) the attitude within mainstream and ecumenical Protestantism was generally friendly to the Jewish state. For the moment, the word "Zionism" rang positively for most Christians.

But much has happened since then in the lives of the Church and the State of Israel. Almost immediately after Israel's war to establish its UN-mandated independence ended, attitudes within the Church establishment shifted towards anti-Zionism. During the weeks previous to the Six-Day War of June 1967, when Nasser, the dictator of Egypt, was rallying the Arab world for a war of liquidation against Israel, the National Council of Churches remained silent. But immediately after Israel's victory, the council came awake and announced that it "cannot condone by silence territorial expansion by armed force." From that day forward, the NCC, in concert with the WCC, has generally portrayed Israel's behaviour in lockstep with Arab rhetoric: all subsequent wars have been fomented by Israel, for the purposes of further territorial gain and for the opportunity to incorporate innocent and abject Arab populations. The NCC pressed constantly through the 1970s and 1980s for American official contact with the PLO and always stood ready to denounce Israel's punitive responses to terrorism and civil disruption. It denounced the Camp David Accords of 1978 for allegedly ignoring the national ambitions of the Palestinian Arabs.

Not surprisingly, this record has embittered relations between the National Council of Churches of the United States, the official voice of mainstream American Protestantism, and the various bodies that speak for the mainstream Jewish community. In his *History of the Jews in*

America (1992), Howard Sachar sums this up (perhaps a bit too stridently): "By 1978, the old collaborative relationship between the Council [National Council of Churches] and the Jewish community had gone by the board ... Without question, the Council's anti-Israel posture was based, at least in part, upon genuine compassion for the Palestinians, who appeared now to be sharing the ordeal of defeated underdogs everywhere. Unlike their millennial right-wing cousins, however, the Christian establishment also seemed to be disoriented by the theological dilemma posed by Jews functioning as victorious conquerors rather than as perennial martyrs and as convenient scapegoats for Christian imperfections."[3]

At the same time, voices could be heard inside every denomination protesting the anti-Zionism reflected in official Church statements. Sometimes groups of the like-minded were formed – lobby groups, within the denominations and within the delegations to the subsequent Assemblies of the World Council of Churches. Little, if anything, was accomplished on this level; clearly, the anti-Israeli trend was growing at the top. Not daunted, Christian Zionists then moved their efforts on behalf of Israel into the great and boundless world of parachurch, where so much that is vital in Christian life – the charismatic movement of the 1970s and 1980s, the new political activism, revivals, moral renewal movements of many kinds (like Promise Keepers) – has been taking place during the last generation, as it has, for that matter, throughout the history of the Church.

In this chapter, I shall consider a number of volunteer movements on behalf of Israel that have appeared in the spaces between the denominations and all around the edges of the historical churches. To anticipate: these movements have spawned powerful international organizations of Christian friends of Israel, whose value has been increasingly appreciated by the State of Israel and to a lesser degree by Jewish Zionists outside Israel. These groups have simply outflanked official ecumenical Christianity to give expression to the pro-Israeli disposition that (public opinion polls consistently report) is characteristic of most Christians outside Israel.[4] Furthermore, they have accomplished this at the same time that the Jewish Diaspora has become a less-reliable, less-constant source of strength for Israel.

CHRISTIAN ZIONISM REVIVED

G. Douglas Young and the Institute of Holy Land Studies

The pioneer of what I will call renewed Christian Zionism was Dr G. Douglas Young. Born in 1910 in Korea, the son of Canadian Presbyterian missionary parents, Young studied at Faith Theological Seminary in Wilmington, Delaware, then completed a PhD in semitic languages at Dropsie College for Hebrew and Cognate Learning in Philadelphia. Short- term pulpit assigments followed, and then a sequence of academic postings in American theological seminaries on the evangelical side of the spectrum. (Unhappy with the theological liberalism taking hold in mainline Presbyterianism, Young eventually settled into the Evangelical Free Church.) Young's considerable reputation as a scholar stood on his many academic articles, his *Grammar of the Hebrew Language* (1951), and his *Ugaritic Concordance* (the latter, published in Rome in 1956, being the fruit of Young's pioneer work, under his teacher Cyrus Gordon, on the hoard of Ugarit documents discovered in 1928 at Ras Sharma). There followed an appointment as dean of Seminary at the National Bible Institute (later Shelton College), at Northwestern in Minneapolis, and later as professor of Old Testament at Trinity Evangelical Divinity School in Deerfield, Illinois. Throughout the 1950s he had a radio broadcast, originating at KTIS in Minneapolis and carried over the American Family Radio Network. His biblical messages turned more and more on themes drawn from Old and New Testament prophecy. He taught that restoration of the Jews to Israel was fulfilment of prophecy, and a vindication of the faithfulness that Jews had shown to their religion over the long centuries of Diaspora. In the spirit of Romans 11, he taught that Christians must "cease their boasting" and see themselves as the "natural branches" grafted onto Israel, the olive tree. The moral corollary of this theological conviction was that Christians must seek reconciliation with the Jews for the centuries of persecution and have an active concern for the present trials of the people of Israel.

During a brief visit to Israel in 1956, Young established contacts with many figures in Israeli government and academic life, including Yigal Yadin, who had recently retired from his position as commander-in-chief of the armed forces to resume his full-time work as an archaeologist; Dr Benjamin Mazar, president of the Hebrew University; and Dr Chaim Wardi, the director for Christian Communities in the Religious Affairs ministry. In the summer of 1957, Young took up Professor Yadin's invitation to participate in the very successful dig at Hazor.

In that same year, 1956–57, Young pursued his idea of founding a postgraduate school for biblical studies in Jerusalem. Here (in the words of his biographer) young Christians from abroad "could study the Bible and the land and also have opportunity to visit Israeli institutions, industries and homes to help build bridges of better understanding where prejudice reigned by the re-education of the Christian world *vis-à-vis* Israel."[5] This led, in 1957, to the founding in Jerusalem of the Israel-American Institute of Biblical Studies (later renamed the Institute of Holy Land Studies, and later still, Jerusalem University College). Originally housed in the American Gospel Church (of the Christian Missionary Alliance) at 55 Rehov Haneviim, the college now occupies the old Bishop Gobat school on Mount Zion, a building that greatly interests archaeologists as its foundations incorporate building blocks from the time of Herod and portions of a city wall that probably goes back much further. From the beginning, the project had the earnest support and cooperation of Dr Wardi, the director of the Department of Christian Communities, and would enjoy the cooperation of that office as well as other branches of the Israeli government and the Jerusalem municipality. In due course, its program was fully approved by the Israeli Ministry of Education and Culture. Nonetheless, while the school could count on the goodwill and active participation of many Israeli government officials, Israeli archaeologists (including such famous names as Nelson Glueck, Ruth Amiran, Yigal Yadin, and Benjamin Mazar) and Israeli religious scholars such as Zwi Werblowski (then cochairman of the Department of Religious Studies at Hebrew University), there was always a need for caution. A vignette from the diary of a student in that first academic year serves to illustrate a theme that would recur throughout the years: "Friday night we started out at 5 on a round of carolling at Christian homes and mission places. We went close to Dr Wardi and decided on the spur of the moment to stop by and sing Jingle Bells. Mrs Wardi came to the door, put her hands to her mouth and said, 'Shush, the Chief Rabbi of Israel lives upstairs.' They invited us in and got quite a charge out of our innocence – the chief Rabbi gives them a bad time on Sabbaths if there is any noise around the place. Anyhow they insisted that we sing a carol before we left so we sang *very softly*, 'Silent Night'! They said they appreciated it very much. But imagine a bunch of loud singing American kids, giving out 'Jingle Bells' underneath the home of the Chief Rabbi of Israel on shabbat evening! "[6] The students at the College were mainly young Americans of evangelical background. Under Dr Young and others (including Jewish scholars, some from Hebrew University), they became fluent in ancient and modern Hebrew and studied a demanding curriculum that was long on archaeology, Hebrew scriptures, and the study of the Jewish context out of which Christianity comes. In 1971 the Institute for Holy Land Studies sponsored the Jerusalem Conference on Bible Prophecy (referred to in chapter 2), which brought in more than twelve hundred people from thirty countries. Carl F. Henry, the editor of *Christianity Today*, was the chairman of the program. Former prime minister David Ben-Gurion gave the welcoming address, which helps explains the satisfying amount of attention that the event received in the secular press.[7]

Young, who had moved his family permanently to Jerusalem by the end of 1963, was by now a passionate Zionist, deeply distressed by what he perceived to be the lack of sympathy for Israel's cause in the secular press abroad and the hostility increasingly emanating from the mainline churches and the WCC. In a letter to the *Jerusalem Post* on 26 October 1975, Young wrote: "I have been accused of being a Zionist – a Christian Zionist – by some of my co-religionists in Israel and in the administered areas. I would like to take this means of thanking them for this compliment. I feel very sorry for Christian friends, and apologize for some of them, who are silent and have not yet identified publicly with Zionism, perhaps because they do not understand or because they fear other consequences. I have always thought it was a grand thing when the King of Denmark and his subjects wore the yellow patch when the Nazis tried by this means to single out the Jews in that country. Now I am glad to be able to wear a similar identifying pin."[8]

In September 1976 Young published the first edition of his *Dispatch from Jerusalem*, a monthly newsletter made up of short passages of news from Israel, modelled on the insiders' newsletters that were then becoming so influential in American academic, business, and political circles. The newsletter was edited by Lois and Bob Blewett of Minneapolis and circulated by a group called *Christians for Israel* in Dallas, Texas. Soon it had a circulation of some twenty thousand.[9] By now Young had many contacts in Israeli governmental, political, academic, and journalistic circles, who were more than ready to help him fill the pages of his newsletter. Soon there was a large arsenal of pamphlets, books, and recorded messages for use on American Christian radio stations. Young's supporters in the US formed study groups and began lobbying on behalf of Israel in Washington.

As it happened, these months when G. Douglas Young was seeking ways to "build bridges" between Christians and Israelis coincide with the moment when the majority of Israelis shifted away from their allegiance to the Labour coalition, making possible the victory of Likud under Menachem Begin in early 1977. In those months, a great dilemma was being created for the newly elected prime minister, Menachem Begin, by the diplomatic initiatives undertaken by Carter administration, also newly-elected. In March 1977 (in what turned out to be the last hours of the first Rabin administration), President Carter had declared publicly his interest in working towards a "Palestinian homeland" – a departure from the previous US official position; then, having reviewed the results of Secretary of State Cyrus Vance's diplomatic mission to the Middle East, President Carter took the politically risky step of issuing the joint US–USSR statement of 1 October 1977, whose purpose was to coax Israel into some unilateral concessions towards Egypt and the Palestinians without first securing from the other side (the various Arab nations) any commitment to recognize the State of Israel. A few weeks later, President Sadat of Egypt did an end run around the US–USSR/Geneva strategy by making his personal visit to Israel, thus priming the pump for bilateral diplomacy between Israel and Egypt, facilitated by the direct mediation of the president of the United States. All this issued, in due course, in the memorable Camp David Accords of September, 1978 and the Egpyt-Israel peace agreement of March 1979.

During his first months as Prime Minister, the media and academics both in Israel and abroad were distinctly unfriendly towards the "right-wing" Menachem Begin. He was still not trusted by American Jews, most of whose leaders had been shocked by his democratically won victory over the Labour regime that had governed official Zionism and Israeli politics from the beginning. It was during that time, the last eighteen months or so of G. Douglas Young's life, that he made his most lasting contribution to the history of Christian attitudes towards the State of Israel, by bringing into the bright light of political day the fundamental pro-Israel spirit of most American Christians, a spirit that he knew to be particularly strong on the evangelical-to-fundamentalist side, the "Bible-believing" side, of the Christian spectrum – thus laying the foundations for a new Christian Zionist activism that, as we shall see, later seemed almost indispensable to the security of Israel.

Among several initiatives taken at the time, there was a full-page ad in the *New York Times* on 1 November 1977 headed, "EVANGELICALS' CONCERN FOR ISRAEL," signed by several of the best-known evangelical theologians, preachers, and other notables, including Hudson T. Amerding, past president of the National Association of Evangelicals; W.A. Criswell, pastor of the First Baptist Church in Dallas; Kenneth Kantzer, dean of Trinity Evangelical Divinity School; Harold Lindsell, editor of *Christianity Today*; and John Walvoord, president of the Dallas Theological Seminary. It read (in part): "We the undersigned Evangelical Christians affirm our belief in the right of Israel to exist as a free and independent nation and in this light we voice our grave apprehension concerning the recent direction of American foreign policy *vis-à-vis* the Middle East. We are particularly troubled by the erosion of American governmental support for Israel evident in the joint US–USSR statement ... While the exact boundaries of the land of promise are open to discussion, we, along with most evangelicals, understand the Jewish homeland generally to include the territory west of the Jordan River ... [W]e would view with grave concern any effort to carve out of the historic Jewish homeland another nation or political entity, particularly one which would be governed by terrorists whose stated goal is the destruction of the Jewish state ... The time has come for Evangelical Christians to affirm their belief in biblical prophecy and Israel's Divine Right to the Land by speaking now."[10]

From 31 January to 2 February 1978, Young hosted the International Congress for the Peace of Jerusalem. Several of the same evangelical notables who had participated in the Jerusalem Conference on Bible Prophecy in 1971 were joined by Jewish academics (including Geoffrey Wigoder, editor of the *Encyclopedia Judaica*) and by Prime Minister Menachem Begin, who gave the opening address. The last session was particularly dramatic: it was held on Masada under a huge sign that read, "Masada Shall Not Fall Again." On that site, an "Act of Affirmation" was read out: "We the delegates of the International Congress for the Peace of Jerusalem in this solemn act of affirmation, guided by the Word of God which tells us that all Israel shall be saved, hereby firmly state our faith and conviction that the nation Israel where Masada stands has been established by God and shall stand forever."[11] Thus was founded "International Christians for Israel."

In 1979 Young retired formally from his position at the Institute for Holy Land Studies, to give his full time to an organization that would bring his philo-Judaic, pro-Zionist message to the United States and elsewhere in the Western Christian world. With the help of Bob and Lois Blewett of Minneapolis, Young put together a board of directors to assist him in launching Bridges for Peace. He turned to Clarence Wagner, Jr, to help him prepare a business plan for the new organization. Wagner was a young MBA graduate of the Oral Roberts University in Tulsa who, since 1977, had been operating the famous Spafford Children's Centre in the Old City of Jerusalem (to which, incidentally, he had been able to direct some generous financial gifts from the Oral Roberts organization). It was while he was going over Wagner's draughts that Dr Young suffered a sudden massive heart attack and died in May 1980. Shortly after that, Clarence Wagner agreed to accept the board's challenge to become the first director of Bridges for Peace, a position he still held in the year 2000.

Bridges for Peace[12]

The mission of Bridges for Peace is to "build bridges of understanding and support between the Christian and Jewish communities – to begin a process of healing ancient wounds and misunderstandings that have long endured between Christians and Jews. We do this by expressing support for the Jewish people in tangible ways and by educating Christians about the Jewish roots of Christianity and the value of interpreting the Bible from a Hebraic perspective. We are also vitally concerned for the present and future well-being of Israel as a Jewish state in the Middle East, and of her citizens. We see this as a biblical, historical and moral mandate for Christians." The "Goals" of the organization include "interpreting Israel to Christians around the world in light of the Bible and today's events. Providing counsel and channels of service for pro-Israel groups and individuals desiring to actively support and bless Israel and the Jewish people. Working to combat anti-Semitism and all forms of prejudice and misunderstanding between Christians and Jews."

While continuing Dr Young's newsletter (*Dispatch from Jerusalem*), Wagner has added an *Update from Jerusalem – The Israel Teaching Letter* (featuring articles on modern Israel, the historical setting of the Old Testament, and the Jewish roots of Christianity), and a lively website. In 1998 Bridges began a series of teaching videos under the series title *Jerusalem Mosaic*, for use on Christian television networks in the United States and Canada; these have been dubbed into Japanese, Portugese, and Spanish for broadcast around the world. Honouring and enlarging on Young's commitment to the importance of familiarity with Israeli life, Bridges for Peace conducts correspondence courses, Bible-study tour programs, conferences, and seminars. In the name of encouraging and expressing love for Israel, the organization carries out numerous large-scale programs of assistance to the local needy (under the name *Operation Ezra*), with a special emphasis on recent immigrants. These include Jerusalem's largest continuing food bank program, which delivers a ton of food every day[13] (for which the organization has been honoured with the "Guardian of Jerusalem" Award, presented by Mayor Ehud Olmert, in the presence of the then prime minister Binyamin Netanyahu, in 1997), and a program that provides volunteers to repair, renovate, and furnish the homes of the poor and elderly. (The inspiration for this last activity was found in Isaiah 58:12: "And they that shall be of thee shall build the old waste places, thou shalt raise up the foundations of many generations; and thou shalt be called, The repairer of the breach, The restorer of paths to dwell in.") "Welcome kits" of groceries, toiletries, kitchen and school supplies, blankets, and other essentials (including a Hebrew-Russian Old Testament) are distributed to immigrants. Under a program called "Operation Rescue," BFP helps poor Jews in the countries of the former Soviet Union to immigrate to Israel. These activities are managed by a volunteer staff of about forty in Jerusalem. Bridges for Peace now has national offices with branches of their own in the UK, Canada, US, South Africa, Japan, Brazil, and dozens of other countries.

All of the Christian Zionist organizations acknowledge Dr Douglas Young as their pioneer and Bridges for Peace, under the leadership of Clarence Wagner, Jr, as the senior organization in the ranks of renewed Christian Zionism.

The International Christian Embassy Jerusalem[14]

On 30 July 1980, the Knesset of Israel passed a new "Basic Law" (tantamount to a constitutional principle) with the title "Jerusalem the Capital City of Israel." In this document, an "integral and united Jerusalem" is declared to be the capital of Israel and the seat of the presidency, the Knesset, the government, and the Supreme Court. The legislation introduced no new principle (the Knesset had declared precisely this on 23 January 1950) and added nothing to reality. Yet editorial opinion in the West was overwhelmingly hostile to Israel's action, and Arab nations threatened an oil embargo against any nation acquiescing in Israel's decision.

In the eyes of the UN, Israel had always been in contempt of the stipulation (part of the partition decision of 29 November 1947) that Jerusalem should be a *corpus separatum* – for the reasons already noted in chapter 2. To keep themselves in line with this principle, all but twenty embassies had located themselves in Tel Aviv. The Netherlands and Yugoslavia were the only two European countries among the twenty. (After the Yom Kippur War of 1973, Yugoslavia and six African embassies had severed diplomatic relations with Israel altogether.)

Why did the Begin government choose this moment to bring the issue of Jerusalem back to the front burner at the UN? Perhaps it was simple cussedness. In the eyes of Menachem Begin's government, the months since Camp David had seen one concession after another for the sake of peace with Egypt. It was time to assert Israel's sovereign right to defend what it had won at painful cost in wars inflicted on her by neighbours who had never acceded to the partition decision in the first place. But among many other motives attributed to the Begin government was the intention of compelling American politicians to declare their loyalty to Israel. Nineteen-eighty was, after all, a presidential election year, and for the first time ever there was good cause for Jews to favour the Republican candidate over the Democratic one: the Republicans were about to nominate Ronald Reagan, who was believed to have a solid pro-Israel disposition, owing to his links to the many friends of Israel in the evanglical-to-fundamentalist wing of Christian life. President Jimmy Carter, the facilitator of the Camp David Accords and the Egyptian-Israeli peace treaty, would need to work hard to recover the confidence of the American Jewish community and the friends of Israel. By putting the Jerusalem issue back on the front burners of the UN Israel would give American politicians an opportunity to declare their confidence in the future of Israel and in Israel's sovereign right to govern the citizens and property that lay within her own declared borders. But Jimmy Carter failed Begin's test. On 20 August 1980, the UN Security Council, with the US assenting, passed Resolution 478, calling on members of the UN to withdraw their diplomatic missions from the city of Jerusalem. All but El Salvador and Costa Rica did so.[15]

On 30 September 1980, a group of evangelical Christians resident in Jerusalem, under the leadership of Dutch theologian and pastor Jan Willem van der Hoeven, announced the opening of the International Christian Embassy Jerusalem. Born in Haarlem in the Netherlands in 1940, a graduate of the Bible College of London University, ordained in the Armenian Evangelical Church, van der Hoeven had already been in Israel for seven years, most recently serving as the warden of the Garden Tomb. He had been active in charismatic/pentecostal fellowships in the city, and in the circles that had formed around Douglas Young. The "Embassy" announced that it would represent what it said was the vast majority of Christian people who wished to see their governments represented in the Israeli capital. The organization would stand with the Jews in affirming what God had said about Israel's right to rule in Jerusalem.

Little notice was paid to this event, and the few commentaries that appeared in its wake were either condescending or mocking. Commentators at the time noted that the full measure of the loneliness experienced in official circles in the wake of the flight of diplomats was proved when Jerusalem's mayor, Teddy Kollek, found the time to attend the official opening. Yet, as we shall see, Israeli leaders have since learned a thing or two about how to make Israel's case before the Christian world, and government leaders of both parties have in recent years considered it well worth their time to visit ICEJ and be photographed with its leaders. Ironically, the founding of the "Christian Embassy" may well be the most important consequence of the Israeli government's announcement of its new Basic Law. ICEJ did *not* wither away after the initial enthusiasm but instead grew from strength to strength. ICEJ opened its embassy in a modest-sized house off Ramban Street and later moved to the vacant Chilean mission at 10 Brenner Street in what was once the residence of Martin Buber), then in 1998 to a large and attractive building of truly ambassadorial proportions at 20 Rachel Imeinu Street, in German Colony. By 1998 there was a permanent staff of sixty people, mostly volunteers, who speak a total of about fifteen languages. This number is augmented by about two hundred more volunteeers during the period of preparation for the annual Succoth event (see below). Today it has active representation in over one hundred countries. It has eighty-two branches worldwide and a supporting membership of many tens of thousands. It publishes a newsletter, *A Word from Jerusalem,* and a monthly commentary on current affairs originally called the *Middle East Intelligence Digest,* now the *Middle East Digest.* In the United States, in addition to having many branches, it plays a role in the lobbying organization "Christians' Israel Public Action Campaign (CIPAC).

ICEJ has explored an astonishing range of ways for Christians to declare their support for Israel and to have a presence in the day-to-day life of the state. In doing so, it has won the goodwill of most citizens and has to some degree alleviated the suspicions that the Orthodox Jewish population of Israel has always harboured towards evangelical Christians. Some of ICEJ's activities resemble those of Bridges for Peace, including programs to assist immigrant Jews. Its International Christian Investment Corporation draws together Christian capitalists to invest in Israeli industry. Although there are no significant differences in theology, ICEJ is more boldly political than is Bridges for Peace. ICEJ has worked harder at cultivating bridges to the Israeli government, while most of BFP's political friends are in municipal politics, and most of its practical activities are carried out in the local life of Jerusalem.

Two areas in which ICEJ has surpassed Bridges are the organization of mass meetings of Christian visitors in support of Israel and active promotion of immigration of Jews to Israel from abroad. ICEJ insists that Christians are duty bound to assist the morale of the people of Israel by visiting their country. This is a duty quite apart from the more generally recognized privilege of visiting Christian holy sites. Christian tourists must be aware that they are visiting *Israel.* In this light, the ICEJ has made the focus of its calendar the organization of a massive rally during the time of *Succoth* (Tabernacles, or "Booths"), a festival that takes place in the fall, several weeks before Christmas, and that is said to be the only major festival not incorporated into the Christian year. In recent years, the number of participants has reached seven thousand, which makes this, according to ICEJ, the largest regular annual tourist event in Israel. ICEJ holds its convention during the festival, and those attending from all the continents of the world march and dance through the city of Jerusalem in demonstration of solidarity with Israel. In this way, not only do Christians "show concern for the Jewish people and the reborn State of Israel, by being a focus of comfort ... ('Comfort ye, comfort ye my people, saith your God' [Isaiah 40: 1]" but they "take part through these activities in preparing the way of the Lord and to anticipate his reign from Jerusalem(Isaiah 2: 2–3.)" All this is seen as fulfilling the prophecy of Zechariah 14: 16: "And it shall come to pass that every one that is left of all the nations which came against Jerusalem shall even go up from year to year to worship the King, the LORD of hosts, and to keep the feast of the tabernacles."

ICEJ literature speaks proudly of its long-standing "Russian Connection" and was, in fact, something of a pioneer in the work of assisting the emigration to Israel of Russian Jews and other Jews within the Soviet Empire. In its earliest years, the ICEJ organized demonstrations at Soviet embassies in various countries calling for the USSR to allow emigration of Soviet Jews to Israel. In those early years, there was an "underground" aspect to this work, as volunteers entered the Soviet Union to provide encouragement to some of the early "refuseniks." Interviews and other information gathered in the early visits was smuggled out for use in a video, *Gates of Brass,* which circulated in churches in the West. In 1990, as the walls against emigration were coming down, a project was developed for busing Soviet Jews into Finland; since then, some ten thousand have been brought to Israel by this route.[16] From the beginning, the project has been carried out with the close cooperation of the Jewish Agency. When asked why a land route should be maintained after the Soviet Union had collapsed and most émigrés were leaving by air, ICEJ spokesmen say that they and the Jewish Agency are agreed that if there should be a political reaction against Jewish emigration – that is, should Russia, or Ukraine, or Belarus relapse into the familiar mode of persecution of Jews – a land route will be needed for escape.[17]

Of the roughly 700,000 immigrants who had come from the former Soviet Union by 1998, roughly 40,000 were assisted by the ICEJ. Some fifty-one flights, in addition to the buses via Finland, were paid for by ICEJ supporters. The organization encourages Jews across the former Soviet Union to consider emigration to Israel. Among other means, its representatives travel about the former USSR, going especially into areas where there have been serious occurences of anti-Semitism, using a double-decker bus that houses a miniature theatre where videos are shown and literature is distributed promoting the hopefulness of a future in Israel. Concerts are held celebrating Israel. At one time, ICEJ sponsored the Exobus project (since taken over by another funding organization) to gather and take to the major airports Jews wishing to emigrate throughout Russia, Ukraine, Moldava, and other parts of the former Soviet Union. In Israel, ICEJ's Soviet Jewry department gives immigrants practical help in matters of health, job-seeking, and so on. By 1995 over forty plane-loads of immigrants had been brought to Israel by ICEJ. ICEJ also provided a mobile clinic to deal with the problem of leprosy among the 14,500 Ethiopian Jews (Falashas) who were airlifted into Israel in a thirty-six-hour period during Israel's "Operation Shlomo" in May 1991. In addition, many hundreds of Falasha families have been supplied with clothing, food, and shelter.

ICEJ does not flinch at the suggestion that its activities are political. As proof of its political seriousness, it proudly displays in its literature the many endorsements of its activities that have been proferred over the years by Israeli leaders – most of them taking the form of public declarations at ICEJ conventions and other gatherings. Prime Minister Menachem Begin made this statement: "Your decision to establish your Embassy in Jerusalem at a time when we were being abandoned because of our faith was an act of courage and a symbol of the close-ness between us. Your gestures and acts gave us the feeling that we were not alone." From Prime Minister Yitzhak Rabin: "Allow me to tell you how much I, and Israel, appreciate your [presence] here in Jerusalem ... Israel has experienced through her existence many diffi-culties. Therefore, whenever we see people that care, that are involved, and who show this by deeds, and by words – we appreciate this." And from Chief Rabbi Shlomo Goren: "Your sympathy, solidarity and belief in the future of Israel – this to us is tremendous. We con-sider you part of the fulfilment of the prophetic vision of Zechariah in chapter 14." In April 1991 ICEJ received the Speaker of the Knesset's Quality of Life Award and, in December 1991, the Brandeis Award of the Zionist Organization of America, for fostering friendship between the United States and Israel.

I shall expand upon the role of Christian Zionists in American poli-tics in chapter 8, but it is worth noting here that one of the best-informed scholars of the Christian Zionist groups, Yaakov Ariel, cau-tions against the tendency to overstate the American connection and goes so far as to claim that the strength of the ICEJ, in particular, lies more with its European and African (especially South African) mem-bership than with its American membership.[18]

ICEJ considers itself as an embodiment (notwithstanding the con-spicuous distinction that it is a Christian organization) of the Zionist movement that Theodor Herzl founded in 1897. Between 27 and 29 August 1985, ICEJ held its own "First Christian Zionist Congress" in Basel, the same city, and in the same building, where the First Zionist

Congress opened in 1897. Five hundred people attended. A message of greeting from Prime Minister Begin was read, and President Chaim Herzog spoke in person to the convention: "When the International Christian Embassy was founded, I do not think that even its devoted leaders expected a mass movement of such dimension to emerge in the course of a few years. Your understanding of the spiritual roots of Zionism and of the special nature of Jerusalem are unfortunately far from universally held in other circles and movements. That you are joining us in celebrating the fortieth anniversary of Israel's establishment is indeed a logical outcome of your attachment to Scripture and to the people who have lived by Scripture throughout the centuries." As was the practice at Herzl's meetings, a declaration was produced: "We congratulate the State of Israel and her citizens for their many achievements in the short span of less than four decades ... We also lovingly implore you: please try to realize more clearly and to acknowledge more openly that it's the hand of God, as prophesied in your Holy Scriptures, which has restored the land and gathered in the Exiles, not just the strength of your own hands ... We call upon every Jew throughout the world to consider making aliyah to Israel, and upon every Christian to encourage and support their Jewish friends in this freely-taken but God-inspired step ... [We urge] the nations which are friends of Israel but whose policies totter between true support and political expediency ... to establish your embassies in Jerusalem ... and to recognize Judea and Samaria as part of the Land ... We warn the nations hostile to Israel, including the Arab nations (except Egypt) and the Soviet Union, to stop the obstruction of peace in the Middle East. We also ask the USSR to let all Soviet Jews emigrate to Israel ... The Congress respectfully asks the World Council of Churches in Geneva to recognize the Biblical link between the Jewish People and their Promised Land as well as the deep Biblical and prophetic dimension of the State of Israel ... We pray and eagerly await the day in which Jerusalem and the Mountain of the Lord will become the center of mankind's attention when our Lord's Kingdom will become a reality. (*Micah* 4: 1, 2)[19]

The Second and Third Christian Zionist Congresses, held in Jerusalem on 10–15 April 1988 and 25–29 February 1996, issued declarations that repeated the positions appearing in the first declaration, while developing in more detail its positions on the current diplomacy between Israel and the Arab states (more or less in line with those of the national religious sector of the right wing of the Likud) and speaking out against the menace of Islamic fundamentalism: "[We affirm] the biblical right of the Jewish people to live freely in the entire land of Israel, including Judea, Samaria, and Gaza as a Jewish state ... We recognize ... that the Arab nations have been granted their own great and eternal promises, for example, as found in Genesis 17: 20 ... and Isaiah 19: 24 & 25. We therefore call upon ... the Arab leaders of Judea, Samaria and Gaza, the leaders of Jordan, Syria and Lebanon, and those of the other Arab nations, to recognize Israel's right to exist ... We encourage Israel, in accordance with the scripture to grant political, economic and cultural rights to all of Judea, Samaria and Gaza who agree to loyally assume their concomitant rights and responsibilities without violence (Ezekiel. 47: 22.)"[20] On 23 August 1997, the ICEJ celebrated the centenary of the First Zionist Congress in the very same hall where Herzl called his founding meeting. The ICEJ's own newsletter comments: "Although the ICEJ event occurred on the eve of the official Jewish commemoration, many of the Jewish visitors present commented that the ICEJ gathering was the true celebration, inasmuch as it acknowledged the sovereignty of God behind the movement to restore the people to their ancient homeland."[21] However, this judgment overlooks the fact that the first congress was a distinctly secular affair.

THE THEOLOGY OF RENEWED CHRISTIAN ZIONISM[22]

By the time that ICEJ came into the world, leaders of the mainstream Protestant churches had gone over *en masse* to the anti-Zionist camp. By the 1980s the official voices of the Church had virtually made rejection of the predictive uses of the Old Testament a test of theological correctness. In the spirit of neo-Marcionism, the ecumenical Church demanded that Christian Zionists prove their case from the New Testament – to prove that it is a *Christian* doctrine that Christian Zionists propound, and not a Jewish doctrine coopted by Christians for the purpose of pursuing pro-Israeli politics. The renewed Christian Zionism of the 1980s and 1990s is characterized, accordingly, by its emphasis on a New Testment defence of Zionism.

Perhaps the best-developed sources for this teaching are the booklets and audiotapes of the teaching of Malcolm Hedding, a South African theologian who has always been close to ICEJ and was at one time its designated "chaplain."[23] Taking as his text Luke 21, Hedding teaches: "Jesus Himself spoke of the scattering and latter-day regathering of the Jewish people [referring specifically to Luke 21:21–24: "They will fall by the sword and will be taken as prisoners to all nations. Jerusalem will be trampled on by Gentiles until the times of the Gentiles are fulfilled"]. Indeed He placed their second regathering in an eschatological setting (Luke 21: 8). Thus Christian Zionists simply seek to give voice to that which Jesus Himself has already said, namely, that the modern day restoration of the State of Israel is not a political accident, or merely the result of a secular political Zionist plot but rather the fulfilment of God's own Word."[24]

Of interest to students of the many-faceted "dispensationalist" tradition is the fact that ICEJ does *not* teach the concept of the Rapture of the church that is such an important feature of the teaching of most popular End Times teachers (including the enormously influential Hal Lindsey), according to which God will snatch away all of his true believers in a moment of time, just *prior to* the worldwide tribulation.[25] (Understandably, Jews who have dipped into Lindsey's books take a dim view of this teaching, as I note later.) "We are not helping Israel in order to bring Jesus back. We do not expect to be absent ... The nations will come against Israel, and Israel's enemies will be destroyed. But this will not be a Holocaust for the Jews. There is no Holocaust ahead for the Jews."[26] Taking these texts together with Acts 15: 13–16 and Romans 11: 25–32, ICEJ teaches: "The completion of God's purposes with the Gentiles marks the beginning of his renewed grace to the people of Israel. After the time of the Gentiles has been fulfilled, after the fulness of the Gentiles has come into the kingdom, then all Israel will be saved ... We are the generation privileged to witness the third homecoming of the people of Israel. This time it will result, as the Bible tells us, in life from the dead for the whole world. The Lord will come down and save this world from all the negative and destructive forces that have caused havoc for so many centuries." Malcolm Hedding blames the "unbiblical teaching of replacement theology" (supersessionism) for the anti-Semitism in the history of the Church, and for the resistance found in the Church in 1948 to the Restoration of Israel and, in 1967, to Israel's enlargement towards its "biblical" borders. "In these last days, as Peter called them 2000 years ago, the struggle between light and darkness will intensify. Israel will be at the heart of this struggle since it is through her that God will establish His reign of righteousness over the world (Zechariah 14: 9). The forces of darkness will always oppose such a reign and they will do it chiefly by seeking to destroy Israel."[27]

There is no mystery about ICEJ purposes and the philosophy. They are elaborated in a number of well-designed booklets and brochures (some of which are noted in the bibliography). To the question why ICEJ was created and why it continues the answer is, "To Love and Comfort Zion" (quoting Isaiah 40: 1.) "The Christian Embassy seeks to demonstrate to Israel that there are Christians all over the world who do care for her and love her." ICEJ teaches that the ingathering of the Jews to Zion is the necessary first step towards the return of the Jews to the understanding of the love of God which is central in their own tradition. "Everything the prophets foretold will be fulfilled, not just the convenient portions of it ... The prophets foretold that there would be a day on earth, under the reign of the Messiah in Jerusalem with His nation when: All wars would cease. Each man would live under his fig tree in equality and justice. The child would play with the viper so that there would be harmony between mankind and the animal world. Nature would be fully restored, the trees would 'clap their hands' and the Dead Sea would become a sweet water lake ... We believe with Paul that the Messiah has come once; and we join him in rejoicing at the restoration of Israel, for we know that it signals the return of the Messiah and the fulfilment of the physically restored nation, and that He has brought them back to be given a new heart and a new spirit, and eventually to become a light and glory to the nations."

Until the day comes when the people of Israel have returned voluntarily and with full hearts to the religion of their fathers, realizing the expectations of Joel, Christian missionary activity among the Jews is not in the will of God. It is this part of the message of the ICEJ – the renunciation of evangelical intention towards the Jews – that the Jews of Israel find hardest to swallow. Yet it is absolutely sincere and without reservation, and in no degree inconsistent with the organization's public declaration of the members' Christian hope. Until Messiah comes, ICEJ believes, it is the supreme work of religious Jews and those Christians who respect the faith of the Jews to keep Israel alive: "The enemy realises only too clearly that natural Israel will ultimately become spiritual Israel and therefore invokes all the political forces of this world to try to destroy her ... Christians must therefore take a stand against this and counter lies with truth. This is not primarily political but a part of the warfare to help protect the Lord's people and to help preserve them for that time when the Lord will fulfil his promises in Ezekiel 37, Zechariah 12 and Joel 3."

Senior leaders of ICEJ have made intense personal commitments to the State of Israel. Most of the present leadership have lived with their families in Israel for many years, although none is an Israeli citizen. Jan Willem van der Hoeven has the status of a permanent resident of Israel. He can get along in Hebrew but is not fluent in the language. Both his son and his daughter, however, have served in the Israeli armed forces. The rank and file of the membership, who remain citizens of the United States, United Kingdom, Canada, Finland, or South Africa, are made to understand that loyalty to Israel is no less a kind of patriotism for them. In season and out, they must defend Israel's actions against her critics.

This does not mean pretending that Israel is entirely a force for sweetness and light; Israel's behaviour as a nation is sinful, as is the behaviour of all nations everywhere. Hendrikus Berkhof (professor emeritus of Dogmatic and Biblic Theology, Leyden State University, and former moderator of the Council of Churches of the Netherlands, 1974–83) has noted that Israel's enemies fasten on publicized acts of cruelty towards Arab Palestinians or the occasional resort to counter-terrorist ugliness, and they say, "People can only be and remain elected and beloved by God, when they act morally. Israel does no longer act morally, because it has expelled the Palestinians or is still oppressing them." But, says Berkhof, "We Christians ... confess for ourselves that our grace does not depend on our moral behaviour, that it is the other way round: we are elected without any merits on our side, we live by grace alone. That is the same miracle which we see in the long history of Israel."[28]

ICEJ's massive public events (the annual Succoth festival and the several congresses) have made it the highest-profile Christian Zionist group. Accordingly, by the mid-1980s, it had become the *bête noire* of Christian anti-Zionists. The mere mention of ICEJ causes Palestinian Christian spokesmen and MECC dignitaries to explode in rage. WCC/MECC literature routinely identifies ICEJ as the embodiment of all that disturbs the peace of the Palestinian Christian community: it is a monstrous, incendiary machine, fuelled by the most disreputable of "fundamentalist" heresies.

Periodically, outsiders would hear rumours of trouble inside the walls of the ICEJ headquarters. From the beginning, there have been differences over the distribution of responsibilities between Jan Willem van der Hoeven (who had the title of spokesman for the embassy) and Johann Luckhoff (who was the director). One source of dissatisfaction for many, it seemed, was the tendancy of the senior leaders to act without consultation with the board, or to make public statements that did not have the wholehearted agreement of the rank and file. Johann Luckhoff is accused by some of having an authoritarian approach to his duties as chief administrator of the organization. Jan Willem van der Hoeven, who used his weekly teaching meetings to set the political position that ICEJ has taken, is regarded by many members as having something of the authority of a prophet. His thoughts on the future rebuilding of a physical temple (as described by Ezekiel) have not always commended themselves to the board.[29] From time to time, leading individuals have left the organization in protest about some incident and have then re-emerged as founders of some new organization – a rib out of the side of ICEJ.[30]

Christian Friends of Israel.[31]   During the First Christian Zionist Congress held at Basle in 1985 there was, behind the scenes, a leadership crisis, followed by defection of some long-serving members. These later founded another organization with a similar purpose, Christian Friends of Israel. This is one of many Christian pro-Israel groups that have headquarters in Jerusalem and active branches around the world. The present International Director is Ray Sanders, one of the original founders in 1985. David Dolan writes the monthly publication for CFI, *Israel News Digest.* CFI also distributes a quartley report on its work (*For Zion's Sake*), the *Middle East Update* (the newsletter of Lance Lambert, whose books on Israel have been widely read by evangelicals over many years), and many educational videos. CFI has over twenty affiliate offices around the world, including two in the United States – one for the East Coast in Charlotte, North Carolina, and the other for the West Coast, in Kirkland, Washington. Its "calling" is "(a) to teach the Church in the nations and (b) to reach out to the Jewish people with Christian love through various outreaches and projects in Israel." CFI characterizes itself as "a humanitarian organization," in contrast to ICEJ, which it sees as "a religious-political organization."[32] Like ICEJ and Bridges for Peace, it carries on relief work in Israel, through its "Distribution Centre" and its "Door of Hope" ministry, and it has actively assisted immigration of Russian Jews to Israel. CFI combines with other like-minded organizations in support of lobbying actions in the United States, and in sponsoring public events in support of Israel.

The National Christian Leadership Conference for Israel.   The original nucleus of this organization was Christians Concerned for Israel, founded immediately after the Six-Day War by a distinguished Church historian, Franklin Littell of Southern Methodist University. CCI was, in a real sense, the residual heir to the legacy of PPF, CCP, and ACPC, which had closed down after the work of establishing the Jewish state. Littell's hope was to keep alive in the mainstream of the Church something of the spirit of concern for Israel that had marked those early pro-Zionist groups, to meet the new situation of defending Israel and Israel's policies in the face of the hostility that increasingly characterized the liberal Protestant and Roman Catholic world. CCI was always something of one-man band – for a while, little more than a letterhead organization, whose work was all done by Franklin Littell. It was he who would call up allies off the letterhead long enough to take out ads in *New York Times,* to meet a crisis. The fact was that constant pro-Zionism was not easy to find in the ranks of mainstream clergy or among Protestant or Catholic academics. It was in the hope of developing a broader base of supporters for Littell's organization that the National Christian Leadership Conference was established in 1978.[33] Its present chairman is Dr David Lewis, of Springfield, Missouri.[34] One example of the organization's activities is an advertisement published in the *New York Times* late in 1992. Here, NCLCI declares that it "fully supports the direct Arab-Israeli peace negotiations begun in Madrid" (differing on this matter with the ICEJ) and that it "celebrates the miracle of return of hundreds of thousands of Jewish refugees from all over the world, especially from Ethiopia and the former USSR," and supports Israel's need for money to absorb these immigrants.[35]

NCLCI can be particularly effective when it joins with other pro-Israeli Christian groups in sponsorship of conferences and other public occasions, because, while its membership is nowhere near as broad as Bridges for Peace or ICEJ, the organization has acquired credibility through the range of academic and clerical leaders that support it. For example, while on a visit coordinated by Inter-Religious Coordinating Council in Israel, and headed by the director of the American Jewish Committee office in Israel, Dr Ron Kronish, the executive of NCLCI met in Jerusalm in January 1992 with Church leaders and with several political leaders in Jerusalem, including Yitzhak Shamir, Natan Sharansky, and Binyamin Begin. On that occasion, Shamir described the group as "among the best friends we have in the world."[36]

Voices United for Israel. Voices United for Israel is a coalition of 162 pro-Israel Christian and Jewish organizations that claim to represent eight million individuals, and that come together for conferences and other public occasions.[37] At its third annual National Unity Conference for Israel, held in Washington, DC, its speakers included Elwood McQuaid, Cal Thomas, Ralph Reed, Ed McAteer, David Lewis, Walid Phares, James Rudin, and David Bar-Ilan. This organization was responsible for putting together rallies in support of Prime Minister Netanyahu on the occasion of his visits to the US, during which President Clinton sought to secure more concessions from Israel on the so-called peace process with Arafat.

Religious Roundtable. Religious Roundable is a rib out of the side of the International Christian Prayer Breakfast for Israel, originally held in conjunction with the annual convention of National Religious Broadcasters, in Washington, DC. On several occasions since, the Annual Prayer Breakfast for Israel has met in Jerusalem. The organization is led by Rev. Ed McAteer and has its head office in Memphis, Tennessee. Its *Proclamation of Blessing* states: "Representing the vast majority of Bible-believing Christians in the United States ... we agree that a secure, strong Israel is in American's self-interest. Israel is a major strategic asset to America. Israel is not a client but a very reliable friend. To weaken Israel is to destabilize the Middle East and risk the peace of the world, for the road to world peace runs through the Middle East. " And in a press statement: "We forcefully assert that we believe the Bible when God declares uncompromisingly that he has given His land Israel, including Judea and Samaria, Gaza, the Golan and all of Jerusalm, to His people the Jews as an everlasting possession."

This organization calls upon other Bible-believing Americans not to vote for any politician "whose policy concerning Israel would be contrary to the mandate of God." The *Jerusalem Post*, 4 March 1992, describes its Eleventh Annual Prayer Breakfast for Israel, held in Jerusalem, which was addressed by Prime Minister Yitzhak Shamir and John Showcroft (governor of Missouri). At the time, the most urgent issue for Christian Zionists on the public agenda was Israel's request of a loan guarantee from the American Congress in support of its massive building program to accommodate recent immigrants from Russia. The Bush administration opposed the guarantee, unless Israel pledged not to build on lands whose ownership was disputed by the Arab-Palestinian side. Speakers at the breakfast said they expected that many evangelicals would vote for any Democrat against President George Bush because of this issue, or would sit the election out in protest of Bush's position. The Fourteenth Annual Christian Prayer Breakfast, held in Jerusalem on 29 February 1996, was held in conjunction with the Third Christian Zionist Congress.[38]

Christian Friends of Israeli Communities. Founded in 1995 by Ted Beckett, a commercial real estate developer from Colorado Springs, this organization tries to provide "solidarity, comfort, and aid" to the Jewish settlements in Judaea, Samaria, and Gaza, by linking them with evangelical churches and groups in the US that raise funds for their support and sponsor cooperative activities between the citizens of these settlements and the churches that sponsor them.[39]

Christians' Israel Public Action Campaign. At the 1991 Prayer Breakfast for Israel a decision was made to form the Christians' Israel Public Action Campaign (CIPAC), to lend the support of Christian Zionist groups to the political activities which are carried out on behalf of Israel by the American Israel Political Affairs Committee.[40] CIPAC is currently headed by Richard A. Hellman, who had worked as minority counsel for the Senate Environment and Public Works committee (under Howard Baker) and had then moved to Israel where he became a businessman active in ICEJ. CIPAC draws its support from ICEJ, Christian Friends of Israel, Christians for Israel, and others and represents "Christians in the US and worldwide who recognize the people and the State of Israel as fulfilment of Biblical prophecy in both the Old and the new Testaments." It seeks to "educate and mobilize Christians on behalf of sound laws and policies toward Israel."[41]

Evangelical Sisterhood of Mary, Darmstadt, Germany. Considerable numbers of American and Canadian Lutherans draw their Christian Zionist sympathies from the literature of the Evangelical Sisterhood of Mary, whose headquarters are in Germany, and which maintains affiliates in North America. The leading figures of this movement are Sisters Basilea Schlinck and Pista, who have appeared regularly at public functions sponsored by the larger Christian Zionist organizations. Originating in the contrition of those German Christians who see a duty to keep the memory of the Holocaust alive, publications of the movement present the history of the creation of the State of Israel in the light of classical Christian Restorationism and urge Christians to understand the need for support of Israel's present cause.[42]

Other Organizations. Several other lesser-known Christian Zionist organizations run ads from time to time in newspapers and participate in cooperative efforts with the larger organizations. To judge from my own efforts to correspond with these organizations, none is in the same league with those just mentioned in terms of financial support and continuity of effort. All of the major Christian Zionist organizations maintain websites and some provide Internet newsletters. In addition, there are innumerable freelancers who maintain websites and newsletters devoted to Christian Zionist perspectives. It is impossible to assess their influence. Among those that might be presumed to have some effect on public opinion are a few that are maintained by some of the better-known evangelical and fundamentalist authors of books on Israel and on biblical prophecy, such as Lee Underwood, David Dolan, Don Feder, and others.

THE THEOLOGY AND PRACTICE OF CHRISTIAN ANTI-ZIONISM

Any believer who tries to justify through his theology the religious right of Israel in Palestine is an infidel who denies God and Christ.

Geries Khoury[43]

The PLO has highjacked the main churches.

Willem van der Hoeven.[44]

MECC as a Source of Christian Anti-Zionism

The Middle East Council of Churches, founded in 1974, is actually a more "ecumenical" body than the WCC. The formally organized voice of the churches in the Middle East, it represents seventeen Christian denominations in the region, belonging to the Eastern Orthodox, Oriental Orthodox, Catholic, and Protestant families – virtually all of the fourteen million Christians of the Middle East.[45] It came into the world announcing that it was "without political or ideological axes to grind, but focusing upon the human needs of individuals and communities for whom Christ died"[46] A major obstacle to this task is the irritating presence of Western evangelicals and fundamentalists: "The presence of western evangelical missions and para-church groups, some of which can be described as fundamentalist, in the Middle East has been a matter of concern to the MECC and its member churches for some years now ... [T]he increase in both their numbers and activities has been augmenting the risks of alienation and division among Christians in the region ... [In the literature of such groups] there is often an ignorance or a deliberate negligence of the ecclesiastical values as well as the life and witness of the local churches of the Middle East, on the grounds that they are not 'Christ-centered,' not 'Biblically-oriented' and 'unable to do mission.'"[47] At its meeting of 16–18 April 1986, the executive committee of MECC denounced the International Christian Zionist Congress held in Basle, August 1985: "We EMPHASIZE that, in spite of many religious references, that meeting had an overtly political character ... We CONDEMN also the misuse of the Bible and the abuse of religious sentiments in an attempt to sacralize the creation of a state and legitimate the policies of a government."[48] After the Second International Christian Congress met in April 1988, MECC's general secretary, Gabriel Habib, sent a letter to Christian churches and organizations throughout the world "warning of the danger of this Christian Zionism, and emphasizing that it must be opposed as a corruption of Christianity and a false claimant to speak in its name."[49]

"Misuse of the Bible," of course, refers to the predictive uses of prophecy. What is astonishing is not the vehemence of the critique – given that the credibility of advanced theological scholarship is at stake – but rather the extraordinary lack of familiarity in these circles with the most basic concepts of historical theology. Thus, MECC declares that "Pre-millenial [sic] and post-millenial [sic] eschatologies are not new to western Protestant Christianity, but the new link between them, conservative-evangelical religion, and extremist political movements make them especially troubling and dangerous."[50] As anyone evenly dimly familiar with the literature on traditional biblical eschatology knows, "pre-millennial" and "post-millennial" positions are mutually incompatible (rather like "continence" and "incontinence"). It is a logical absurdity to speak of "the new link between them" on the one hand, and anything else at all on the other. The people who write the MECC/WCC position papers on this theme simply will not stoop to enter into the thought-world of the adversary, even for purposes of understanding their arguments or learning how to spell them. Why should they – given that every department of religion in every major university of the Western world, followed by most of the theological seminaries, long ago cast into outer darkness the belief in predictive prophecy? Their concern is not with scholarly dialogue but with ecclesiastical politics. In that spirit, a letter from the general secretariat said of the congress that the International Christian Embassy had planned for Jerusalem in March 1988: *"There is no room for ill informed and biased 'Christian' Zionist ideologies that are dangerous distortions of the Christian faith* ... In essence, we are concerned that the presence of 7–10,000 western Christians in Jerusalem to support Israel's policies from their understanding of the Bible will be *anathema to the intent of Christian faith* and will be detrimental to Christian presence and witness in our region."[51] In another document of 1988 we read:

The peculiar Zionist tendency in Christian thought represents the most recent *outside intrusion into the region.* Churches that have been living the Christian faith in an unbroken continuity since the Pentecost consider this tendency as *anathema to the Christian faith.* The International Christian Embassy in Jerusalem, which embodies Christian Zionism in the region, by sanctifying Revisionist Zionism, has allowed little room for Christian principles to become an incentive for justice in the region ... [At its Basel Congress, ICEJ] adopted the Zionist principles that are based more on Israeli political and military policies as signs of prophecies in the Arab world [*sic*] than on authentic Christian Biblical faith. This makes them absolutely unable to recognize through any suffering people the sign of the liberating cross of our Lord Jesus Christ. As such, they represent the consistent tendency to force the Zionist model of theocratic and ethnocentric nationalism upon the Middle East ... The churches of the west must recognize Christian Zionism as their responsibility as well, and join the Christians of the Middle East in portraying a correct interpretation of the gospel of Jesus Christ and role of the Christian in these societies.[52]

In a document of 1994, we read: "No group can *presume to speak* on behalf of the Christians of the Middle East except the Churches of this region."[53]

There is no room for ... we condemn ... uninformed ... anathema ... correct interpretation ... No group can presume to speak. This is not the vocabulary of scholarly argument or dialogue. It is the vocabulary of inquisition. Indeed, the commanding assumption in all MECC/WCC literature on this theme is that there is no need for dialogue with the enemy – only that all people of goodwill should be advised of the "correct interpretation." Thus, "Key to this theological task is the need to help Christians avoid confusing the biblical stories related to the divine election of Israel with the notion that the modern state of Israel is the fulfilment of prophecy or is an eschatological entity ... Finally, it is necessary to counter the notion of 'mission to the Islamic world' with more enlightened notions of mission and evangelism, pointing out that peacemaking is at the core of the Great Commission."[54]

It is curious that while dialogue with Muslims is always viewed as an unqualified good in this circle, dialogue with "fundamentalists" (that is, *Christian* fundamentalists) is unthinkable. "Christian Zionists are our first enemy, " Geries Kouhry declaims. "They are more dangerous to Palestinian Christians than the Israeli occupiers." He speaks in anger of the trouble caused for Palestinian Christians by publicity attaching to the activities of the ICEJ – their demonstrations and rallies, their Succoth parades, their sponsorship of immigration of Russian Jews. "These forces," he insists, "compell us to concentrate on our nationalist identity."[55]

Evangelical Anti-Zionism

Christian Zionists are well aware of the contempt there is for "fundamentalism" within the liberal church. They are certainly not less aware than the churchmen who lead MECC that laymen without the least learning in theology or Church history can be struck dumb by fear of association with fundamentalism. Though it operates all along the ecclesiastical spectrum, the fear of being thought a fundamentalist is, ironically, most potent in evangelical circles. For that reason, Christian Zionists are particularly concerned by the appearance of anti-Zionist forces on the evangelical side of the Church. These forces draw their materials from the same sources as do the churches of the WCC, but they direct their arguments as closely as they can to the fear of association with fundamentalism that haunts so many evangelicals.

Within the International Congress on World Evangelization (also called the Lausanne Congress) – an organization that has sought for a quarter-century to become to conservative Protestants what the WCC is to the Protestant mainstream, and whose original honorary chairman was Billy Graham – there is a group called Evangelicals for Middle East

Understanding. Founded in October 1986 at a meeting hosted by John Stott of the Lausanne Congress on World Evangelization, it now has a mailing list of something over one thousand. It is not an awe-inspiring number when compared to the membership figures of the principal Christian Zionist groups; nonetheless, it does reflect a certain defection in what has always been its stronghold. Many believe that the great rush of popular End Times literature has subsided, accompanying a decline of the influence of traditional dispensationalism, and with it a declining interest in locating the events of recent history around the adventures of Restored Israel.

In his book *Who Are God's People in the Middle East?* Gary M. Burge describes himself as an evangelical Christian who, typically, began life predisposed to a Christian Zionist understanding of this question and its proper answer. But having visited Israel and interviewed the leaders of the Palestinian Christian community, Burge is brought to another answer. His conversion began when he was told by Father George Makhlour of St George's Greek Orthodox Church in Ramallah: "The church has inherited the promises of Israel. The church is actually the new Israel. What Abraham was promised, Christians now possess because they are Abraham's true spiritual children just as the New Testament teaches."[56] Burge thus came to understand that "Jesus uprooted the assumption that the benefits of land permanently came to Israel. Now he says that these benefits come to someone else, men and women living in concert with his dawning kingdom."[57] Burge's ingenious exegesis of the New Testament Letter to the Hebrews, chapters 3 to 5, draws out the proposition that the "land" that was the desire of the hearts of the patriarchs is a "metaphor for discipleship." The "promised rest" that the patriarchs sought in Canaan has now been won by the spiritual inheritors of that promise, namely the followers of Jesus. But this spiritualized understanding leads to a paradoxical result: "Followers of Jesus were the new people of God. And they would inherit the history and the promises known throughout the Old Testament ... Whatever the 'land' meant in the Old Testament, whatever the promise contained, this now belonged to Christians."[58] Thus, *the land itself belongs to the Christians.* This is not a manner of speaking or a metaphor. The land *literally belongs* to the People of God, the Christians. And the Christians on the land are *Palestinians.* "There has been a continuous Arab Christian population in Palestine for almost two thousand years."[59] And it is these Arab Christians – and only they in all the world – who are "reliving for the first time in history the conditions of the first-century church, in which a Christian minority is suffering under the rule of a Jewish majority."[60]

Unlike Burge, Donald Wagner indicates some discomfort that the anti-Zionist case seems to require Christians to endorse "replacement theology." What is needed instead is a spiritualized understanding of such key words as "nation," "people," and so on. Thus: "This is not to argue a replacement theology. God ultimately has a role for the Jews (Romans 11), but it will undoubtedly be one consistent with biblical history (i.e., *hesed* – steadfast love and faithfulness), not necessarily a nation state."[61] Like all Christian anti-Zionists, Wagner insists that Jesus never anticipated the restoration of the Jews. Thus, "there is no sense in awaiting a future fulfilment of biblical promises, a form of interpretation that Jesus counseled against."[62]

Speaking to liberal Christians in the West and to Christian Arabs in the East, Christian anti-Zionists dwell on the allegedly uncritical support that Christian Zionists give to the State of Israel and their abject philo-Judaism. Donald Wagner says that Christian Zionists are victims of a "religious game" played by the governments of Israel: "If the Western churches sing the praises of Zionism, they will be viewed positively by the government."[63] When the opportunity arises to talk to Jewish audiences, the Christian anti-Zionists take another line – namely, that Jews should avoid the Christian anti-Zionists like the plague, because their fundamentalist scenario requires that all the Jews be drawn back to Zion, preliminary to an ultimate global conflict (World War III) in which the Jews will be destroyed, the champion of the Christians will return (Jesus/Messiah), and the Christians will inherit Zion. This canard can be put very crudely by pamphleteers, or it can be put more elegantly, by scholars like Wagner and theologians like Naim Ateek. In "An Arab-Israeli's Theological Reflections on the State of Israel After 40 Years," for example, Canon Ateek writes "The Christian so-called [*sic*] Fundamentalists ... these self-styled [*sic*] Evangelicals ... see in Israel the fulfilment of their eschatological interpretation of certain texts in Scripture. The existence of the State fits in with their concept of the end of times and the Second coming of Christ. Some in Israel may consider them useful friends both financially and psychologically, but those in Israel who know something about what these Fundamentalists actually believe would, I am sure, abhor and reject them. As part of their biblical understanding of the last events in history is the annihilation of two thirds of the Jews and the Christianization of the last one third."[64]

Whatever one may find in pamphlets or in the books of popular End Times pamphleteers or on freelance websites, none of the Christian Zionist organizations I have spoken of in these pages holds such a view. The ICEJ speaks of its expectation, based primarily on the apocalyptic sections in the synoptic Gospels, that a final war faces *the whole of mankind*, and that its driving force will be hatred of the Jews, and its main motive will be the eradiction of Israel. Furthermore, Christian Zionists believe that a clear-minded reading of the daily newspapers indicates that such an outcome is imminent. But, as we have seen, these same organizations also insist that according to the very same biblical prophecies, Israel's "tribulations" are over now that the Jews have returned to Zion. It is Israel's enemies that face tribulation and annihilation. A person of goodwill might deduce an unlovely spirit from some of the speculation about the outcome of this war between Israel and its enemies. That is another matter. The fact is, however, that some such false notion of the theology held by Christian Zionists is common among Jews and is used by many of them to excuse their rejection of the company of the "fundamentalists." (I shall offer examples in chapter 8.) How much of this is owing to ignorance and how much to avoidance is difficult for an outsider to Judaism to say. But Naim Ateek, a Christian theologian, should know better than to misrepresent the theology of the Christian Zionists in this way.

Echoing the spirit of Count Leo Tolstoy's Christian anarchism (as proposed in his *The Kingdom of God Is Within You* [1893]), Christian anti-Zionists put the sin of possession at the centre of Israel's betrayal of its God. Zionism, we are told, is about *possessing*. It is therefore inevitably about governing (that is, oppressing) others. Christian Zionists, they say, are guilty of a terrible literalism in their insistence that God's promise to make the Jews a people was a promise that they would be a nation – that is, that they would possess a land. In their revolt against the God of Love, the Jews have "grasped the land." But Christians know that God could not be with the Jews in this matter; on the contrary, "In the economy of Jesus' kingdom, those who weep shall rejoice, those who want to be first must become last, those who grasp at life will lose it – and those who grasp onto the land as if it were their property will find it going to others ... [Jesus] announced that his kingdom was inaugurating a new people of God. Jesus uprooted the assumption that the benefits of land permanently came to Israel. Now he says that these benefits come to someone else, men and women living in concert with his dawning kingdom."[65]

In the light of divine teaching, Christian anti-Zionists see clearly that the Jews really do not need a state. Surely they should be content with being a religious community, "practising *hesed*, steadfast love, faithfulness" – something that they could do with less distraction and less compromise were they not also trying to run a government. It will help the Jews in coming to these Christian truths (suggests Donald Wagner) to review their own history and reflect on how they have profited spiritually from exile: "The Jews of Judah were forced by the exile in Babylon (587–586 BCE) to search for new personal and corporate systems by which to sustain worship and hope. Many came to recognize that God gave them 'new wineskins' of faith and worship in the synagogue and the invitation to a covenant faith written 'on their hearts' (Jer. 31:31–4). Psalm 137:4 asks painfully, 'How could we sing the Lord's song in a foreign land?' No doubt many had given up on God when the temple was destroyed and they were carried into Babylon. Others came to recognize that God had met their needs in a profound manner, through spiritual resources that had actually been there all along if they only had the eyes of faith to see them."[66]

It is striking that so long as the immediate purpose is to discredit the claims of the Jews to the land, Christian anti-Zionists can go on for pages in this Tolstoian vein. The People of God, we are told – in contrast to the Jews – are *not* possessers, owners, asserters, of self. Israel's salvation will come the day that Jews learn this truth. Yet the spiritual benefits that accompany exile are never recommended to the "Palestinians," who suffer the agonies of "landlessness, dispossession," etc. Indeed, it is clear that the Tolstoian spirit presides over this circle only long enough to establish God's disappointment in the Jews for their desire to possess the land. Once that point is made, the argument shifts immediately to the historical right of the Palestinians to possess the same land!

Wes Michaelson, one of the editors of *Sojourners*, a journal for politically liberal evangelicals, writes: "Holding the belief that the real estate of Israel is divinely sanctioned, and that their cause is righteously ordained, will only make evangelicals accomplices to the injustice and sufferings of the status quo in the Middle East."[67] In Christian anti-Zionist circles it is thought both witty and profound at the same time to intone that God is not in the real estate business. This dictum comes quickly to the mind of every anti-Zionist when he asks us to consider the claims of the Jews to *Eretz Israel*. But when the subject turns to the dispossessed and landless Palestinians, there is no more talk of mere real estate. Then, without any warning or change of theological warrant or philosophical authority, the same authors tell us *the land belongs to the Arabs*. The Tolstoian mask comes off, and an entirely different spirit takes over.

A great gap separates the two kinds of argument – the spiritualizing and the historical. But the anti-Zionists never seem to notice that they have moved from one to the other. They vehemently deny that there is anything "political" in their reasoning: it is the Christian Zionists who are the politicians. But one has to be utterly tone-deaf to the language of politics to imagine that we are still in the realm of "religion" when we read a document like the First La Grange Declaration, May 1979, which emerged from a meeting at Lagrange, Illinois, of Christian anti-Zionists:

> Forthrightly, we declare our conviction that in the process of establishing the state of Israel, a deep injustice was done to the Palestinian people, confiscating their land and driving many into exile and even death. We are further grieved by the ongoing deprivation of basic civil rights to those Arabs who live today in the state of Israel. Moreover, for 13 years large portions of the holy land and its people, including the West Bank of the Jordan River, Gaza and East Jerusalem, have suffered under foreign military occupation, even as in our Lord's time ... We extend out hearts to our Jewish brothers and sisters, common sons and daughters of Abraham. Like us in the United States, their corporate national spirit [*sic*] is being corroded by the weight of their government's reliance on rampant militaristic policies and actions ... The Arab people and their land have been plundered for centuries by Western Christendom. We acknowledge and confess a continuing legacy of prejudice evidenced today toward Arab people, both Christian and Moslem.[68]

This line of argument leads immediately to the call for a sovereign state of Palestine.

ODIUM THEOLOGICUM: THE WAR BETWEEN PRO- AND ANTI-ZIONISTS WITHIN THE CHURCH

The numbers of adherents to Christian anti-Zionism may or may not be growing. What is clear is that the Christian anti-Zionists are becoming more brutal in their indictment against Israel and Israel's friends every day. Given the magnitude of contemporary Israel's sins, the Christian anti-Zionists say, we should begin to prepare ourselves for the thought that Israel will be thrown out of the land she presently imagines that she "possesses." Elaborating on Leviticus 25:23 ("The land shall not be sold in perpetuity, for the land is mine; with me you are but aliens and tenants"), Gary Burge insists that Israel is "a tenant in the land, not a landlord. Israel is a renter, a visitor, an alien ... Israel must hold this land loosely, because God will always determine the tenure of its occupants."[69] Burge notes that in the first six books of the Bible there is no reference to the land of Israel but only and consistently to "the land of Canaan," a title that "preserves an important reminder that the land has a heritage that is larger than Israel's own history ... To be sure, the nation of Israel is promised possession of the land as an everlasting gift, but this promise is conditional; it depends on Israel's fidelity to the covenant and its stipulations ... Modern Israel must be judged by the standards that the prophets applied to biblical Israel ... Today Palestinian Christians in the land, Christian relief agencies (evangelical and mainline), and secular agencies (such as the Red Cross, the United Nations, and Amnesty International) all offer the same complaint: Israel is not promoting justice ... They appealed to their Scriptures to justify their privileged position as God's people to reject what God was saying to them through Jesus ... God's displeasure will be stirred and his judgement will be swift."[70]

Confident that he speaks only out of Christian love unstained by political motive, the Christian anti-Zionist is impelled to denounce the sins of the Zionists. An impressive example is John W. Stott, a preacher and writer widely esteemed in evangelical Church circles today, who abruptly announced in 1987: "I have recently come to the conclusion that political Zionism and Christian Zionism are anathema to Christian faith ... The true Israel today is neither Jews nor Israelis, but believers in the Messiah, even if they are Gentiles ... The Old Testament promises about the Jews' return to the land are [accompanied] by promises of the Jews' return to the Lord. It is hard to see how the secular, unbelieving state of Israel can possibly be a fulfilment of those prophecies." Later, he elaborated: "Israel today is a sinful nation. Her human rights record in Jerusalem, the West Bank, and Gaza is shameful. Many Christians are suffering under this occupation. Israel may be seeking physical and military security through nationalism, but she is not seeking the heart of the Lord."[71] In the same spirit, Donald Wagner says that the ICEJ "has ... surrendered the central doctrines of Christianity for a nationalist political ideology – Zionism – whose very morality is inconsistent with biblical teachings. Examination of the essential doctrines and practices of the ICEJ suggests that it should be declared a heretical cult."[72]

Declared by whom?

Even the most liberal churchmen – those who move in WCC circles and who will normally go to any length to avoid theological, as distinct from religious, vocabulary (allegedly because of theology's tendency to put up walls impeding intra-Church and inter-religious dialogue) – make an exception in this matter of Christian Zionism: they never miss an opportunity to denounce Christian Zionists for the absolutism of their theological interpretation and do not hesitate to cast them out of the Church as "heretics ... blasphemers ... infidels."

But ours is a secular age, and there are crimes much worse than heresy. The worst crime of all is "racism." Picking up on a theme very close to secular hearts, Christian writers like Donald Wagner denounce the ICEJ for its putative contempt for Arabs, quoting many nasty remarks alleged to have been made off the record by its leaders.[73] Charges that ICEJ ignores the plight of the Palestinians are simply false. ICEJ literature proclaims its desire to promote goodwill among the Arab population, noting, for example that its social assistance program is intended to meet many practical needs of Jews and Arabs in Israel, and to promote a positive image of Christians. Wagner simply throws these statements back in the face of the ICEJ: " Goal five in the ICEJ strategy states that they will be engaged in services regardless of race, etc. However, in the 'holy' land, Palestinian churches and Muslim organizations will not accept grants or donations from the ICEJ."[74] In the eyes of organizations like the MECC and EMEU, to oppose, as ICEJ does, the creation of a sovereign Arab state of Palestine is the same thing as "working toward the ultimate demise of the local Christian community ... [taking] the side of the powerful, of the oppressor, of the Zionist political elites, in direct opposition to all Palestinians, including the churches."[75] And this simply *must be* motivated by *racism*. The denunciation of Christian Zionist racism is always accompanied by condescension to Arab nationalism, which is always described in positive and virile terms. Needless to say, there is never a glimmer of recognition of the possibility that their anti-Zionist attitudes might ever be touched by another variation of racism.

Evangelical anti-Zionists believe that their efforts to rally Christians of goodwill everywhere in denunciation of Israel's sins is the most effective and wholesome way of moving the whole People of God into the more perfect ecumenical Church, which they see as prefigured in MECC. "It is time American evangelicals stood in solidarity with the church of the Middle East," says Gary Burge.[76] Similarly, Donald Wagner, the leader of Evangelicals for Middle East Understanding, takes note of the exceptional inclusiveness of the MECC, and declares: "The next major challenge is that of the Western evangelical churches and movements, a matter being discussed already through Evangelicals for Middle East Understanding."[77] Sensing the softening of support for Israel in evangelical ranks, MECC officials have directed at least two "Open Letters to Western Evangelical Leaders" and held workshops and conferences for their benefit.

No well-informed student of this scene would argue that the recent appearance of a lively anti-Zionist presence within evangelical ranks has so far overturned the generalization noted first in connection with the events of 1967: today, as before, the majority within the evangelical-to-fundamentalist end of the ecclesiastical spectrum understand the creation of the modern state of Israel to be a fulfilment of God's promise to the Jews and expect that God will bless the nations as they continue to bless Israel. What is different now from the situation of fifty years ago, when the State of Israel came into existence, is that everywhere else on the ecclesiastical spectrum a virtually monolithic anti-Zionism is taking hold. At the same time, aggressively anti-Zionist voices, like those of John W. Stott, Donald Wagner, and Gary Burge, are now heard on the right wing (theologically speaking) where Israel has been accustomed to hearing only friendly noises.

As this situation goes on, it becomes increasingly easy for Israelis to appreciate the distinctiveness of the constituency of Christian Zionists.

8 Christian Attitudes towards Israel: The Issue in Current American Politics

Israelis and Jews of the diaspora simply do not know what to make of Christian attitudes toward Israel. On the one hand, there is the phenomenon of "Christian Zionism," which, some say, provides the most reliable, the most *constant* voice in defence of Israel, and which indeed, in recent years, has been a more constant political resource for Israel than the "Jewish vote." On the other hand, there is the attitude of the World Council of Churches, generally reflected in the conventions of its constituent denominational bodies, where a consistent anti-Zionism has been the keynote for decades.

WCC AND ISRAEL SINCE 1967

It is easy to trace a hardening of WCC attitudes towards Israel from year to year and from document to document since 1967. In a Faith and Order Commission Report, dating from a few days after the Six-Day War of June 1967, we read that the creation of the State of Israel "is of tremendous importance for the great majority of the Jews; it has meant for them a new feeling of self-assurance and security. But this same event has also brought suffering and injustice to Arab people. We find it impossible to give a unanimous evaluation of its formation and of all the events connected with it, and therefore in this study do not make further mention of it. [*Sic!*]" At the head of the document is another telling disclaimer: "To avoid misunderstanding, in this document we have used the term 'Israel' only when referring to the people in the Old Testament and New Testament times; no present-day political reference is intended or implied."[1]

Even in those early days of the WCC, says a disenchanted insider, "the people of the Middle East Office had been at the game for quite a while. As most of them were representatives of missionary interests in Arab countries, their basic view of the Middle East was one that left no room for Israel as an integral part of the region. Whenever a governing Board or National Council of Churches Executive Committee was approaching, a small group of 'Middle East Desk' and 'Justice and Liberation' people would get together to work on a draft statement. It was, of course, important that the proposed announcement be 'prophetic,' which in that particuar context usually meant that the critique of some alleged Israeli sin would be severe while Arab countries were spared any kind of condemnation in order not to jeopardize Christian missionary interests there."[2] As I have noted, by the time the WCC held its meeting at Uppsala, Sweden, in 1968, the hearts and minds of the activists had wandered far from their original affirmation in favour of "order" towards the virtues of "revolution." In the wake of the Six-Day War, Israel was fixed in the minds of most WCC activists as an outpost of capitalist imperialism. As the American Church historian Martin Marty observed, "Being anti-Israel has become part of the anti-Establishment gospel, the trademark of those who purport to identify with the masses, the downtrodden and the Third World."[3]

Shortly after the UN adopted its Resolution 3379, equating Zionism with racism (10 November 1975), General Secretary Philip Potter asked the UN to "re-consider and rescind" it. Zionism, Potter suggested, "has historically been a movement concerned with the liberation of the Jewish people from oppression, including racial oppression." Potter's statement and others in a similar vein caused Jews and friends of Israel to hope that perhaps the WCC had begun to reconsider the company it was keeping on the issue of Zionism. The *Christian Century*, for example, declared about this time: "Many Jews, as well as Christians, opposed the creation of a state based on the Jewish faith. But that was 30 years ago. The existence of Israel is no longer debateable. Israel is a reality ... [The Resolution] is a hostile propagandistic action that has nothing to do with the question of racism."

In the summer of 1975, WCC officials contemplated the possibility that resolutions might be brought forward at the upcoming Fifth WCC Assembly in Nairobi, seeking to align the WCC with the recently passed UN declaration. Planning meetings were held. Although not one Jew was invited to participate in the planning, a PLO representative was: this was Clovis Maksoud, an editor from Beirut, Lebanon, later a representative of the Arab League at the UN, not a member of any church affiliated with the wcc. Maksoud's presentation was described by Isaac Rottenberg (who was there as chairman of the Office on Christian-Jewish Relations of the ncc) as containing "some of the vilest anti-Zionist rhetoric I had heard since living [in wartime Holland] under Nazi occupation."[4] At the Nairobi General Assembly, beginning 23 November 1975, the plo showed up and distributed its literature, and Arab and Communist bloc delegations declared their support for the un resolution. The permanent bureaucracy of the organization managed to maintain a degree of peace by heading off a debate on the resolution. But in so doing, it also prevented the accomplishment of what most observers believed was the desire of the majority – to have the wcc publicly declared *against* the Arab-inspired denunciation of Israel.

It seems that whenever wcc bodies face the prospect of division over other issues, the spirit of unity is achieved by raising the Arab-Israeli conflict. Thus, at the meeting of its Central Committee in 1980, delegates found that they could not get the issue of the Soviet Union's recent annexation of Afghanistan on the agenda; but the Jerusalem issue did get discussed, and Israel got denounced for preventing movement towards peace in the Middle East by establishing Jerusalem as it capital. Indeed, denunciation of Israel for its rule over united Jerusalem is a standing agenda item. At the Sixth wcc Assembly, held in Vancouver in 1983, the Assembly was met with a draft statement prepared in secret by the mecc. The document (writes Rottenberg) "no longer even gave the appearance of being fair. In short, they came, not for dialogue, but to pull off a political coup. The climate they found was sympathetic (or, at least, indifferent) enough for them to succeed." Even the *Christian Century*, whose editorial policy has always been anti-Zionist, "observed in an editorial (Aug. 17–24, 1983) that the Vancouver resolutions could just as well have been formulated at the U.N. [where the Zionism-is-racism declaration was still in force] and indicated 'a total lack of concern for Christian-Jewish relations.'" At a press conference, wcc general secretary Philip Potter, responding to reporters' questions about its imbalance, said: "The Jews have other voices speaking on their behalf." At the same Assembly, the leaders removed from the agenda motions criticizing the Soviet Union for its presence in Afghanistan, having been told in advance by the Russian churches that they would not be permitted to attend unless assured that there would be no anti-Soviet statements made from the Assembly. The same assurances prevented discussion of the situation of Christians imprisoned in the Soviet Union.[5]

Critics of the wcc – Christians and others – were quick to point out the hypocrisy in steadfastly avoiding criticism of the Soviet Union and its satellites while being ready and eager to denounce Israeli persecution of Palestinians. Less noted at the time but of much greater long-term importance (since the Soviet Empire *did* collapse) was the similarly inspired avoidance of criticism of Muslim persecution of Christians. An example is the situation of the Coptic Christians (discussed in chapter 5). Isaac Rottenberg describes the futile efforts of the Coptic Christians of Egypt to get some attention to the matter of their persecution by Muslims in Egypt, abetted or condoned by the successive governments of Anwar Sadat and Hosni Mubarek. But, Rottenberg writes, "oppression of the Coptic Christians did not fit into the priorities of the Council's social agenda." The problem (according to Rottenberg) was *not* concern about the attitude of Egypt, but concern about the attitude of the MECC, whose leaders insisted that making a fuss about Muslim persecution of Christians would aggravate relations between Muslim and Christian Palestinians. With the MECC lending its full weight to suppression of the story of the Copts, the WCC felt it could not afford to highlight it.[6]

J.A. Emerson Vermaat, a Dutch journalist, speaks of WCC leaders as "the radicalized ecumenical elite which has estranged itself from the very essence of theology in order to commit itself to political causes." After a careful study of WCC documents on human rights issues, he notes: "Only rarely has the WCC criticized the human rights situation in Islamic countries in the Middle East ... I am not aware of the issue of oppressed Jews in Arab countries ever being seriously considered by the WCC."[7]

Beginning in the 1970s the WCC and, to a lesser degree, the Vatican became more attached to the "Palestinian" and "anti-Zionist" interpretation of the history of the Middle East conflict. One major reason for this was that the historic pre-Chalcedonian communities, hitherto virtually ignored by both camps, were being brought into the WCC camp and friendlier relations were developing between those same Churches of the East and the Vatican. Beginning with the Nairobi Assembly of 1975, WCC documents on Middle East matters increasingly reflected the anti-Zionist worldview of these Eastern Churches. On political issues, the "Palestinian" position is embraced without challenge.[8] The WCC supported the PLO's need to train its "liberation armies" in various places through the Middle East. It denounced the Camp David Peace Accords for having shunted aside the national aspirations of the Palestinian people in favour of mere "autonomy." It reacted strongly against Israel's intervention in Lebanon in 1982, seeing no merit in Israel's argument for intervention against PLO terrorism. In the wcc booklet *Invasion of Lebanon*, we read: "This [Israeli intervention] was a premeditated, carefully planned, ruthlessly executed aggression. The objective was to exterminate Palestinian nationalism." But no reference is made to Syria's presence in Lebanon, nor to its responsibility for the deaths of many thousands of Christian civilians. In December 1982 Ninan Koshy, director of wcc's Commission of the Churches on International Affairs (ccia), spoke of the plo as "one of the most viable liberation movements in recent history in genuiness of motivation, grass roots appeal, organizational structure and international support and standing" but called on the plo "to recognize Israel's right to exist as a state, in order to strengthen the present political momentum for achieving a genuine peace."9

At Nairobi the wcc supported "the rights of the Palestinian people to self-determination." At its Sixth Assembly in Vancouver, 1983, the wcc called for the establishment of a Palestinian state, and it repeated this position at its next Assembly in Seoul. The wcc welcomed the Oslo Accords of 1993 and spoke hopefully of prospects for peace; but as it became clear that the "peace process" was going to be a rocky one, the wcc consistently and exclusively blamed Israel, dismissing the Israeli government's complaints about violations from the other side. Konrad Raiser, secretary of the wcc, visited the Holy Land in June of 1996 and returned to say that the peace process in the Middle East was in "severe crisis." As always, Israel was entirely to blame, the Palestinian side being helpless to affect the situation. (This, it should be noted, was at the time of the Rabin-Peres government, not yet the Netanyahu government, which would later be consistently blamed for falling short of the commendable record of courage and imagination shown by the Rabin and Peres governments.) Yassir Arafat explained the situation to Raiser during the latter's visit to the scene: there was a complete impasse in the peace process due to Israeli intransigence, he said, and a sense of abandonment by the international community. Raiser reported: "We heard warnings from many on the Palestinian side that, unless the peace process is brought back on track, a general uprising and possibly uncontrollable violence will be the result."10 (Raiser did *not* note, either to Arafat at the time or to the wcc later, that such "warnings" about "violence," which go on all the time, publicly and privately, are in themselves violations of the Oslo Accords.)11

RECENT HISTORY OF CHRISTIAN ZIONIST
SUPPORT FOR ISRAEL

In contrast to the wcc/mecc front, Christian Zionist support for Israel has in recent years been so fulsome as to be, on occasion, almost embarrassing to many Israelis. It is important to note that, in addition to the organizations devoted entirely to Christian Zionist activity, which I described in chapter 7, there is a much larger evangelical milieu within which concern for Israel and Israel's interests prevails. Occupying an important corner in this milieu are the Christian radio and television broadcasters in the United States and Canada. Their services to Zionism take many forms. Life in Israel is frequently a theme of special segments in the programs of the television evangelists, as are remote broadcasts covering special events in Israel. Current affairs segments on Israel's ongoing struggles appear with regularity in the programming of Pat Robertson's Christian Broadcasting Network. Several widely syndicated television Bible teachers (notably Jack Van Impe and Bernice Gerrard) illustrate their lectures about End Times with footage of current scenes in Israel and interviews with Israeli religious and political leaders. All of this attention to the Holy Land is shaped by a confidently pro-Israel viewpoint that is in striking contrast to the viewpoint informing the coverage provided by the major news organizations.

Most of the television evangelists promote Christian pilgrimages to Israel; some (notably Jerry Falwell, Pat Robertson, and David Mainse of Crossroads Ministries, which originates in Canada), personally conduct tours to Israel from time to time, typically including many hundreds of visitors at a time. The good relationship existing between the Christian broadcasters and the Government of Israel assures special treatment for these visitors in Israel, often taking the form of friendly visits by government figures to their public events. The whole constituency of Christian pro-Zionists is therefore many times larger than the membership lists of the Christian Zionist organizations and should be numbered in the tens of millions. We can suggest this without concluding that the enthusiastic pro-Zionism of the television evangelists is shared by *all* of their listeners.

Not coincidentally, the major Christian television broadcasters are all identified as well with what might be called patriotic conservatism – that is, that particular sector of the coalition that Ronald Reagan led to victory in the 1980s whose conservatism is driven primarily by concern about the alleged neglect of the nation's military and strategic strength, the alleged decline of self-confidence in American foreign policy, and the alleged truckling to internationalism. This last item has figured increasingly in the minds of patriotic conservatives since the collapse of the Soviet Empire. It is a fact of great significance that the television evangelists are, at the same time, strong on patriotic national assertion, suspicious of internationalism and especially of UN-sponsored efforts, and faithful towards Israel. At a time when the political left is seeking to relativize the virtues and values of the two sides in the Middle East struggle, while declaring itself keen on reducing the range of actions that the United States may take outside its obligations to the UN or to NATO, patriotic conservatives find natural allies in the Christian Zionist camp. (Patrick Buchanan is a notable exception to this generalization.) Christian Zionists believe that there is still a war of fundamental values going on between the two sides in the Arab-Israeli contest, despite the peace process that was supposed to have begun with the Oslo Accords of 1993, and that depends to some degree on international participation and monitoring.

Since declaring her independence on 14 May 1948, Israel has seen to a dramatic enlargement, not merely of her legal boundaries – that is, the boundaries that the publishers of atlases allow to appear as those of "Israel" – but also of her sphere of responsibility in what until the Oslo Accords she called the "Administered Territory" (Judaea and Samaria). On 19 December 1981, Israel formally extended its jurisdication to Golan, without the approval of its former occupier, Syria, and without the approval of the UN or the US. Beyond that there is southern Lebanon, where Israel maintained a "security zone" (until the end of May 2000) and where she still asserts a right to intervene against Muslim forces that conduct acts of terror against her. Liberal historians and ecumenical churchmen tell the story of Israel's expanding sphere of action in the same language that is used for the wars of Napoleon or Nebuchadnezzar. Christian Zionists prefer the vocabulary of self-defence and national security that the Israeli government itself employs.

Millions of Christian Zionists look upon Israel as one key to the survival of the Judaeo-Christian civilization. As I have already noted, conservative Christians are impressed by the achievement of the Orthodox religious forces in Israel, in such matters as securing observance of the Sabbath and the important religious festivals, public financing of religious education, and generally more of a stand-up presence of traditional religion in the public life. Evangelicals and fundamentalists are aware, of course, that daily life in Israel remains secular, and that the orientation of most Israelis is probably no more "religious" than that of most Americans. Yet it helps the morale of conservative Christian forces in the United States to think that there exists in Israel living proof that the model of radical separation of church and state is not the only model available for consideration by people of goodwill who are concerned about recent trends in respect to the public role of religion in the United States and about public morality.

THE AMERICAN POLITICAL CONTEXT
SINCE 1980

The American presidential election of 1980 was a testing time for American Jews. Even though Jimmy Carter was perceived as being the least sensitive of all recent presidents to the security needs of Israel, a slight majority of Jews voted for him against Ronald Reagan, whose sweeping victory was made possible by the defection from the Democratic party of every other component of the old New Deal coalition – except blacks. Contributing to Reagan's victory, although by no means deciding it, was the defection of evangelicals from Jimmy Carter, who had presented himself as one of their own in 1976 but had since pursued policies out of line with the evangelical consensus (for example, on the homosexual challenge to the family, on abortion, on school prayer, and many other issues of domestic concern). Jerry Falwell's Moral Majority movement was a response to the challenge of mobilizing the evangelical-to-fundamentalist vote, now liberated from the spell of Jimmy Carter.

It is not true that the Israeli government's embrace of the Christian Zionists began with Menachem Begin. Yet all in all, the Likud governments of Begin, Shamir, and Netanyahu have been more forthcoming than Labour governments in their contacts with the Christian Zionist organizations. In 1980 Prime Minister Begin conferred the Jabotinsky Medal upon Jerry Falwell for his constant friendship towards Israel, and others have been honoured in one way or another. A longtime American Zionist leader, Alexander M. Schindler (president of the Union of American Hebrew [Reform] Congregations and past chairman of the Conference of Presidents of Major American Jewish Organizations), writing in the *Jerusalem Post*, asked at the time: "Is Jerry Falwell good for the Jews? Is the Moral Majority a political force with which Israel and her American supporters should make alliance? At first blush the answer to these questions is a clear *yes*. After all, Falwell ranks among Israel's staunchest supporters. Israel has too few friends as it is. Moreover, the Moral Majority is an emerging political force of some consequence. Why not cooperate with them? A more careful consideration of the ends and means of America's new right prompts an entirely different response ... This new political force – which gained considerable strength in the campaign just past [1980] – seeks nothing less than to Christianize America, to make it a republic ruled by Christ ... Such a climate, in my judgement, is bad for civil liberties, human rights, social justice, interfaith understanding, and mutual respect among Americans. Therefore, it is bad for Jews." More significant to Schindler than the presidential election victory was the defeat of several Senate liberals (Bayh, Nelson, McGovern, Church) who had been among Israel's most stalwart friends. "One result of the success of the Christian right is the replacement of Frank Church as chairman of the Senate Foreign Relations Committee by Charles Percy, who told the Kremlin last month how important is was for Yasser Arafat to have a state to rule over before he died. Is that good for Israel?"

(When the defeated Senator Church visited Israel a few weeks later, the *Jerusalem Post* noted that he seemed to be in pain when reminded of Menahem Begin's recent award to Jerry Falwell of the Jabotinsky Medal. "The evangelist group advocates 'clear secular positions wrapped in religious garb,' said the senator, 'and sends people to the voting booth with the belief that they are carrying out the will of God.'") Schindler's intemperate letter to the *Jerusalem Post* received a response from Shmuel Katz, a longtime ally of Begin in the *Herut* party. "The Moral Majority movement in the US has shown its support for Israel, and this sympathy deserves to be reciprocal," was Katz's reply to Schindler.[12]

The Missionary Issue

On the Israeli side, as well, there were countervailing domestic pressures at work. Prime Minister Begin was under steady pressure from some elements in his coalition to devise new legislation to restrain Christian missionaries. Although the legislation that emerged had little effective meaning, it had to be opposed on grounds of free exercise of religion by Begin's allies in the evangelical camp. The painful irony is that the effective Christian Zionist groups (ICEJ, Bridges for Peace, and the others) have a rigorous policy of not seeking conversions, as already noted. Jewish organizations in North America that focus on the challenge of Christian missionaries are even harder to convince on this matter than are the Israelis. The American group "Jews for Judaism" stated: "There is more to this group of 'Christian Zionists' than meets the eye. There is an agenda and methodology to their 'unconditional love' for Israel and the Jewish people often overlooked and ignored by the Jewish community because of the 'good work' they do ... We found a deliberate pattern of proselytizing by the ICEJ, its staff and volunteers over a long period of time ... in spite of their protests to the contrary. We also found that the ICEJ allies itself with 'Jews for Jesus' type groups which are actively involved in deceptively proselytizing the Jewish community." A report to this effect was conveyed to ICEJ, which replied: "You have failed to cite one example of a Jew who has converted to Christianity as a result of our alleged missionary agenda."[13] Nomi Winkler, vice-president of the Toronto Zionist Council, joined in the debate:

These people [Canadian Friends of ICEJ] possess to an uncommon degree a quality which we have found sadly lacking in the community at large: their actions give life to their words! When we held demonstrations against the *Toronto Star* for its anti-Israel bias, they were with us; when we publicly protested Arab terrorism, they stood with us; when we demonstrated at the US Consulate for Jonathan Pollard's freedom, they marched with us ... Last week, when we asked various Jewish organizations to lend their names to our letter of concern for the Settlers' security, we were asked "Who else is signing?" Not Al Lazerte: he promptly faxed a letter – far stronger than ours – to the Prime Minister on behalf of the Canadian Friends of ICEJ ... If ICEJ wishes to convert Jews to hasten the coming of the Messiah, let us produce an educational system, a religious and cultural milieu that will render our people impervious to their "agenda and methodology." In the meantime, for their generosity and actions on behalf of our people, I am beholden to Christian friends such as Canadian Friends of ICEJ who came to Israel when the Scuds were flying (and Jews were re-routing to Florida) and who, God Willing, will be joining our mission into Judea and Samaria because they believe, as we do, that it is a sin to create an Arab terrorist state in Eretz Yisrael.[14]

Lenny Davis, formerly AIPAC's chief of research, makes the same point, but more crudely: "Sure, these guys give me the heebie-jeebies. But until I see Jesus coming over the hill, I'm in favor of all the friends Israel can get."[15]

JEWISH ATTITUDES TOWARDS CHRISTIAN ATTITUDES TOWARDS THE STATE OF ISRAEL

The attitude of most North American Jews towards Christians in general is governed first of all by the fact that Jews are a small and steadily declining minority in the population in which they find themselves.

The culture of North America is not Christian today and arguably never was – even though most Jews have been under a different impression from the beginning. One hundred years ago, when the grandparents and great-grandparents of today's American Jews arrived, America had a secular culture that allowed a certain place for attenuated expressions of Christian purpose. Today, it is a post-Christian culture. But that post-Christian culture is being challenged by Christian political activists, most of whom believe the rumours that

America once had a Christian culture and must have one again if it is not to perish. In this setting, inertia seems to dictate that Jews should work in cultural and political alliance with elements that belong to the post-Christian ascendancy. American Jews are a declining, some say a vanishing, community. *The actual number of people identifying themselves as Jews in the United States has declined* from 5.7 million in 1985 to about five million today. In percentage terms, Jews were about four percent around 1960 and are now two percent of the population. One-third of all Americans of Jewish ancestry no longer report Judaism as their religion. The principal reason for this trend is the increasing tendency of Jews to marry non-Jews. As late as 1959, only 7.2 percent of Jews married non-Jews; but of all Jews who have married since 1985, the *majority* (fifty-one percent) have married non-Jews. Only twenty-eight percent of the children of these inter-marriages are raised as Jews. At the same time, the reproduction rate among Jews is declining, to the point where it now figures among the lowest in the West: at less than two percent, it has passed ZPG (zero population growth) – a marker corresponding to the point where non-human species are declared to be "endangered."[16] Compounding this bad news, many Jewish commentators speak of a drastic decline of the sense of Jewish community in general, owing (among other factors) to a lessening willingness to be identified with the Jewish state. This is said by some to follow from a decline of confidence in the political leadership of Israel (in part following, as I have already argued, from the rightward shift in Israeli politics, which, taken all in all, seems to be the principal feature of the period since the mid-1970s). Many Jewish commentators in the United States speak of declining confidence in the justice of Israel's cause in ongoing conflicts with internal and external enemies. Some trace this back to the Lebanon incursion of 1982, while others see the outbreak of the Intifada in December 1987 as the turning-point. The issue of support for Soviet Jews (the "refuseniks" of the 1980s) briefly gave a renewed lease to Jewish solidarity. This issue had the great advantage that the Jews involved were among the oppressed, not (by anybody's definition) the oppressors, so that generalized humanitarian concern was engaged among non-Jews and could be recruited, almost as in the old days when the British were turning back Jewish refugee ships. But since the collapse of the Soviet Union and Soviet Empire at the outset of the 1990s this cause has gone, and none like it has come to fill its place. Therefore, it is not surprising to see a lessening of restraint among American Jews in their criticism of Israel – this exacerbating other divisions within Jewish ranks that turn on American domestic-policy matters.

Since the end of the Second World War, giant strides have been made towards reconciliation between the churches and the Jews. Roman Catholic and Protestant official bodies have undertaken review of the underlying theology. All the major Christian churches in the West have explictly retracted their age-old commitments to Replacement theology. As we have seen, it is now Roman Catholic teaching that "the Jewish faith, unlike other non-Christian religions is already a response to God's revelation in the Old Covenant."[17] In public statements, Pope John Paul II has made this even clearer, saying to Christians, "It is not lawful to say that the Jews are repudiated or cursed ... [for] the Jews are beloved of God, who called them with an irrevocable calling", and to Jews: "Continue your particular vocation, showing yourselves to be still the heirs to that election to which God is faithful."[18] Likewise, all the major Protestant denominations have within the last twenty years or so taken the trouble to explicitly repudiate Replacement theology. All have found time for statements of regret for Christian responsibility for anti-Semitism. All have put much energy into honest programs of Christian-Jewish dialogue. Elliott Abrams concludes: "In most Christian denominations, a two-thousand-year-old war against Judaism is being called off and its direct connection to anti-semitic violence admitted ... The historical role of Judaism has been appreciated and reaffirmed, and in many cases its ongoing covenant with God has been acknowledged. Efforts to convert Jews to Christianity have been questioned in some churches and brought under strict control in others. This is revolutionary."[19]

What do American Jews make of this new world in which liberal Christians (represented, to their minds, by the National Council of Churches, which stands with most Jews on the liberal side of all domestic matters of importance) have become champions of the PLO, while the only steady friends of Israel are the "right wing" Christians?

Most American Jewish religious leaders and Jewish community activists seem to be aware, at least to some degree, that mainstream Protestant churches and the Roman Catholic church have repudiated and rejected the Replacement theology and anti-Semitism of the past. At this level of leadership there are few who fear a return to the evil days of persecution in the name of religion. Yet even those Jews who are aware of these positive developments find it impossible to reconcile the apparent transformation of attitudes towards Jews and Judaism with the hostility toward the State of Israel that is characteristic in the most respectable Church circles. It occurs to many Israelis and Jews throughout the world today that the resistance that the Christian nations still offer to the existence in peace of Israel owes something to the legacy of Christian resentment about the continuance of Israel after its rejection of the Messiah in the person of Jesus of Nazareth. Is it not obvious, they say, that, beneath all the rhetoric of secular complaint against Israel – its alleged territorial aggressions, its allegedly cruel behaviour towards its "Palestinian" population, and the whole catalogue of its alleged sins against its neighbours and against the world community – there is a far deeper cause of complaint that draws from the same theological source as did the medieval libels against the Jews of Europe? Most spokesmen of the mainstream Protestant and the Roman Catholic churches seem not to appreciate the place that allegiance to Israel has at the centre of Jewish self-understanding. Jews are right to ask: if it is true that Protestants and Catholics cannot yet accept that the Jewish state has at least the same "legitimacy" as the homelands of the Italians, Greeks, and Turks, is it because Protestants and Catholics cannot accept that Jews have the same right to call themselves a people? And if so, from what does this refusal follow? Is this neo-anti-Zionism not a genteel reincarnation of the old anti-Semitism?

Jews understand that there is a theological issue that tends to affect, if not govern, Christian attitudes towards the State of Israel. Yet when they look to Church documents for clarification on the matter they usually find double-talk. An example is this 1990 statement of the United Church of Christ of the US: "We do not see consensus in the United Church of Christ … on the covenantal significance of the State of Israel. We appreciate the compelling moral argument for the creation of modern Israel as a vehicle for self-determination and as a haven for a victimized people; we also recognize that this event has entailed the dispossession of Palestinians from their homes and the denial of human rights." This same United Church document refers throughout to "the State of Israel-Palestine." A Lutheran statement on the same subject reads: "It seems clear that there is no consensus among Lutherans with respect to the relation between the 'chosen people' and the territory comprising the present State of Israel." When they look for an affirmative commitment to the survival of Israel they find instead expressions of commitment to the other side: "We stand in solidarity with Palestinians as they cry for justice as the dispossessed," says a recent official Presbyterian statement.[20] Christian churchmen imagine that statements like these reflect a creditable spirit of even-handedness, but to most Jews the tone is one of menace towards Israel.

By the 1950s, as we have seen, mainstream liberal Protestantism and evangelical/fundamentalist Protestantism were speaking with strongly contrasting voices on the subject of Israel. To state it plainly: the respectable leadership had backed away from Israel; all of her constant friends were seated below the salt. Yet it is very unusual to find an American Jew who feels any gratitude for this moral and political support from Christian Zionists. In fact, American Jews remain suspicious of Christian Zionists; so much so, that there is a real risk that American Jewish organizations might eventually create conditions that make it impossible for Jewish and Christian friends of Israel to cooperate. Christian Zionists are drawn, for the most part, from the ranks of that part of the American and European Church that stands outside the consensus on world issues that informs the position papers generated by study commissions of the Roman Catholic church and the World Council of Churches. This is the constituency that Howard Sachar, with the typical contempt of the liberal American academic, calls "the millennial right-wing cousins" of mainstream Protestantism. A less-patronizing term might be "Christians of conservative theology." This constitutency includes many millions who are members of churches that belong to the WCC (for example, Methodists, Presbyterians, Lutherans, and even Episcopalians) but whose own personal theology or religious philosophy puts them at odds with the public statements of the WCC on political, economic, social, and international issues. And it would include many more millions belonging to denominations not included in the WCC. In this combined camp, loyalty to Israel is constant and of long standing. It is rooted in the nineteenth-century tradition called "Restorationism."

The general attitude towards Christian Zionists is not the same in Israel as it is among American Jews. American Jews, like the rest of us, are affected by the anti-Christian stereotypes promoted in the nominally Christian culture that surrounds them. They are conditioned to look upon the conservative side of the Christian religious spectrum with loathing: these are the Bible thumpers, whom everyone is permitted to despise, regardless of race, sex, or creed – whom *not* to despise is a sign of cultural deficiency. Occasionally, the public is afforded a glimpse at this reality. Such an occasion occured in January 1998 during Prime Minister Netanyahu's visit to the United States, in the course of which he attended a meeting of evangelical Protestant leaders who sought to help him gird up his loins for the meeting with the Clinton administration. Prominent at the meeting was Jerry Falwell – to most American Jews a self-caricaturing Bible thumper, whose very name it is difficult to resist giggling at. At the meeting, Falwell called upon Southern Baptist preachers to speak out against Israel's giving away any more land to the Palestinians. He declared: "There are about 200,000 evangelical pastors in America, and we're asking them all through E-mail, faxes, letters, telephone, to go into their pulpits and use their influence in support of the state of Israel and the Prime Minister." As noted earlier, a rally in support of Netanyahu followed the Falwell visit. Organized as the "National Unity Coalition for Israel" mainly through the efforts of Voices United for Israel and featuring speakers from the Christian Coalition and the National Religious Broadcasters, it was attended by about one thousand people. The theme of the rally was that American Christians oppose any further concessions of territory to the Palestinians.[21] (Conveniently for Mr Netanyahu, the media suddenly lost interest in the matter as first news of the Monica Lewinsky affair broke.)[22] When Netanyahu visited the president again in April 1998, another, even larger, rally was got together by the same organizations, where speakers included several of the televangelists and leaders of Christian Zionist organizations, as well as such heavyweight political leaders as Dick Armey (majority leader in the House), Dick Gephardt (minority leader in the House), and Tom Delay, Republican whip in the House.[23]

The leaders of most American Jewish organizations are aware that the evangelical leaders who were present that day are active in the domestic political arena in support of many causes that they, the leaders of the major American Jewish organizations, oppose – including restriction of abortion, school prayer, and taxpayer support for alternative schools. *On these grounds alone,* the American Jewish leaders were hostile to the idea that Israel's Prime Minister should be giving them the time of day. In the particular case of Jerry Falwell, the offence was compounded because he is regarded as one of the public figures whom the president was known to detest most. The outcome was that the Israeli prime minister was publicly scolded for his association with these disreputable evangelicals by the American Jewish leaders.

The dilemma for Mr Netanyahu, explained the *New York Times,* was that he had been given to understand that such Bible thumpers are somehow an asset for Israel: "On the issue of Israel, there is no one stronger than evangelicals," said an Israeli official. In the manner of a visiting anthopologist from Mars, the reporter explains:

Evangelical Christians who interpret the Bible literally regard Israel as a land given by God to the Jews ... The Israeli Government and evangelical Christians may appear to be strange bedfellows, but they are old ones. Regardless of party affiliation, prime ministers from Menachem Begin and Yitzhak Shamir, both Likud leaders, to Yitzhak Rabin, or Labor, have broken bread with evangelical Christians vocal in their support for the Jewish state. In the book of Genesis [the reporter has not taken the trouble to make the citation more precise], often cited by evangelicals as the basis for their loyalty to Israel, God promises to bless the nations that bless the Jews, and curse the nations that curse the Jews ... Some evangelicals read certain Biblical passages to mean that an "ingathering" of Jews to Israel is a prerequisite to an apocalyptic war that will usher in the second coming of Christ. But some Jewish leaders who have been active in reaching out to evangelicals said yesterday that they have rarely heard evangelicals mention that as a reason for supporting Israel.[24]

A major misperception of many Christian Zionists is that those Jews who stand with themselves in support of Israel would be likely to see eye to eye on other matters as well. The logic is that since liberal Christians clearly tend to the anti-Israel side, and since Jews are always presumed to be pro-Israel, it would follow that most Jews must be naturally disposed to the same side of the *domestic* agenda as the conservative Christians who make up nearly the whole constituency of pro-Zionists. Efforts by conservative Christian groups to unite Jewish leaders with themselves on domestic issues have not met the degree of success that such thinking promises. When Christian conservatives lapse into this assumption an outcry emerges from the other side. Not long before the Netanyahu visit, the Voices United for Israel group had sent out a mailing that claimed, "Your average, hard-working, family-oriented, church and synagogue-going American is getting involved in the political process and helping Republicans win race after race. Liberals and Democrats are using scare tactics in a smear campaign to discredit these Americans by labelling them the 'Religious Right.' This is dirty politics at its worst." This had led Abraham Foxman, executive director of the Anti-Defamation League, and Rabbi Leon Lenicki, director of the Anti-Defamation League's Interfaith Affairs department, to resign from the Voices United executive committee in 1994. Rabbi Yechiel Eckstein, founder and president of the International Fellowship of Christians and Jews, also resigned from the board of Voices United because of its "anti-Rabin, pro-Likud" posture.[25]

American Jews are hesitant to embrace or be embraced by the evangelical and fundamentalist supporters of Israel. Whereas in Israel the focus of concern is the matter of the menace of conversion, in America the focus of Jewish concern is more the declared intention of evangelicals/fundamentalists to re-establish, somehow, the Christian character of American public life. American Jews, for the most part, are not keen on such matters as constitutional amendments to return prayers to the school, to open the schools to Bible study groups, and so on. Most American Jews are only dimly aware of the extent of the transformation of Christian attitudes towards Jews that has taken place almost across the Christian community (but not extending to the Orthodox or Eastern churches). The perception that the Christians are a threat to the peace of the Jews is a legacy of the experience of Central European Jews. Perversely this now anachronistic phobia is fixed almost exclusively on "the Christian right" – evangelicals and fundamentalists. This follows from a completely false perception that anti-Semitism was always especially characteristic of the conservative side of Christianity in America, and that it still thrives there, while reduced, if not eliminated, on the left side of the Christian spectrum. The patent fact that anti-Zionism flourishes on the left while pro-Zionism flourishes on the right of the Christian house does not seem to affect this judgment. Pro-Israelism in the conservative world is seen as the perverse result of an unhealthy theological obsession: the Second Coming of Jesus, related to the expectation of the eventual conversion of the Jews to Christian faith, and also to much bad news about Armageddon.

This obsession is carried to the extent that "the Christian Right" is routinely defamed by Jewish organizations, notably by the American Jewish Committee and (with least excuse) by the Anti-Defamation League. Nathan Perlmutter of the ADL, admits that "our image of the Fundamentalist and the Evangelical is a kind of collage assembled out of bits and pieces from Theodore Dreiser, Sinclair Lewis, and Erskine Caldwell ... memories of that great swarm of sex-ridden, Bible-thumping caricatures."[26] In any other context, as Elliott Abrams points out, this would be recognized for the bald-faced prejudice that it is: "Bias against black or Hispanic citizens is automatically and roundly condemned in the Jewish community as plain bigotry, and so it should be. It seems to be another matter when the target is religious Christians. Anti-Christian bias is apparently the only form of prejudice that remains respectable in the American Jewish community."[27]

The mentality described by Abrams recalls the better-dead-than-red mentality of the Goldwater years. An example of this irrational hostility towards the Christian right is the ADL publication *The Religious Right: The Assault on Tolerance and Pluralism* (1994), which denounces the "religious right"' for its alleged "hostility to tolerance and pluralism ... hostility to difference ... basic rejection of the modern democratic state ... rhetoric of fear, suspicion, and even hatred ... [They are] prophets of rage ... paranoia and scapegoating ... [and allies of] homophobes, conspiracists, and concerted foes of church and state separation." ADL and American Jewish Committee literature has been known to resort to ugly McCarthyite guilt-by-association logic to link the best known leaders of the Christian right (Pat Robertson, Jerry Falwell, and Ralph Reed) with racists, Ku Klux Klan figures, and old-time Judeophobes like Gerald L.K. Smith and Father Coughlin.[28]

ADL thinking does not control the field, of course. In June 1984 an organization called *Toward Tradition* sponsored an ad in the *New York Times* headed: "Should Jews Fear the 'Christian Right?'" It denounced the ADL report just cited for using "such discreditable techniques as insinuation and guilt by association ... [in fact,] defamation ... Insofar as the objections to the religious Right are honestly presented in the ADL report, they are mainly political ones: Christian conservatives advocate positions that run counter to many people's beliefs about such issues as abortion, school prayer, homosexual rights, and the meaning of the First Amendment ... The separation of church and state is not the same thing as the elimination of religious values and concepts from political discourse. Moreover, Judaism is not, as the ADL seems to suggest, coextensive with liberalism ... Above all, on the issue with which this community does speak with one voice, namely, the survival of Israel, the Jews have no more stalwart friends than evangelical Christians. Judaism teaches the principle of *Hakarat Hatov*, that we have the duty to acknowledge the good done to us. In attacking *The Religious Right* the ADL has among other things seriously violated that principle." Signatories included several rabbis, Midge Decter, Gertrude Himmelfarb, Milton Himmelfarb, Irving Kristol, Michael Medved, Jacob Neusner – all distinguished figures in American cultural life. In September 1994 *Commentary* magazine, published by the American Jewish Committee, printed a long article by Midge Decter that develops the themes to be found in the ad in the *New York Times*.[29] Subsequently, numerous letters to the editor documented the resentment that many American Jews felt at seeing the ADL virtually equating current Judaism with the domestic agenda of the political left. Among others, Egal Feldman commented on the irony that alarm about the alleged threat posed by remnants of Christian presence in public life comes mainly from Reform Jews whose religious practice is so marked by liberal-minded accommodations that they are unable to keep their children from marrying out of the Jewish ranks. "Orthodox Jews," Feldman noted, "rarely sit around fretting about the conspiratorial designs of the Christian Right. Secure in their adherence to Torah, they have erected an armor of religious conviction that cannot be pierced as easily as that of the liberal Jew. My suggestion to the members of the liberal Jewish community is to learn from their Orthodox brethren: that is, to worry less about the Christian Right and to spend more time raising their children in homes deeply permeated with love and appreciation of Judaism."[30]

There are many signs that the mainstream Jewish organizations are as remote from the hearts and minds of most American Jews as are the bureaucrats of the WCC/NCC from the hearts and minds of most church-going Christians.

The worst of this situation is that it seems to be about the obsessions of the élites. Elliot Abrams says: "For decades, leaders of mainline Christian denominations and of the National Council of Churches who were unvaryingly hostile to Israel were viewed as appropriate partners for the Jewish community in interfaith dialogues and political endeavors ... because they were graduates of the finest seminaries and were men and women of social prestige, and because they were people of liberal political bent ... The preference [of such Jewish organizations as the ADL and the American Jewish Committee] for a more liberal political agenda over the one embraced by most devout and observant Jews [in such matters as homosexuality, abortion, sex education in schools] is perfectly proper, but it should not be dressed up as a concern for the future of American Jewry ... It is wrong to decry – on grounds of separation of church and state – the intrusion of the Christian right into politics while the intrusions of the Christian left are accepted and indeed celebrated."[31]

In the past, it could have been said that Jewish prejudices against evangelicals owed something to lack of familiarity. Until the last thirty years or so, Jews were mainly Northeasterners, especially New Yorkers, while evangelicals were disproportionately rural and southern. But the sociological profile has changed dramatically. Jews are much more evenly distributed throughout the country than in the past, and so are evangelicals. (Forty percent of those who identify themselves as Jewish by religion now live in the southern and western regions of the country, as compared to only twelve percent in 1930.) No longer can lack of personal acquaintance be accepted as an excuse for this particular prejudice. It is a case of cultural inertia – of wilful refusal to become acquainted. In any case: if it is true that most evangelicals generally don't know many Jews, they are certainly better informed *about Judaism* than are mainstream Protestants and certainly better informed than Roman Catholics. Intensive surveys of attitudes conducted by Jewish organizations in recent years document the fact that fundamentalism does not promote anti-Semitic attitudes – contradicting the myth that still grips the Jewish community in general.[32]

The truth of the matter seems to be that evangelicals attract fear and contempt because they use a forthright language of piety, which offends the ears of secular Jews, as it offends the ears of most nominal

Christians (not to mention secularized post-Christians), and probably more than it does the ears of most pious Jews. At the root of this phenomenon is a simple fact: that evangelicals are evangelical! That is, they are committed to sharing their faith and thus have (or should have) a missionary attitude towards all their neighbours, including Jews. For mainstream churches, which have virtually stifled explicitly missionary work and are now falling all over themselves in embarrassment about the "Eurocentrism" and "cultural imperialism" that allegedly characterized missionary enterprises of the past among heathen populations, it costs nothing to take the pledge of abstinence from missionary enterprise to the Jews. Evangelical organizations, on the other hand, have a harder time swearing off the missionary enterprise, whether in North America or in Israel. A number of Christian Zionist organizations, like ICEJ (as we have noticed) and Bridges for Peace, have made principled declarations to the effect that missionary enterprise to the Jews is not the will of God – and have abstained in the best of good faith. Others have set limits to the missionary enterprise – for example, confining their sharing of the gospel to contexts of discussion and dialogue, and forbidding streetcorner or door-to-door ministry. Refraining from seeking conversions of the Jews does not require evangelicals to cease talking like first-century Christians. It is their unblushing use of *the language that belongs to their faith* that offends secular Jews: the language of being "born again," of "sharing," of "God's love in their lives," etc. Still, only a minority of the evangelical churches and missionary organizations remain committed to evangelism among the Jews, conducted on the old lines. But this commitment is a principled one and follows not from a desire to destroy Judaism but from studied conclusions about the missionary command with which Jesus of Nazareth left His followers.[33]

Paradoxically, many Jews are suspicious of the very fact that evangelicals show a greater interest in having contact with Jews than do the mainstream Protestant or the Roman Catholic churches (not to mention the Orthodox and Eastern Christians). Few seem to have the historical knowledge to appreciate the tradition of philo-Semitism that has always existed among evangelicals and thus are taken aback to hear of the interest in Jewish language, history, and customs that flourishes in Baptist Sunday Schools. Jews can be caught off guard by an evangelical neighbour who seeks an invitation to participate in a *seder*. But this sort of interest is genuine and should not be presumed to be a patronizing cover for a missionary intention. Instead, it probably reflects a conviction of the special favour under which Jewish believers live. This conviction was the basis of Restorationist thinking from Puritan times forward.

CHRISTIAN ATTITUDES TOWARDS THE ISSUE OF ISRAEL'S "LEGITIMACY"

Long ago, the American Christian Palestine Committee, the principal body of pro-Israel support among liberal Protestant clergymen, dissolved, and with it went the friendly alliance between Israel and the ecumenical Protestant mainstream. The effort to establish a pro-Zionist presence in this company has never brought more than meagre returns, as we saw in chapter 7. Because it was not grounded in a transcendent theology, the liberal-ecumenical attitude simply shifted when the political scenery shifted. This reality can be explained in secular terms, and it can be explained in religious terms. Deep down, the two sets of explanations have common ground.

Among secular and religious liberals alike, the Jewish cause is affected by the disdain for "the establishment" that possesses the generation trained in the universities in the 1960s and since. Israel is a sovereign state, founded on the rule of law and the consent of the governed – a perfect target for the anti-institutionalism that informs the present intellectual world. Bureaucrats of the WCC were taught in university that Israel came into the world as a nuisance, a creation of American Cold War policy, an obstacle in the path of the liberation of oppressed colonial peoples. The reverse side of the liberal's negative attitude towards the inherited culture is a disposition to celebrate other remote cultures, with special preference for those that can be presented as having been victimized by the liberal's own civilization. From this comes a disposition to patronize. In the Manichean worldview of American and European liberals, the Palestinian/Arab cause is aligned with the generalized cause of the "oppressed" everywhere, capable of serving the ingrained need of liberals to condescend.

The history of the missionary effort of Western churches in the Middle East has made the churches of the West patrons of the Arab cause. This is a variation on the phenomenon that diplomatic historians call "clientitis," the tendency of foreign service people sent abroad to serve their country to come to see the world from the perspective of the client country to which they are sent. Beginning in the mid-nineteenth century, Christian missionaries from the West – Protestant, Catholic, and evangelical – sought the conversion of the Jews of Palestine for about a century, with only the most modest results. On the other hand, missionary efforts among the Arabs did win substantial conversions in the latter half of the nineteenth century and a modest number since. Not unreasonably, Church organizations have been much more open to the political aspirations of their clients than to those of their clients' adversaries. This reality reinforces the tendency to adopt the "Third World" perspective already noted.

The creation and the perseverance of the State of Israel has, in a most paradoxical way, provided a new lease on life for age-old antipathies towards Jews and Judaism. "Anti-Zionism" (a preposterous term, historically speaking, since the Zionist program was accomplished a half century ago) provides respectable camouflage for hostility towards Jews and towards Judaism that cannot be admitted to oneself or to others. Belonging to the "Anti-Zionist" side gives one plenty of company among progressive people, allowing one to use the noble-sounding rhetoric that surfaces easily when one speaks of "the oppressed." It serves as the perfect cover for anti-Semitism – all the more perfect for the fact that many Jews themselves employ it.

THE RELATIVE JUSTICE OF THE ZIONIST CAUSE IN 1948–1998

Israel's cause escapes people who have the congenital habit of stooping. At the same time, Jews do not take well to being patronized. Although the Zionist program was launched as long ago as 1897, and although the state was founded as long ago as 1948, many people still have not got used to the idea of Jews as peers. Many still tend to remember statehood as our gift to the Jews, rather than as a hard-earned, long-denied right, won against all the predictions and the predelictions of the politically and militarily informed.

Today Israel is a sovereign state; yet there are still many people who cannot think of it as a state like other states – a peer of the United States. A peer of Canada! People still talk of Israel as though it were a freshly begun experiment, as though it were still too early to say whether it will succeed – even though the present state, founded in 1948, is in fact older than most of the nearly two hundred present member states of the UN, including most of those that still withhold recognition. We recall that, at that time, the other superpower, the Union of Soviet Socialist Republics, held one of the five permanent seats on the UN Security Council. Without the approval of the USSR (whose motives in this matter still baffle scholarly commentators) the State of Israel would never have been allowed to be born. Since then, not Israel but the USSR has gone into the "dustbin of history."

Before long, Israel emerged as victor over her enemies. Immediately, a change of attitude came over many who had formerly shown her goodwill – including, of course, the USSR and its satellites, who went over to the other side when it became clear that Israel was not going to line up, under Soviet example, in a policy of hostility towards the West. No less than the Soviets, many Christian liberals have found it hard to get along with victors. In contrast, it could not occur to Christian Zionists to question the "legitimacy" of Israel. In a profound sense, Israel is the most legitimate state of all – maybe the *only* legitimate one, in a theological sense.

Why does the question of "legitimacy" occur only with respect to Israel, never with respect to the scores of nations that have come into the world since 1948 and been admitted as full members of the UN, despite the atrocious performance of most of them in matters of human rights, despite so many unfinished issues regarding borders, and regarding the unsatisfied nationalist hopes of minorities within those boundaries? Israel is one of a most select company of states that existed in 1948 and whose constitutional system has not since been overthrown or drastically rewritten under the effects of military intervention or popular uprising. (This larger company includes all the nations of Africa, most of the Asian ones, and of course the used-to-be-Soviet Bloc.) Why, in the light of this, is Israel constantly singled out for her "illegitimacy"?

When the State of Israel came into the world in 1948, world opinion was in great part moved to support the deed by conviction that justice was on the side of the Jews. It is precisely for that reason that we must stress that no conscientious friend of the Jews has ever claimed that the argument for the creation of Israel was an absolutely just one – that is, that the deed caused no suffering to others. No conscientious friend of Zionism has ever denied that the case for creation of a Jewish state, if expressed exclusively in terms of justice, was a relative one – a compelling case, maybe even an overwhelmingly compelling case, but still, like all other such matters, a relative one. Similarly, the argument for Israel's continuing in possession of the territory that she governs today is an argument that can be defended in terms of justice; but no conscientious friend of Israel claims that nobody on the other side has ever suffered some degree of injustice because of it.

The history of the relations between the Church and Israel has been shaped by the fact that, somewhere along the line since the war for Israel's independence in 1948–49, most official spokesmen of most of the churches reworked the moral arithmetic and came to find more "justice" in the claims of the Palestinian Arabs and less in the cause of Israel than they saw in 1947. In contrast, most Christians who define themselves as theologically conservative have remained constant in their preference for Israel's claims. That is because for "Christian Zionists" the case for the Restoration of the Jews in the first place, even though it was manifestly defensible in terms of "justice," actually stood upon a firmer ground: namely, that it was predicted and ordained by

Scripture. To have resisted it would have been sin, and in any case would be futile. To support it, brought blessing: "He who blesses thee, I will bless; he who curses thee, I will curse" (Genesis 12:3).

Christian Zionists *can* make a case for the justice of Israel's regime – in doing which they are helped by pointing to certain powerful extenuating facts : that Israel has always had to contend with the very denial of her right to exist – a minimum condition of peace among neighbours; that she remains beset by hostile neighbours (most of them formally at war with her until very recently), and all of whom have had a hand in sponsoring terrorist activities against her and against her citizens throughout the world; and that all of Israel's enemies outside and inside the territories she governs could have had peace with Israel – a much smaller Israel – in 1948, had they been willing to abide by the world's decision, embodied in the UN resolutions of 1947.

Going beyond this calculation of the relative justice of her claim, Christian Zionists argue that Israel has much to commend her stewardship of the land since 1948. She has created and sustained the only democratic system in the region, while being surrounded by hostile authoritarian regimes. She has achieved a remarkably high standard of living (education, health, economic opportunity, etc.) for all of her citizens, including the Arab citizens, while providing for those in the disputed territories (not citizens) standards higher than those enjoyed by the Arab citizens of any of the neighbouring Arab states. She has carried out honourably her responsibilities in terms of access to and respect for Christian and Muslim holy places. She can demonstrate the highest levels of cultural and scholarly accomplishment, including conscientious attention to the archaeology of the Holy Land, and has maintained the basic freedoms of speech, assembly, religion, and so on.

Yet for Christian Zionists none of this is really the heart of the matter. The Christian Zionist is not knocked off his perch when Israel is denounced for rough treatment of the Palestinians, or when a politician is found to have his hand in the till, or when the Mossad, the Israeli intelligence outfit, carries off a dirty trick, or when instances of brutality occur in her prisons, etc. The Christian Zionist does not have to rework the ethical arithmetic all over when bad news appears, in order to reckon whose side he is on. To the Christian Zionist, it is a requirement of faith to prefer the blessing of Israel above all passing things. Doing this, he believes, cannot, by definition, ever be incompatible with the will of God.

Jews understand that there will be fluctuations from time to time in the relative justice of the case that Israel can present before world opinion – as, for example, with regard to what the state perceives to be her security needs *vis-à-vis* internal and external foes. But Jews cannot understand how Christians, who parade their sensitivity to the situation of the oppressed, can even for a moment toy with the thought that Israel has a doubtful right to exist within the borders that have resulted from her original acceptance of the partition of 1947, improved by result of her enemies' recurring appeal to the god of war. Yet today Jews hear leading voices of the official churches announcing that the decision to permit Israel to come to birth in the first place was "unjust" and should be reconsidered.

Anti-evangelical prejudice on the part of so many American Jewish leaders is best seen as a product of historical confusion, compounded by élitist disdain, tending to phobia. More important: it is at the root of a profound political miscalculation. Jews who take the time to review the history of the politics of the quarter-century that led to the creation of their state in 1947–48 will learn that the sturdiest champions of the restoration of the Jews to Israel were the evangelicals and fundamentalists. In the years when Britain was turning away from her commitments under the Balfour Declaration, and was supported in so doing by mainstream Christianity, evangelicals sustained the Zionist cause. In the same spirit, "the [evangelical] movement on the whole recognized at an early date that the Holocaust was impending and believed that six million Jews had been murdered at a time when most liberal Christians were denouncing 'Jewish atrocity propaganda'."[34]

Elliott Abrams puts the matter in plain terms: "As the ability and willingness of American Jews to promote pro-Israel policies erode, support from evangelical groups that are growing in size and political influence should be viewed with gratitude, not suspicion, by Americans who are concerned about Israel's future."[35] The problem, as Abrams clearly perceives, is that American Jews, who are overwhelmingly "liberal" in their attitudes on domestic issues, cannot bring themselves to recognize that the "liberal" (that is, mainstream) Church is as genuinely hostile to Israel as is plainly stated in the policy pronouncements of the WCC and the NCC. "This is not a matter of theology," says Abrams. " Few Jews know or care much about where Israel fits in the theology of mainline Protestantism. What they *do* know is that among the mainline Protestant denominations there is a lack of will to understand what Israel means to American Jews."[36]

But perhaps Jews *should* pay more attention to "the matter of theology" involved. Christian anti-Zionism is not merely a subtype of a generic neo-anti-Zionism. Just like Christian Zionism, it follows from alleged spiritual and theological insights; and, no less than Christian

Zionism, it imposes religious duties on people – making it far more powerful than the secular sort of anti-Zionism. The real contest within Christianity – on which the survival of Israel may well depend – is over one of the oldest theological issues in the Church: How the destiny of the Jews is related to the destiny of the Church. It is simply too soon to know whether the work done by forces dedicated to Jewish-Christian reconciliation – a work that involves repudiation of "replacement theology" – will stand against the flanking effort of the neo-Marcionists, whose heart is in the different work of accomodating the secular liberals, the Churches of the East, and the Muslims.

Notes

INTRODUCTION

1 Heschel, *Israel: An Echo of Eternity,* 49–51.
2 Gildersleeve, M*any a Good Crusade,* 49.
3 Ibid., 181–2, and 409–12.

CHAPTER ONE

1 Combined population of the states of the the Arab League was then about 140 million people and covered about five million square miles. Israel's population in May 1948 was about 650,000 and the State of Israel as described by Resolution 181, 29 November 1947, was to be about ten thousand square miles.
2 Meir, *My Life,* 257–71.
3 Compensation was paid under the Luxembourg Treaty of 1952 by the Federal Republic of Germany, as acknowledgment of German responsibility for the Holocaust. Sachar, *Israel and Europe,* 32–51.
4 Quoted in Sachar, *A History of Israel,* 335.
5 *Encyclopedia of Zionism and Israel,* 1971 ed., s.v. "Declaration of Independence."
6 Meir, *My Life,* 223–4.
7 Eban, *An Autobiography,* 93–4, citing Isaiah 11: 12.
8 Rose, *Chaim Weizmann,* 267.
9 Raphael, *Chaim Weizmann,* 5–6.
10 Quoted in ibid., 17.

11 Weizmann, *Trial and Error*, 569.
12 Teveth, *Ben-Gurion: The Burning Ground*, 9.
13 Ibid., 479.
14 Kurzman, *Ben-Gurion*, 24–7.
15 Quoted in Nixon, *Leaders*, 280.
16 Weizman, *The Battle for Peace*, 220.
17 *Bulletin of Associated Christian Press*, no. 375 (May–June 1993): 11.
18 Quoted in *MED* (November 1995).
19 Clyde Habermas, "The Cohorts of David Smite Rabin," *NYT*. 15 December 1993.

CHAPTER TWO

1 Quoted in Croner, ed., *Stepping Stones*, 3.
2 Ariel, "Born Again in a Land of Paradox," 35–49; "Christians in Israel pledge 'nonaggression,'" *CC*, 22–29 April 1998, 426.
3 See "Foreign Intervention in anti-Missionary Activity," *Arutz7* 11 November 1999.
4 The examples that follow are drawn mainly from Fishman, *American Protestantism*, 142–4.
5 H.S. Coffin, "Perils to America in the New Jewish State." *Christianity and Crisis* (21) February 1949, 9–10.
6 Burge, *Who Are God's People in the Middle East?*, 118–9.
7 Laqueur, *A History of Zionism*, 586.
8 *CT*, 24 December 1956.
9 Fishman, *American Protestantism*, 178–9.
10 See sections 3 ("Barthianism and the Kingdom," 140–93), and 5 ("The Church and the Churches: The Ecumenical Movement," 265–94), in Niebuhr, *Essays in Applied Christianity*.
11 Smith, *The Fraudulent Gospel*, 1–2.
12 Lefever, *Amsterdam to Nairobi*, 63–9.
13 Lefever, *Nairobi to Vancouver*, 21–2.
14 Ibid., 30–1.
15 Ibid., 2–3.
16 Ibid., 34.
17 Lefever, *Amsterdam to Nairobi*, 1–3. See also ibid., Appendix F, "Program to Combat Racism: Grants, 1970–1978," 91–6, and Appendix G, "Grants to Groups Combating Racism: Facts and Rationale – A Statement by the WCC, 1978," 97–101.
18 Ibid., 56–7.
19 Smith, *The Fraudulent Gospel*, chapter 2, "Education for Liberation," where Smith describes a meeting of the WCC executive at Geneva in 1973, to discuss "Education and Theology in the Context of the Struggle

for Liberation," and where Smith reviews WCC publications inspired by liberation theology.

20 Belli, *Breaking Faith*, 151–65.

21 Quoted in Smith, *The Fraudulant Gospel*, 134–5.

22 Lefever, *From Amsterdam to Nairobi*, 48.

23 Ibid., 135.

24 This paragraph draws in part on Lefever, *Nairobi to Vancouver*, especially 70–5.

25 Smith, *The Fraudulant Gospel*, 128–30.

26 Ibid., 4.

27 Hudson, *The World Council of Churches*, 17.

28 Banki, *Christian Reactions*; Fishman, *American Protestantism*, 166–7.

29 Banki, *Christian Reactions*, 5.

30 See "8 Church Leaders Ask Aid to Israel/Call on Johnson to Honor 'Commitment' on Straits," *NYT*, 28 May 1967, 4; and advertisement, signed by the same individuals, on behalf of "American for Democracy in the Middle East," *NYT*, 4 June 1967, sec. 4, p. 5.

31 Banki, *Christian Reactions*, 2.

32 Letter to the Editor, *NYT*, 7 July 1967, 32. See also many responses in the letter section on 13, 22 and 26 July.

33 Brickner, "No Ease in Zion to Us"; John C. Bennett, "A Response to Rabbi Bricker," 204–5; Niebuhr, "David and Goliath"; Geyer, "Christians and 'The Peace of Jerusalem,'" 160–4.

34 Walter I. Wilson, quoted in Malachy, *American Fundamentalism and Israel*, 148.

35 "I will also gather all nations, and bring them down to the Valley of Jehoshaphat; And I will enter into judgement with them there, on acount of My people, My heritage Israel, whom they have also scattered among the nations; they have also divided up My land" (Joel 3: 2.)

36 Quoted in Malachy, A*merican Fundamentalism and Israel*, 149.

37 Quoted in Boyer, *When Time Shall Be No More*, 210–11.

38 Quoted in Fishman, A*merican Protestantism*, 145–6.

39 The most convenient source for this material is Boyer, *When Time Shall Be No More*, chapter 6, especially 187–99.

40 Ibid., 188, citing *Moody Monthly* (October 1967).

41 Cited in O'Neill and Wagner, *Peace or Armageddon?*, 81.

42 *NYT*, 6 April 1980, sec. 7, p. 27.

43 Woodward. "The Way The World Ends."

44 Martin, *Prophet with Honor*, 210, 368, and 593.

45 Malachy, *American Fundamentalism*, 158; Boyer, *When Time Shall Be No More*, 196–9.

46 Banki, *Christian Reactions*, 18.

47 Kelso, *CT* 11 (21 July 1967): 1051–2.

48 *Inter alia*: Sidey, "For the Love of Zion"; Weber, "How Evangelicals Became Israel's Best Friend"; Morgan, "Jerusalem's Living Stones."

49 "What Is Israel," *CC* 84 (30 August 1967): 1091–2.

50 See, *inter alia*, "Israel and the Christian Dilemma," *CC* 84 (12 July 1967): 883–4; and "Israel Annexes Old Jerusalem," *CC* 84 (12 July 1967): 884–5.

51 Among the anti-Israeli pieces are McLeod, "Isaac and Ishmael"; Oxtoby, "Christians and the Mideast Crisis"; Sanders, "Urbis and Orbis: Jerusalem Today." Among the pro-Israeli pieces are Polish, "Why American Jews Are Disillusioned"; Eckardt and Eckardt, "Again, Silence in the Churches."

52 Sachar, *History of Israel*, 658; compare with Flint et al., *The Arab-Israeli Wars*, 14.

53 See, for example, "The Priority of Human Need."

54 ACPC Report to Hearings of Joint Anglo-American Committee of Inquiry. US Dept. of State. Washington. DC, 1946.

55 Quoted in Croner, ed., *Stepping Stones*, 69–72.

56 See, for example, Third Assembly of the WCC, New Delhi, India, 1961, "Resolution on Anti-Semitism," in ibid., 72–3; Report to the Faith and Order Commission of the WCC, Geneva, 1968, in ibid., 73–85.

57 Rottenberg, *The Turbulent Triangle*, 49–50; Drinan, *Honor the Promise*, 195–7.

58 Rottenberg, *Turbulent Triangle*, 43–58.

59 Ibid., 97–107.

60 See Fishman, *American Protestantism*, chapter 7, "The Internationalization of Jerusalem," 108–26.

61 ACPC to President Truman, 20 October 1948.

62 H.M. Sachar, *History of Israel*, 433–4.

63 Statement of the National Executive Council of ACPC, 30 December 1948, and press release, 20 October 1949.

64 H.M. Sachar, *History of Israel*, 434.

65 Fishman, *American Protestantism*, 123–6.

66 From Report of Policy Reference Committee III, in Paton, ed., *Breaking Barriers*, 164–5. Emphasis added.

67 Ecumenical Considerations on Jewish-Christian Dialogue, Executive Committee of the WCC, Geneva, 1982, in Croner, ed., *More Stepping Stones*, 172.

68 Central Board of the Union of Evangelical Churches in Switzerland, 1977, in ibid., 204.

69 "Reflections on the Problem 'Church-Israel'," issued by the Central Board of the Union of Evangelical Churches in Switzerland, 1977, in ibid., 204.

CHAPTER THREE

1 A major source for this chapter is the two sets of interviews, noted in the acknowledgements, that I conducted in 1995 and 1998.

2 Too busy with the life-and-death issues of its earliest years, the First Knesset decided not to undertake right away the work of drawing up a full and formal constitution. Instead, beginning in 1950, the Knesset worked out a series of "Basic Laws," each of which deals with a single aspect of public life. Technically, these Basic Laws are subject to revision at any time by a mere majority of the Knesset, and some have, indeed, been revised along the way. The consensus today seems to be that a complete and definitive codification of the Basic Laws in a constitution (on the American model) would create perhaps too inflexible a situation for the good of the citizen. Americans, who are nurtured in the concept of separation of powers and the related concept of fundamental rights embodied in a written constitution and amendable only by an extraordinary process, claim to find this situation perilous. Yet the constitutional situation in Israel is really no different from that in the UK, where basic "rights" of citizens similarly stand on statutes (for example, the Petition of Right, 1628 and 1680, and the Habeus Corpus Act, 1679), which, while having a special standing in the eyes of the courts, could technically be overturned in a moment by a mere majority in any elected parliament. The Palestinian National Authority, similarily, has passed a number of "Basic Laws," pending the enactment of a constitution, and religious rights are for the time being defined under these. See Rolef, ed., *Political Dictionary,* s.v. "Religious Pluralism" and "Basic Laws"; *Religious Life in Israel.*

3 Sfeir. "Education in the Holy Land."

4 Holy Land Foundation, *Crisis in the Holy Land,* n.p.

5 "Diminishing number of Christians in Jerusalem topic of concern for International conference." *United Methodist News Service* (Internet: www.umc.org/umns.html), 26 June 1996.

6 Bishop Slams Israel's 'evil.'" *Ottawa Citizen,* 27 December 1997.

7 The principal source for these numbers and those that follow is the Israeli Central Bureau of Statistics, whose authors note that they have not included the whole population of the West Bank and Gaza Strip (counting only the 130,000 Jewish people there). A second source is Sabella, "Palestinian Christians." No census was conducted in the West Bank and Gaza between 1967 and December 1997–February 1998, when one was held under the Palestinian Authority. The Palestinian census takers reported a total population of 2,890,631 (including East Jerusalem), a figure that Israel believes to be greatly exaggerrated (*New York Times, Jerusalem Post, Jerusalem Times,* and *Arutz7* files).

8 The Druze are a sect deriving from another sect – the Ismailiyya wing of Islam. They look to a Syrian mystic, al-Darazi (d. 1019) and to a certain al-Hakim bi-Amrih Allah (985–1021), the sixth Fatimid caliph, whom the faithful believe to have been an incarnation of God and the giver of an

esoteric wisdom regarding the principles that govern the cosmos. Considered heretical by the dominant branches of Islam, they have been subject to brutal persecution in Moslem lands and thrive today only in a virtually autonomous pocket in mountainous Lebanon and the adjacent region of Syria – and in the Northern Galilee region of Israel. The Druze of Israel have multiplied in number since 1948 and are now reckoned at 100,000. Israeli adherents of Baha'i are much fewer and do not constitute a substantial localized community with a fully developed way of life of their own. Their founding prophet, Mirza Hoseyn Ali Nuri (1819–1850), known as Baha Ullah, the Glory of God, appeared much later on the scene than the founding prophets of the Druze. The Persian government put the prophet to death by firing squad in 1850 and followed this up with a general massacre in which an estimated 20,000 died. This was the first of many assaults on the movement, that culminated in the virtual liquidation of its home community in Iran under the Ayatollah Khomeini (1980). The world centre of the main branch of the movements is on Mount Carmel, in Haifa, Israel. This movement, unlike the Druze, teaches a boldly universalistic message that follows, it says, from the essential identity of the messages of all the world religions. It is believed to have over five million adherents worldwide, its largest following being in the United States, where about 110,000 persons meet in some seventeen hundred assemblies.

9 *MED*, January, 1999.

10 "Christendom's Holy Destinations: Bethlehem," *NYT*, 27 December 1998.

11 In the years of her regime in Jerusalem (1948–67), Jordan wilfully obliterated all traces of Jewish presence. The Jewish population of the Old City was removed and the "Jewish Quarter" was demolished. Thirty-four synagogues were destroyed or desecrated. The Jewish cemetery on the Mount of Olives was vandalized and desecrated. In total contradiction of an explicit pledge contained in the 1949 Israel-Jordan Armistice Agreement, Jews were barred from visiting their holy sites, the most important of which is the Western Wall. Christians fared much better. They were allowed to remain in Jerusalem, Bethlehem, and elsewhere in the West Bank, but their churches now came under a new set of restrictions. Christian institutions were forbidden to purchase land in or near Jerusalem. Mosques were built next to churches to prevent their expansion, and the teaching of the Qur'an by Muslim teachers was now an obligatory part of the curriculum in Christian schools. (This paragraph draws in part on material in the *Bridges for Peace Teaching Series*, especially the excerpt "Jerusalem: Myths and Reality.")

12 *Christians and Israel* 4, no. 4 (Autumn 1995): 6.

13 The Israeli census indicated that there were 99,000 Christians altogether under Israeli rule in 1985; 101,0000 in 1986; 103,000 in 1987; 107,000 in 1989; 114,000 in 1991; 128,000 in 1992; 140,000 in 1993; 188,000

in 1998. Palestinian spokemen insist that these recent increases are owing to the immigration of Russian Christians, and they ask us to deduct some 30,000 from the total "Christian population" on the same line of thought that would have us deduct "expatriates" from the Jerusalem population (Salim Munayer lecture to EMEU-Open Doors group, 13 May 1998, Bethlehem Bible College). Complicating the picture further is the fact that hundreds of Palestinians have applied for Israeli citizenship since the Oslo Accords were signed.

14   During 1998, the population of Israel grew by 133,000 inhabitants, of which number forty percent was owing to immigration and the rest to natural increase (at a rate of 2.5 percent). Of the 60,000 new immigrants in 1998 alone, about 45,000 were from the former Soviet Union. Altogether between the mid-1980s and 1998, 460,000 immigrants came to Israel from the USSR and its successor state. Of the 58,000 immigrants to Israel in the period from May 1998 to April 1999, 45,000 were from the former USSR.

15   This account combines information from *Christians and Israel* (Spring 1996) and *MED* (November 1996).

16   *Bulletin of Associated Christian Press*, no. 387 (August/September 1995): 10; compare with Prior and Taylor, *Christians in the Holy Land*, 31–52.

17   Ariel, "Born Again in a Land of Paradox."

18   Moffett, *A History of Christianity in Asia*. Vol. I: *Beginnings to 1500*; Atiya, *A History of Eastern Christianity*.

19   Schwartz. "Towards Understanding Churches in the Middle East, 205.

20   Atiya, *Eastern Christianity*, 389–423.

21   This paragraph draws on chapter 20 of Ariel, *Evangelizing the Chosen People*, which I had the opportunity to read in manuscript in late 1999, prior to its publication by the University of North Carolina Press.

22   The ministry's view of the ongoing relationship between Christians and the State of Israel can be discovered by reading its quarterly publication, *Christians and Israel*, published in six European languages by the Association of Christians and Jews in Israel, and distributed through the various embassies of Israel.

23   The issue was still unresolved in 1999. See *JPost*, 23 May 1999.

24   Letter, jointly signed by the Greek, Latin, and Armenian patriarchs to Prime Minister Netanyahu, 12 April 1997 (copy provided by Ministry of Religious Affairs); conversation with Sami Musallam, 11 May 1998.

25   *ICEJ*, "Wolves in Sheep's Clothing"; Colbi, *A History of the Christian Presence*, 217–18; Betts, *Christians in the Arab East*, 217–18.

26   Quoted in Irani, *The Papacy and the Middle East*, 50–4.

27   *CT* 19 (11 October 1974): 15–18, 3 January 1975, 24 & 36; *Time* 100, 2 September 1974, 33–4; Yeshayahu Ben-Porat et al., *Entebbe Rescue*, 7–8. New York: Delacorte Press, 1977.

28 Weigel, *Witness to Hope*, 708 (and 931n.57).
29 "Palestine/Israel on the MECC Agenda." MECC VI GA/GS 9.
30 Suermann, "Palestinian Contextual Theology," 10.
31 Ibid., 12–13.
32 As quoted in *ICEJ*, "Wolves in Sheep's Clothing."
33 Conversation with Geries Khoury, Bethlehem, 7 November 1995.
34 Suermann, "Palestinian Contextual Theology," 13.
35 Raheb, *I Am a Palestinian Christian*, 13, cited by ibid., 15.
36 Ateek, *Justice and Only Justice*, quoted in Suermann, 16.
37 Younan, "Palestinian Local Theology," 56–7.
38 Conversation with Mitri Raheb, 16 May 1998, Bethlehem.
39 Conversation with Munib Younan, 12 May 1998, Jerusalem.
40 Oddly, though, the Anglican church in New Zealand has proved itself more Palestinian than the Palestinian Anglicans by removing references to Israel and Zion from *its* prayer book. Comment by Malcolm Lowe (on the lecture "An Arab-Israeli's Theological Reflections on the State of Israel After 40 Years," by Naim Ateek), in *People, Land and State of Israel*, 114–15.
41 Meier, "Conference on Palestinian Theology."
42 *Theology and the Local Church in the Holy Land, Nazareth*, 9.
43 Younan, "Palestinian Local Theology," 51–2.
44 Ateek, *Justice and Only Justice*, 81–2, quoted in Suermann, "Palestinian Contextual Theology," 17–19.
45 Giulia Clementi, letter to the editor of *Avenire* (Rome), 31 December 1995, quoted in *Christians and Israel* 5, no. 2 (Spring 1996).
46 *Theology and the Local Church in the Holy Land*, 5–6.
47 Suermann paraphrasing Khoury in Suermann, "Palestinian Contextual Theology," 22–3.
48 Interview with Geries Khoury, November 1995, Bethlehem.
49 Pryce-Jones, *The Closed Circle*, 283.
50 Sociologist Bernard Sabella states that there are 50,000 Christians in the West Bank and Gaza – about two percent of the total population living under the aegis of the PA. The *PASSIA Diary* counts in the Christian population of Jerusalem (10,910) and arrives at three percent of the whole "Palestinian population." Virtually all the rest of those living under the PA are Muslims.
51 *Palestine Report*, 27 March 1998; compare with Aburish, *Arafat*, 318–19.
52 From a paper delivered by Radwan Shaban to the International Conference on Employment, Ramalla, 11–13 May 1998, excerpted and translated into English, *Jerusalem Times*, 15 May 1998, 11.
53 *Arutz Sheva* Internet newsletter, 17 March 1998.
54 *MED*, January 1999, citing stories in the *London Sunday Times*, *Associated*

Press, and *Washington Times*. Also, Klaidman and Rees, "Something Rotten in Palestine."

55 Conversation with Zoughbi Zoughbi, 13 May 1998, Jerusalem.

56 Conversation with Bernard Sabella, 12 May 1998, Jerusalem.

57 Converstion with Jack Khasmo, 12 May 1998, Jerusalem.

58 Conversation with Ghassan Khatib, 14 May 1998, Jerusalem.

59 Conversation with Bishop Younan, 12 May 1998, Jerusalem. The same suggestion comes from Mitri Raheb and Geries Khoury, among others.

60 Conversation with Zoughbi Zoughbi, Bethlehem, 13 May 1998.

61 Conversation with Joudeh Majaj, Jerusalem, 11 and 15 May 1998.

62 Youssef M. Ibrahim, "Palestinian Religious Militants."

63 *Inter alia: Time*, 23 April 1990; *JPost*, 2 May 1991 and May 6, 1994; CNN broadcast, 20 December 1995.

64 See, for example, Morgan, "Jerusalem's Living Stones"; Sudilovsky, "Crossing the Line"; Steven Rodan, "Report: Christians Persecuted by PA," *JPost*, 24 October 1997; Rodan and Mohammed, "At The Boiling Point"; Haim Shapiro, "Catholic Official Repudiates Report on PA Persecution of Christians, *JPost*, 5 November 1997; Jay Bushinsky, "Patriarch: Palestinian Christians Not Mistreated under PA," *JPost*, 28 December 1997; Purcell, "Fighting on Two Fronts"; "Christian Converts on Run from Arafat's Men," *Daily Telegraph*, 21 December 1997; Schmemann, "Palestinian Christians"; "Christendom's Holy Destinations: Bethlehem," *NYT*, 27 December 1998; Editorial, "Fleeing Bethlehem," *Commentary*, 19 December 1997. See also "West Ignorant of Palestinian Christian Presence," *Jerusalem Times*, 5 April 1996; Koltermann, "Church Heads accused." Zipperer, "Palestinian Christians Hopeful." See also LAW, *The Myth of Christian Persecution*, Annex 1, 41–2.

65 Sudilovsky, "Crossing the Line."

66 Author's notes of a lecture, "Religious Status of Christians in Israel and Palestine-controlled Areas," given by Salim Munayer to Evangelicals for Middle East Understanding/Open Doors Christian Leaders Group, Bethlehem Bible College, 13 May 1998.

67 Halevi, "Squeezed Out."

68 LAW, *The Myth of Christian Persecution*, 1.

69 *NYT*, 10 October 1998.

70 Klein, 18; *Myth of Christian Persecution*, Annex 4: "LAW's Statement on the Prohibition of Sale of Palestinian Land to Jews," 49–50.

71 LAW, *Myth of Christian Persecution*, 23.

72 Jesus said: "For I have come to set a man against his father, a daughter against her mother, and a daughter-in-law against her mother-in-law, and a man's enemies will be those of his own household. He who loves father and mother more than me is not worthy of me" (Matthew 10: 34–7).

73 Conversation with Uri Mor, 10 May 1998, Jerusalem.

74 Halevi, "Squeezed Out."

75 Rodan and Najib, "At the Boiling Point"; *Arutz7*, 29 October 1997.

76 *Arutz7*, 19 October 1997. A similar case is the PLO's expropriation of the Jericho Garden Monastery of the Russian Orthodox Church (*Arutz7*, 28 January 2000).

77 LAW, *Myth of Christian Persecution*, 7–18, and conversations with Abdul-Hadi (Jerusalem), Zoughbi (Bethlehem), and Musallam, May 1998, Jericho.

78 Conversation with Ghassan Khatib, 14 May 1998, Jerusalem.

79 Conversation with Dr Abdul-Hadi, 12 May 1998, Jerusalem.

80 Conversation with Sami Musallam, 11 May 1998, Jericho.

81 Conversation with Zougbhi Zoughbi, 13 May 1998, Bethlehem.

82 Abu-Amr, *Islamic Fundamentalism in the West Bank and Gaza*, 17–18 and *passim*.

83 Esposito, *The Islamic Threat*, 73–4.

84 Bat Ye'or, *The Dhimmi*, 114.

85 "Arafat's Declaration of War," full-page advertisement documenting recent Arafat statements, paid for by Zionist Organization of America, *NYT*, 28 September 1997. Quoted in Brinkley, *The Unfinished Presidency*, 469.

86 *JPost*, 4 August 1999.

87 "Arafat's Declaration of War," quoted in Brinkley, *The Unfinished Presidency*, 469.

88 Isma'il Raji al-Faruqi, in al-Faruqi, ed., *Trialogue of the Abrahamic Faiths*, 57–8.

89 "Holy City Liberated, Arafat Declares," *NYT*, 24 December 1997.

90 *MED*, February, 1995.

91 Basic Law Draft Resolution, translated from the Arabic by LAW and quoted in LAW, *Myth of Christian Persecution*, 9.

92 Quoted in the article "Christians under Threat: 'Come Back to Islam," *MED* (March 1998); see also LAW, *Myth of Christian Persecution*, 26–7.

93 LAW, *Myth of Christian Persecution*, 8 and 26–7. See also the article "PA denies persecuting Arab Christians," *MED* (February, 1998).

94 This proved to be more of a challenge than I expected. Reference sources and scholarly sources all echo the line that we find, for example, in the *Encyclopaedia Britannica*, which in its 1998 edition, under "Palestine Liberation Organization," states: "The movement is dedicated to the creation of a 'democratic and secular' Palestinian state." This does not settle the matter, however, as the encyclopaedia rightly only reports what it is told by authorities. The "Palestine National Covenant" of 1964, still in force, makes no promise of a secular state, nor of a democracy. (This document appears as Appendix 1 in Becker, *The PLO*, 230–4.) At a meeting of the Palestine National Council in 1977, there was declared to

be agreement in principle to "a democratic state of Palestine," which would be established following Israel's withdrawal behind the lines she held following the war of 1948–49. Western commentors have amplified this and other passing references to "democracy" or "a democratic state," in order to speak of the PLO's commitment to a "secular democracy" (see, for example, Quandt et al, *The Politics of Palestinian Nationalism*, 100–12). Speaking to Arab-Muslim audiences, Arafat has said (6 January 1979): "We did not use the slogan for the establishment of a secular state ... I am certain ... that this is a distortion of the expression of democracy we proclaim." But speaking to Western audiences Arafat was saying at the same time that Palestine will be a "democratic, non-Zionist secular state where we would all live in peace and equality, as we did for a thousand years" ("Palestine: A Case of Right v. Right," *Time* 96 [21 December 1970]: 28–9). Michael Field cites from a 1968 PLO declaration that speaks of the goal of a "multiracial, secular, democratic state in Palestine," (Field, *Inside the Arab World*, 347–8). Jillian Becker argues that when the word "secular" occurs in internal PLO debates it comes from the left-wing, originally Marxist, flanks of the movement, which are mainly of Christian background. Their vision of a secular state has no appeal to the majority in the movement, who are aware of the necessity of accomodating the Islamic viewpoint of the vast majority of the people.

95 Interview with Dr Sami Musallam, 11 May 1998, Jericho.

96 Rosenthal, "Cruelty and Silence."

CHAPTER FOUR

1 As quoted in Bennett, *Philistine*, 137.

2 Morris, *Righteous Victims*, 83 and 674n.71.

3 Lewis, "The Palestinians and the PLO," *Commentary* (January, 1975): 32–48.

4 Lewis, *The Middle East*, 31.

5 Rashid Khalidi, a professor of History at the University of Chicago and at one time adviser to the Palestinian delegation to the Middle East peace negotiations, reviews all the documentary evidence that suggests that there was a powerful local allegiance among Arab-speaking people living in the the "region" (qutr) of Palestine prior to and during the Mandate period and proposes that out of these loyalties would eventually develop a "Palestinian identity." A cautious scholar, he distances himself from the PLO's offical historians and propagandists who locate the beginnings of the Palestinian nation in the "aboriginal" population (Canaanites, Philistines, Jebusites, etc.) See Khalidi, *Palestinian Identity, passim*, especially chapter 3: "Cultural Life and Identity in Late Ottoman Palestine," 35–62.

6 Quoted in Peters, *From Time Immemorial*, 139.

7 8 March 1974, as quoted in Peters, *From Time Immemorial,* 140

8 26 December 1981, as quoted in Bennett, *Philistine,* 139.

9 Speech to United Nations General Assembly, New York, 13 November 1973, as quoted in Bat Ye'or, *The Dhimmi,* 397–8.

10 Quoted in Osband, *Famous Travellers,* 71–2. The accounts of the other authors represented in this collection bear out the impression of abandonment of the land and of poverty in the cities.

11 Lowdermilk, *Palestine: Land of Promise.* See also the file "Walter Lowdermilk," in the Franklin Delano Roosevelt Presidential Library, Hyde Park New York.

12 Lowdermilk, *Palestine,* 5, and 74–6.

13 Lewis, *The Arabs in History,* 17.

14 Ibid., 15.

15 Quoted from Dutch daily *Trouw,* March 1977, in Peters, *From Time Immemorial,* 137. Compare "Reference Books Are Promoting a Bogus Middle East History," *Jerusalem Post,* 16 October 1992.

16 A sermon at the *Al Aksa* mosque, 11 July 1997, from "Voice of Palestine" (radio), as quoted in *Arutz7,* 13 July 1997.

17 In 1870 the figures were: 11,000 Jews, 8,500 Muslims, 4,500 Christians – a total of 24,000.

18 The two previous paragraphs draw in part on *Bridges for Peace Teaching Series,* especially the item "Jerusalem: Myths and Realities," 3d Quarter, 1990; and on Hoade, *Guide to the Holy Land.*

19 Peres, *The New Middle East,* 165–6.

20 In Bennett, *Philistine,* 224–5, citing *JPost,* 4 June 1994.

CHAPTER FIVE

1 Faraj al-Sarraf, quoting Mustafa al-Dabbagh, in Prior and Taylor, *Christians in the Holy Land,* 62–3.

2 A.L. Sachar, *A History of the Jews,* 155–6. The portion quoted is from the historian David Samuel Margoliouth.

3 *Holy Qur'an,* 51n.121, 62n.160.

4 Ibid., Appendix 2 to Sura 5, 282–5.

5 Guillaume, *Islam,* 43.

6 Watt, *Muhammad at Medina,* 47–50. Watt, *Muhammad: Prophet and Statesman,* 166–75.

7 See the explanation of these events in footnotes 3701–9 in Holy Qur'an.

8 The quotations are from interviews on Egyptian television, 18 April 1998, and in the newspaper *Al-Quds* (Jerusalem), 10 May 1998, as cited in *Arutz7,* 27 April and 22 May 1998.

9 Bar-Illan, "If This Be Peace."

10 Bat Ye'or, *The Dhimmi,* 87.

11 Awan, "The Faith Community," 83–4.

12 Field, *Inside the Arab World*, 8.

13 The latter are troubled by the movement's racism and also by such distinctly non-Muslim teaching as Point 12 in the statement of the faith, which appears in every issue of their official paper, *The Final Call:* "(Allah) God appeared in the Person of Master Wallace Fard Muhammed, July, 1930, the long-awaited Messiah of the Christians and the 'Mahdi' of the Muslims." See Morey, *The Islamic Invasion*, 161–4. In appreciation for its political correctness, the movement receives patronage and massive funding from the Muslim dictator of Libya, Muammar Qadhafi, from the radical Muslim regime of Sudan, and doubtless from other sources not publicly known. For Farrakhan's friendship with the Sudanese regime, see Marshall, *Their Blood Cries Out*, 19–22.

14 Ellul, "Preface," 27–8.

15 Runciman, *The Great Church in Captivity*, 77–81.

16 Ellul, Preface to Bat Ye'or, *The Dhimmi*, 30–1.

17 Shafaat, *Islam, Christianity and the State of Israel*, 80.

18 Abbad, "The Current Situation," 115.

19 Quoted by *Voice of Palestine*, 15 May 1998, as reported in *MED*, June 1998.

20 al-Faruqi, "Foreword," *Trialogue of the Abrahamic Faiths*, n.p.

21 Field, *Inside the Arab World*, 50.

22 Abbad, "The Current Situation," 112–15.

23 Ibid.

24 Ibrahim, "Islam's Fury."

25 Hanania, "Churches of the Holy Land," 204.

26 Gillquist, *Metropolitan Philip*, 136–8. In this passage, as in those that follow, Gillquist is paraphrasing the views of his subject, Metropolitan Philip.

27 Ibid., 132–3.

28 Ibid., 136.

29 Bat Ye'or, "Judeophobia and Christophobia In the Arab World."

30 Reuven Firestone's scholarly new book, *Jihad*, describes the circumstances attending the birth of this doctrine and demonstrates its inseparability from the tenets of Islam as laid down by the Prophet.

31 This document appears as Appendix 7 in Becker, *The PLO*, 230–4.

32 *MED*, June 1994.

33 *MED*, November 1998.

34 Cited in Morey, *Islamic Invasion*, 6.

35 Martin Kramer, "Politics and the Prophet," review of Fatima Mernissi, *Islam and Democracy: Fear of the Modern World* (1992), in *New Republic*, 1 March 1993.

36 Rosenthal, "Cruelty and Silence."

37 Abu-Amr, *Islamic Fundamentalism in the West Bank and Gaza*, 130.
38 Joshua Muravchik, "What Use is the UN?" American Enterprise Institute Web Page (www.aci.org/oti/oti6461.htm).
39 Henningsson, "Contemporary Understandings," 47.
40 Article 18 of the Universale Declaration of Human Rights, 10 December 1948, declares that "everyone has the right to freedom of thought, conscience, and religion; this right includes freedom to change his religion or belief, and freedom, either alone or in community with others and in public or private, to manifest his religion or belief in teaching, practice and worship." The complete text is published in *First Things*, no 82 (April 1998): 28–30. The UN Declaration on the Elimination of All Forms of Intolerance and Discrimination Based on Religion or Belief (1981) declares that "the right to replace one's current religion" and "the freedom to adopt a religion" are "protected unconditionally" (as quoted in Marshall, *Their Blood Cries Out*, 244–7).
41 Henningsson, "Contemporary Understandings," 48.
42 *Agence France Press*, as quoted in Bennett, *Philistine*, 57.
43 *MED* (June 1994).
44 Marshall, *Their Blood Cries Out*, 23–8.
45 Henningson, "Contemporary Understandings," 43–4.
46 *MECC News Report* 6, nos. 11 and 12 (November/December 1993).
47 "Importance of Teaching Islam at Christian Schools of Theology Stressed by MECC Committee on Christian Muslim Dialogue," *MECC News Report* (September/October 1993).
48 Marshall, *Their Blood Cries Out*, 49–51.
49 Henningsson, "Contemporary Understandings," 48; Ibrahim, "Muslims' Fury Falls on Egypt's Copts."
50 Wagner, *Anxious for Armageddon*, 57.
51 Hamza Hendawi, "Visiting Church Leaders Fear For Their Survival," *Associated Christian Press Bulletin* (Jerusalem), no. 399 (January/February 1998): 3.
52 al-Rauf, Mohammed Abd, "Judaism and Christianity," 29.
53 Mawdudi, *Towards Understanding Islam*, 75–7.
54 Ibid., 74–9.
55 Lester. "What Is the Koran?"
56 Shafaat, *Islam, Christianity and the State of Israel*, 11.
57 Ibid., 13–14, 17.
58 Ibid., 16, 29m, 30–1.
59 Cardinal Francis Arinze, "Christian-Muslim Relations in the 21st Century," an address given at the Center for Muslim-Christian Understanding at Georgetown University, Washington, DC, 5 June 1997," as excerpted in *Associated Christian Press Bulletin* 397 (August/September) 1997: 8–9.

60 John Paul II, *Crossing the Threshold of Hope*. Emphasis in original.

CHAPTER SIX

1 Quoted in Lapide, *The Last Three Popes*, 282.
2 *Torat Eretz Israel*, 318.
3 Speaking to the Jewish community of Berlin, quoted in O'Brien, *The Hidden Pope*, 315–16.
4 Drinan, *Honor the Promise*, 87.
5 Ibid., 88.
6 Ibid., 33.
7 Herzl, *Complete Diaries*, vol. 4: 1, 589–93. Pawel, *The Labyrinth of Exile*, 518–19.
8 Minerbi, *The Vatican and Zionism*, 94–6.
9 Herzl, *The Jewish State*, 30.
10 Herzl, *Complete Diaries*, vol. 4: 1, 593–4. (23 January 1904).
11 Ibid., 1, 601–5 (26 January 1904).
12 Pragai, *Faith and Fulfilment*, 151–2, citing Sokolow, *History of Zionism*.
13 Lapide, *The Last Three Popes*, 271.
14 Pragai, *Faith and Fulfilment*, 153; Lapide, *The Last Three Popes*, 277.
15 Lapide, *The Last Three Popes*, 83–84, 272.
16 Drinan, *Honor the Promise*, 34–5.
17 Both cited in ibid., 66–7; compare Rokach, *The Catholic Church*, 22–6.
18 As quoted in Drinan, *Honor the Promise*, 65–6.
19 Quoted in Gannon, *The Cardinal Spellman Story*, 354–5.
20 Quoted in Lapide, *The Last Three Popes*, 284.
21 Francis Cardinal Spellman to President Truman, 10 June 1949, HSTL.
22 Gannon, *The Cardinal Spellman Story*, 356–7.
23 Pragai, *Faith and Fulfilment*, 163–4, citing John M. Oesterreicher, *Internationalization of Jerusalem*, South Orange, NJ: Seton Hall University, 1971.
24 Pragai, *Faith and Fulfilment*, 163–4, citing Oesterreicher and Sinai, eds., *Jerusalem*.
25 Pragai, *Faith and Fulfilment*, 169, citing Jacques Maritain, *Le Mystère d'Israel*. Compare Maritain, "The Mystery of Israel."
26 Herzog, *Living History*, 69–70.
27 Pragai, *Faith and Fulfilment*, 154–6; Meir, *My Life*, 406–10; Irani, *Papacy and the Middle East*, 37–41.
28 Pragai, *Faith and Fulfilment*, 155; Meir, *My Life*, 406.
29 The full text is to be found in Croner, ed., *Stepping Stones*, 1–2.
30 *Cathecism of the Church*, paragraphs 839–40 (pp. 184–5).
31 From the record of the discussion at the Plenary Session on *Nostra Aetate*, in Croner, ed., *Stepping Stones*, 2–6. The quotation is from Bouyer, *La Bible et l'Evangile*.

32 *Holy Qur'an,* 230 and notes 663–4.

33 Betts, *Christians in the Arab East,* 156–60.

34 Pragai, *Faith and Fulfilment,* 239–49.

35 Ibid., 239, where he gives examples.

36 Bernstein and Politi, *His Holiness,* 30.

37 A recent book deals entirely with this friendship: O'Brien, *The Hidden Pope.* See also., Szulc, *Pope John Paul II,* 70–1 and 75–6, and many references in Weigel, *Witness to Hope.*

38 Bernstein & Politi, *His Holiness,* 442–4; Weigel, *Witness to Hope,* 484–5.

39 Szulc, *Pope John Paul II,* 40–1, 454–5.

40 H.M. Sachar, *Israel and Europe,* 314–15; O'Brien, *Hidden Pope,* 320–1; Irani, *Papacy and Middle East,* 41–9; Kreutz, *Vatican Policy on the Palestinian-Israeli Dispute,* 158–60.

41 Weigel, *Witness to Hope,* 697–713; *Christians and Israel* 1, no. 4 (Autumn 1992).

42 *Fundamental Agreement between the Holy See and the State of Israel,* 30 December 1993. Text provided by Embassy of Israel, Ottawa.

43 Szulc, *Pope John Paul II,* 453–4.

44 Herzog, *Living History,* 387.

45 Ibid., 386–7; *JPost International Edition,* 15 August 1998.

46 Mordechai Waxman, "The Dialogue, Touching New Bases?" in Croner, *More Stepping Stones,* 24–32.

47 Weigel, *Witness to Hope,* 711.

48 *MED* (January 1999). Among those who maintain this aggressive posture is Pierre Mualem, the Greek Catholic Archbishop of Akko.

49 Weigel, *Witness to Hope,* 824–6.

50 Haim Shapiro, and Lisa Palmieri-Billig, "Dismay at Vatican Apology," *JPost International Edition,* 28 March 1998.

51 Thomas O'Dwyer, "Just a Little Confession," *JPost International Edition,* 28 March 1998.

52 *Christians and Israel* 5, no. 3 (Summer, 1996).

53 These two paragraphs draw on a number of news reports during the week beginning 13 March 2000, including *NYT, JPost,* and on the internet, *Arutz7* and the newsletters *ICEJ* and Bridges for Peace.

54 *Arutz7,* 16 February, 2000.

55 These two paragraphs draw on a number of news reports during the period 18–27 March 2000, including *Time, NYT, JPost,* and on the internet newsletters of *Arutz7,* and the *ICEJ* and Bridges for Peace Newsletters. Also, Weigel, "With John Paul in the Holy Land."

CHAPTER SEVEN

1 This is the subject of chapters 10 through 12 of my book, *The Politics of Christian Zionism, 1891–1948*.

2 Ibid., 123–43, 168, 171.

3 H.M. Sachar, *A History of the Jews in America*, 875.

4 For example, a *NYT* poll taken early in 1998 showed that fifty-seven percent of the American people had a "generally favourable" opinion of Israel, and that fifty-eight percent said that they sympathized with Israel over the Palestinians. Almost half said that they see Israel as a "special place." Reported by *Arutz*7, 27 April 1998. Detailed examination of attitudes can be found in Sheffer, ed., *US-Israeli Relations at the Crossroads*, especially 109–127, and 147–169.

5 Hanson, *A Gentile with the Heart of a Jew*, 74.

6 Ibid., 112–13.

7 Boyer, *When Time Shall Be No More*, 188. See "Prophets in Jerusalem," *Newsweek*, 28 June 1971, 62.

8 Quoted in Hanson, *A Gentile with the Heart of a Jew*, 294–5.

9 Ibid., 301.

10 Quoted in ibid., 344–7.

11 Quoted in ibid., 352.

12 This section is based on a discussion with Clarence Wagner, Jr, Jerusalem, 18 May 1998, and other correspondence with him, and on literature of Bridges for Peace, including files of *Dispatch from Jerusalem, Update, Israel Teaching Letter, Bridges for Peace Teaching Series. Special Edition* (1995), promotional video, "*For Such a Time as This*," 1998, and the pilot video for the television series *Jerusalem Mosaic*, 1997.

13 Halevi, "Squeezed Out," 16.

14 This section is based on discussion and correspondence with Stan Goodenough, until recently the editor of *Middle East Digest*, the ICEJ newsletter; on several personal visits to ICEJ offices; and on ICEJ literature, especially: *Christians and Israel: Essays on Biblical Zionism and Islamic Fundamentalism* ; *Christian Zionism and Its Biblical Basis* ; *The Ministry of the International Christian Embassy Jerusalem; A Word from Jerusalem* (Newsletter); *Middle East Intelligence Digest* (later re-named *Middle East Digest*), a monthly commentary on news of Israel and Middle East). Among the few published sources of worth are: Ariel, "A Christian Fundamentalist Vision," and Melman and Raviv, *Friends in Deed*, 349–61.

15 In 1984 a resolution was introduced into the US House of Representatives urging the government to move its embassy back to Jerusalem, but this was rejected by the Reagan government. In November 1995 a Resolution was passed by Congress ordering the transfer of the US embassy back to Jerusalem. In late July 1999, eighty-four members of the US Senate sent a

letter to President Clinton expressing their "deep disappointment" that he was continuing to exercise the national security waiver provisions in the act in order to stall the move (*Arutz7*, 30 July 1999).

16 Inspiration for this mission was drawn from many passages where the prophets speak of God's intention to bring the scattered people of Israel back from "the North," which has always been taken as the furthest of the four corners of the world. For instance, Jeremiah 31:6, "I [God] will say to the North, 'Give up … my sons … and my daughters"; and Isaiah 49:22, "Behold I will lift up mine hand to the Gentiles, and set up my standard to the people; and they shall bring thy sons in their arms, and thy daughters shall be carried upon their shoulders."

17 ICEJ special newsletter: "Soviet Jewry Newsletter," Autumn 1997.

18 Ariel, "A Christian Fundamentalist Vision."

19 Reprinted in full in MECC, *What Is Western Fundamentalist Christian Zionism?*

20 "It shall be that you will divide it by lot as an inheritance for yourselves, and for the strangers who sojourn among you and who bear children among you. They shall be to you as native-born among the children of Israel; they shall have an inheritance with you among the tribes of Israel." Declaration of the Second International Christian Zionist Congress, Jerusalem, 10–15 April 1988. Reprinted in full in MECC, *What Is Western Fundamentalist Christian Zionism?*

21 *A Word from Jerusalem* (ICEJ newsletter), January/February, 1998.

22 For economy of space, I focus on ICEJ sources, while noting that the same emphases are to be found in Bridges for Peace literature. For example, see the items in the first section of the *Bridges For Peace Teaching Series* ("Israel and the Jewish People").

23 See his essay "Christian Zionism," in ICEJ, *Christian Zionism and Its Biblical Basis.*

24 ICEJ, *Christian Zionism and Its Biblical Basis*, 8.

25 I am indebted to Stan Goodenough for help on this point. He writes: "We do not dispute the biblical foretelling of the moment when we will be caught up to meet Y'shua in the air.… [But,] we do not subscribe to the traditional version of this snatching away, which holds that Israel will be left to go through tribulation while we enjoy the Wedding Feast of the Lamb up in the heavenlies." (Stan Goodenough to the author, 9 November 1998.)

26 From my notes of Malcolm Hedding's lecture, Jerusalem, 13 May 1998, entitled, "The Triumph of Israel."

27 ICEJ, *Christian Zionism and Its Biblical Basis*, 10.

28 Berkhof, "The Link between the People of Israel and the Land," 17.

29 Van der Hoeven's theological and philosophical perspectives are developed in his book *Babylon or Jerusalem?*

30 In May 1998, unhappiness with van der Hoeven's leadership led the board to insist on his resignation. A few months later, van der Hoeven and others announced the formation of the "International Christian Zionist Center."

31 This section is based in part on literature published by Christian Friends of Israel, and some correspondence with the US East Coast office in Charlotte, NC.

32 Hannelle Sorensen, director of East Coast office, to the author, 15 October 1998.

33 The story is told by its first executive director in Rottenberg, *The Turbulent Triangle*, 15 and 26–8.

34 The mailing address is National Christian Leadership conference for Israel, 134 East 39th Street, New York, NY, 10016.

35 The ad was signed by Rt Rev. John H. Burt, NCLCI president (Episcopalian); vice presidents Rev. Edward H. Flannery (RC), Mrs Nancy G. Carroll (Evangelical Covenant), James H. Doherty (RC), Rev. Dr William H. Harter, secretary treasurer (Presbyterian), Franklin Littell (president emeritus) David Lewis, chairman of the board of directors (Assemblies of God), and Sister Rose Thering, the executive director (RC).

36 *JPost*, 15 January 1992.

37 Weber, "How Evangelicals Became Israel's Best Friend," 39–49. The reference to Voices United for Israel is on 48–9. See also *Christians and Israel* 5, no. 2 (Spring 1996): n.p.

38 Ibid.

39 Weber, "How Evangelicals Became Israel's Best Friend," 48.

40 Wagner, *Anxious for Armageddon*, 108. Thorough discussions of AIPAC are to be found, *passim*, in Blitzer, *Between Washington and Jerusalem* ; Goldberg, *Jewish Power* ; Melman and Raviv, *Friends In Deed;* Tivna, *The Lobby*.

41 "Christian Zionists," *JPost*, 24 March, 1992.

42 This organization has headquarters in Darmstadt, Germany, and offices in the US and Canada. Among the books that it publishes or promotes are: Sister Pista, *The Guilt of Christianity;* Michael L. Brown, *Our Hands Are Stained With Blood: The Tragic Story of the "Church" and the Jewish People,* Shippensburg, PA: Destiny Image, 1992; Schlink, *Israel, My Chosen People.* See also "The Evangelical Sisterhood of Mary: A German Confession," *Christians and Israel* 5, no. 3 (Summer 1996): n.p.

43 Quoted in "Wolves in Sheep's Clothing."

44 Quoted in Nellhouse, "Go Tell it on the Mountain."

45 I noted in chapter 2 the collaboration of the Roman Catholic church in certain deliberative proceedings of the WCC. MECC takes this process a step further, as Roman Catholic churches are full members.

46 Founding Assembly of the MECC, May 1974. See MECC, *The MECC: An Introduction*.

47 "Background on MECC's Mandate and Organization,"
    MECC/VI/GA/GS/2.

48 Ibid.

49 MECC/1994/VI/GA/GA6, page 3

50 MECC/1994/VVI/GA/GS9, p. 30

51 MECC/1994/VI/GA/GS 9, pp. 41–43, emphasis added.

52 MECC, *What Is Western Fundamentalist Christian Zionism?*, 12–13, emphasis added.

53 MECC/1994//VI/GA/GS/9, 44. Emphasis added.

54 Ibid., 29–30.

55 Conversation with Geries Khoury, Bethlehem, November 1995.

56 Burge, *Who Are God's People in the Middle East?*, 127–8.

57 Ibid., 132.

58 Ibid., 135–6

59 Ibid., 149

60 Ibid., 154.

61 Wagner, *Anxious for Armageddon*, 80.

62 Ibid., 84.

63 Ibid., 158.

64 Ateek, "An Arab-Israeli's Theological Reflections," 180.

65 Ibid.

66 Wagner, *Anxious for Armaggedon*, 71–2.

67 *Sojourners* magazine (March 1997), cited by David Rausch in "Evangelical Protestant Americans."

68 Reprinted as Appendix E in Wagner, *Anxious for Armaggedon*, 215–7.

69 Burge, *Who Are God's People?*, 64–5.

70 Ibid., 65, 67, 119–20.

71 Quoted in Wagner, *Anxious for Armaggedon*, 80–4.

72 Ibid., 104.

73 Quoted in ibid., 70. Wagner draws on the Jerusalem newspaper *Al Fahr* for accusations of anti-Arab spirit among the ICEJ's leading lights (106–7, and 233n.20). Wagner does not note that Willem van der Hoeven, whom he singles out for his anti-Arab spirit, was married to Widad, a Lebanese Arab woman, the mother of his two children, until she died a few years ago.

74 Ibid., 105.

75 Ibid., 109.

76 Burge, *Who Are God's People?*, 157.

77 Wagner, *Anxious for Armaggedon*, 187.

CHAPTER EIGHT

1 Croner, ed., *Stepping Stones*, 76.

2 Rottenberg, *The Turbulent Triangle*, 12.

3 Quoted in ibid., 50.

4 Ibid., 13–14.

5 Ibid, 53–4.

6 Ibid., 61–2.

7 Vermaat, "The World Council of Churches." Vermaat notes in particular the WCC publication *Human Rights in the West Bank*, WCC Background Information, 1983, no. 1, WCC, Geneva.

8 See the report of Section 5: "Structures of Injustice and Struggles for Liberation," the Report of Policy Reference Committee III: "The Middle East."

9 In Paton, *Breaking Barriers*, 97–119, 162–5.

10 *Ecumenical News International Service* internet newsletter, 18 June 1996.

11 The Interim Agreement (Oslo 2) of 28 September 1995 (Article 22) states that Israel and the PA "shall seek to foster mutual understanding and tolerance and shall accordingly abstain from incitement, including hostile propaganda, against each other and, without derogation from the principle of freedom of expression, shall take legal measures to prevent such incitement by any organizations, groups or individuals within their jurisdiction."

12 Files of *JPost*, December 1980 and January 1981, and Tivnan, *The Lobby*, 116.

13 Csillag, "Report."

14 Nomi Winkler, "Letter to the Editor," *Canadian Jewish News*, 23 November 1993 (reprinted and distributed by Canadian Friends of ICEJ).

15 Tivnan, *The Lobby*, 181–2.

16 This draws principally upon Abrams, *Faith or Fear*, 1–10, which in turn draws on the National Jewish Population Study of 1990 and other surveys.

17 Catechism, paragraph 839.

18 Cited by Abrams, *Faith or Fear*, 41.

19 Ibid., 61.

20 Ibid., 59–60.

21 Laurie Goldstein, "Falwell to Mobilize Support for Israel." *NYT*, 21 January 1998.

22 One particularly zealous and imaginative religious teacher in Israel called on Israelis to think of Miss Lewinsky in the light of Esther 4:14 and to bless her name.

23 Weber, "How Evangelicals Became Israel's Best Friends," 39 and 49.

24 The *New York Times* reported that President Clinton was angered to hear of Netanyahu's meeting with Falwell, who "has used his television program to sell a widely-discredited videotape that accuses the President of peddling drugs and being involved in murders of political opponents in Arkansas. But in continuing to sell the tape, Mr Falwell has lost credi-

bility even with some evangelicals" (Goldstein, "Falwell to Mobilize Support For Israel").

25 Ibid.

26 Abrams, *Faith or Fear*, 64–5.

27 Ibid., 69–70.

28 Ibid., 72–3.

29 Decter, "The ADL vs, the 'Religious Right,'" and letters to the editor on her article in *Commentary* 99 (January 1995): 10–14.

30 Egal Feldman, Letter to the Editor, *Commentary* 99 (January 1995): 10–14.

31 Abrams, *Faith or Fear*, 70, 75–6.

32 Ibid., 56.

33 Ariel, "Born Again," and "A Christian Fundamentalist Vision."

34 Rausch, *Communities in Conflict*, quoted in Abrams, *Faith or Fear*, 69. This generalization is borne out in Ross, *So It Was True*.

35 Abrams, *Faith or Fear*, 69.

36 Ibid., 60–1.

Bibliography

PERIODICALS, JOURNALS, NEWSLETTERS

Al-Liqa' Journal and *Al Liqa' Newsletter.* Published by Centre for Religious and Heritage Studies in the Holy Land, Bethlehem.

Arutz7/ Arutz Sheva Newsletter. Daily Internet newsletter of *Arutz Sheva* (Channel7), Israel.

Associated Christian Press Bulletin. Published by Christian Information Centre, Jerusalem.

Christian Century. Chicago

Christian Friends of Israel Newsletter. Monthly newsletter of Christian Friends of Israel, Charlotte, NC

Christian News From Israel. Published by Ministry of Religious Affairs, Israel, Jerusalem.

Christians and Israel. Published by the Association of Christians and Jews in Israel, Jerusalem.

Christianity and Crisis. New York.

Christianity Today. Carol Stream, Illinois.

Commonweal. New York.

Commentary. New York.

Dispatch from Jerusalem, Israel Teaching Letter, and *Update.* Published by Bridges for Peace, Jerusalem.

First Things. New York.

Israel News Digest. Newsletter of Christian Friends of Israel. Jerusalem.

Jerusalem Post. Jerusalem.

Jerusalem Report. Jerusalem.

Jerusalem Times. Independent Palestinian weekly. Jerusalem.

The Link. Published by American Friends of the Middle East, New York.

MECC News Report. Published by Middle East Council of Churches, Limassol, Cyprus.

Middle East Intelligence Digest. Renamed *Middle East Digest*. Published by International Christian Embassy Jerusalem.

New York Times.

Newsweek. New York.

Palestine Report. Published by Jerusalem Media and Communication Center, Jerusalem.

Time. New York.

A Word from Jerusalem. Published by International Christian Embassy Jerusalem.

BOOKS AND MAJOR ARTICLES

Abbad, Abd Rahman, "The Current Situation: A Muslim Perspective," in Williamson. *The Holy Land in Monotheistic Faiths*, edited by Roger Williamson. Uppsala: Life and Peace Institute, 1992.

Abrams, Elliott. *Faith or Fear: How Jews Can Survive in Christian America*. New York: Free Press, 1997.

Abu-Amar, Ziad. *Islamic Fundamentalism in the West Bank and Gaza*. Bloomington: Indiana University Press, 1994.

Aburish, Said K. *Arafat: From Defender to Dictator*. London: Bloomsbury, 1998.

Aghazarian, Albert, Bernard Sabella and Afif Safieh. *Christian Voices from The Holy Land: Out of Jerusalem?* Jerusalem: Palestinian General Delegation to the United Kingdom Office of Representation of the PLO to the Holy See, December 1997.

Ariel, Yaakov. "Born Again in a Land of Paradox: Christian Fundamentalists in Israel." *Faith and History* 28, no.2 (Summer 1996): 35–49.

– "American Fundamentalists and the Emergence of a Jewish State." In Jay P. Dolan, and James P. Wind. *New Dimensions in American Religious History*, 288–309. Grand Rapids: Eerdmans. 1993.

– "A Christian Fundamentalist Vision of the Middle East: Jan Willem van der Hoeven and the International Christian Embassy." In R. Scott Appleby. *Spokesmen for the Despised: Fundamentalist Leaders of the Middle East*, 363–97. Chicago: University of Chicago Press, 1996.

– "Protestant Attitudes to Jews and Judaism During the last Fifty Years." In *Terms of Survival: The Jewish World Since 1945*, edited by Robert S. Wistrich. London: Routledge, 1995.

– *Evangelizing the Chosen People: Missions to the Jews in America, 1880–2000*. Chapel Hill: University of North Carolina Press, 2000.

Ashi, Arafat El. *A Brief History of Palestine*. N.p.: Muslim World League Canada Office, n.d.

Ateek, Naim. "An Arab-Israeli's Theological Reflections on the State of Israel After 40 Years." *People, Land and State of Israel: Jewish and Christian Perspectives.* Vol. 22/23 of the journal *Immanuel.* Jerusalem: Ecumenical Theological Research Fraternity in Israel, 1989.

– *Justice and Only Justice: A Palestinian Theology of Liberation.* Maryknoll, NY: Orbis, 1989.

Ateek, Naim, Marc H. Ellis, Rosemary Reuther. *Faith and the Intifada: Palestinian Christian Voices.* Maryknoll, NY: Orbis, 1992.

Atiya, A.S. *A History of Eastern Christianity.* London: Methuen, 1968.

Awan, Mahmud. "The Faith Community and World Order in the Perspective of Islam." In al-Faruqi, Isma'il Raji, (ed.). *Trialogue of the Abrahamic Faiths,* edited by Isma'il Raji al-Faruqi. 3d ed. Alexandria, VA: Al Sadawi Publications/United Arab Bureau, 1991.

Badawi, Jamal. *Jesus (Peace be upon him) in the Qur'an and the Bible: An Outline.* Pamphlet. Ottawa: Islamic Information Foundation of Canada.

Ball, George W., and Douglas Ball. *The Passionate Attachment: America's Involvement With Israel, 1947 to the Present.* New York: Norton, 1992.

Banki, Judith H. *Anti-American Influence in American Churches: A Background Report.* Pamphlet. New York: Interreligious Affairs Department, American Jewish Committee, Institute of Human Relations, 1979.

– *Christian Responses to Yom Kippur War.* Pamphlet. New York: Interreligious Affairs Department, American Jewish Committee, n.d.

– *Christian Reactions to the Middle East Crisis [of 1967]: A New Agenda for Interreligious Dialogue.* Pamphlet. New York: American Jewish Committee, November 1967.

Bar-Ilan, David. "If This Be Peace." *Commentary* (February 1995): 30–5.

Bat Ye'or. *Dhimmi Peoples: Oppressed Nations.* Pamphlet. Geneva: Editions de l'Avenir, 1978.

– *The Dhimmi: Jews and Christians Under Islam.* London: Associated University Presses, 1985.

– "Judeophobia and Christophobia in the Arab World." A lecture delivered at an International Conference on "Education Toward Tolerance: The Case of Resurgent Antisemitism," organized by UNESCO and the Simon Weisenthal Centre, 23 June 1992.

– *The Decline of Eastern Christianity under Islam: From Jihad to Dhimmitude.* Translation from the French. London: Associated University Presses, 1996.

Becker, Julian. *The PLO: The Rise and Fall of the Palestine Liberation Organization.* London: Wiedenfeld and Nicolson, 1984.

Bell, J. Bowyer. *The Myth of the Guerrila: Revolutionary Theory and Malpractice.* New York: Knopf, 1971.

Belli, Humberto. *Breaking Faith: The Sandanista Revolution and its Impact on Freedom and Christian Faith in Nicaragua.* Westchester, IL: Crossways/Puebla Institute, 1985.

Bennett, John C. "A Response to Rabbi Bricker," *Christianity and Crisis* 27 (18 September 1967): 204–5.

Bennett, Ramon. *Philistine: The Great Deception.* Jerusalem: Arm of Salvation, 1995.

Bercuson, David. *Canada and the Birth of Israel.* Toronto: University of Toronto Press, 1985.

Bernstein, Carl, and Marco Politi. *His Holiness: John Paul II and the Hidden History of Our Time.* New York: Doubleday, 1996.

Bernstein, Richard. "Evangelicals Strengthening Bonds with Jews." *New York Times,* 6 February 1983.

Betts, Robert Brenton. *Christians in the Arab East: A Political Study.* London: SPCK, 1979.

Billingsley, K.L. *From Mainline to Sideline: The Social Witness of the National Council of Churches.* Lanham, MD: University Press of America/Ethics and Public Policy Center, 1990.

Blitzer, Wolf. *Between Washington and Jerusalem: A Reporter's Notebook.* New York: Oxford University Press, 1985.

Bloomfield, Arthur E. *The End of Days: the Prophecies of Daniel Explained.* Minneapolis: Bethany, 1961.

Bombay, Cal R. *Let My People Go!* Sistera, OR: Multnomah, 1998.

Boyer, Paul. *When Time Shall Be No More.* New York: Harvard University Press, 1992.

Brickner, Balfour. "No Ease in Zion to Us: Christian-Jewish Relations after the Arab-Israeli War." *Christianity and Crisis* 27 (18 September 1967): 200–4.

Bridges for Peace Teaching Series. Special Edition. Jerusalem: Bridges for Peace, 1995.

Brinkley, Douglas. *The Unfinished Presidency: Jimmy Carter's Journey Beyond the White House.* New York: Viking, 1999.

Burge, Gary M. *Who Are God's People in the Middle East? What Christians Are Being Told about Israel and the Palestinians.* Grand Rapids, MI: Zondervan, 1993.

Cambridge Encyclopedia of the Middle East and North Africa. Edited by Mostyn, Trevor. New York: Cambridge University Press, 1988.

Carter, Jimmy. *The Blood of Abraham.* New York: Houghton, Mifflin, 1985.

– *Keeping Faith: Memoirs of a President.* New York: Bantam, 1982.

Catechism of the Church. Toronto: Canadian Council of Catholic Bishops. 1994.

Chomsky, Noam. *The Fateful Triangle: The United States, Israel, and the Palestinians.* Boston: South End Press, 1983.

Cockburn, Alexander, and Leslie Cockburn. *Dangerous Liaison: The Inside Story of the US-Israel Relationship.* New York: HarperCollins, 1991.

Coffin, H.S. "Perils to America in the New Jewish State." *Christianity and Crisis* 21 (February 1949): 9–10.

Colbi, Saul P. *Christianity in the Holy Land.* Tel Aviv: Am Hessefer, 1969.

– *A History of the Christian Presence in the Holy Land.* Lanham, MD: University Press of America, 1988.

Cragg, Kenneth. *Muhammad and the Christian.* Oxford: Oneworld, 1999.

Crisis in the Holy Land: The Christian Exodus. Pamphlet. Washington, DC: The Holy Land Foundation, n.d. (c. 1995.)

Croner, Helga, ed. *Stepping Stones to Further Jewish-Christian Relations : An Unabridged Collection of Christian Documents.* London and New York: Stimulus Books, 1977.

– *More Stepping Stones to Jewish-Christian Relations.* London and New York: Stimulus Books, 1985.

Decter, Midge. "The ADL vs. the 'Religious Right.'" *Commentary* 98 (September 1994): 45–7.

Drinan, Robert. *Honor the Promise: America's Commitment to Israel.* Garden City: Doubleday, 1977.

Duvernoy, Claude. *Controversy of Zion.* Green Forest, AR: New Leaf Press, 1987.

Dwyer, Kevin. *Arab Voices: The Human Rights Debate in the Middle East.* Berkeley: University of California Press, 1991.

Eben, Abba. *An Autobiography.* New York: Random House, 1977.

– *Personal Witness.* New York: Putnam's, 1992.

Eckhardt, A. Roy *Elder and Younger Brothers.* New York: Scribner's, 1967.

Eckhardt, A. Roy and Alice Eckhardt. "Again, Silence in the Churches." *Christian Century* 84, Part 1 (26 July 1967): 970–3; Part 2 (2 August 1967): 992–5.

Ecumenical Theological Research Fraternity in Israel. *People, Land, and State of Israel: Jewish and Christian Perspectives.* Vols 22 and 23 of *Immanuel.* Jerusalem: Ecumenical Theological Research Fraternity in Israel, 1989.

Ellisen, Stanley A. *Who Owns the Land?.* Portland, OR: Multnomah. 1991.

Encyclopedia of Zionism and Israel. New York: Herzl Press, 1971.

Epp, Theodore H. *The Times of the Gentiles.* Lincoln, NE: Back to the Bible, 1969.

Esposito, John L. *The Islamic Threat: Myth or Reality?* New York: Oxford University Press, 1995.

al-Faruqi, Isma'il Raji, ed. *Trialogue of the Abrahamic Faiths.* 3d ed. Alexandria, VA: Al Sadawi Publications/United Arab Bureau, 1991.

Feinberg, Charles L. *Millennialism: The Two Major Views.* 3d enlarged ed. Chicago: Moody Press, 1982.

Feldman, Egal. "Reinhold Niebuhr and the Jews." *Jewish Social Studies* 46 (Summer-Fall 1984.): n.p.

Field, Michael. *Inside the Arab World.* Cambridge, MA: Harvard University Press, 1994.

Findley, Paul. *They Dare to Speak Out: People and Institutions Confront Israel's Lobby.* Chicago: Lawrence Hall Books, 1989.

– *Deliberate Deceptions: Facing the Facts about the US–Israel Relationship.* Brooklyn: Lawrence Hill Books, 1993.

Firestone, Reuven. *Jihad: The Origins of the Holy War in Islam.* New York: Oxford University Press, 1999.

Fishman, Hertzl. *American Protestantism and a Jewish State.* Detroit: Wayne State University Press, 1973.

Flint, Roy K., Peter W. Kozumplick, and Thomas J. Waraska. *The Arab-Israeli Wars, the Chinese Civil War, and the Korean War.* Wayne, NJ: Avery Publishing Group and West Point Military Academy, Department of History, 1971.

Fox, Richard W. *Reinhold Niebuhr: A Biography.* New York: Harper, 1987.

Gannon, Robert. *The Cardinal Spellman Story.* New York: Scribner's, 1962.

Geyer, Alan. "Christians and 'The Peace of Jerusalem." *Christianity and Crisis* 15 (10 July 1967): 160–4.

Gildersleeve, Virginia. *Many a Good Crusade: Memoirs.* New York: Macmillan, 1954.

Gillquist, Peter. *Metropolitan Philip: His Life and His Dreams* Nashville: Thomas Nelson, 1991.

Goldberg, J.J. *Jewish Power: Inside the American Jewish Establishment.* New York: Addison-Wesley, 1996.

Grose, Peter. *Israel in the Mind of America.* New York: Schocken, 1984.

Gould, Allan, ed. *What Did They Think of the Jews?"* Toronto: Stewart House, 1991.

Grabill, Joseph L. *Protestant Diplomacy and the New East.* Minneapolis: University of Minnesota Press, 1971.

Graham, Billy. *Approaching Hoofbeats.* Waco, TX: Word, 1983.

Guillaume, Alfred. *Islam.* 2d rev. ed. 1956, London: Cassell, 1963.

Halevi, Yossi Klein. "Squeezed Out." *Jerusalem Report* 10 July 1997, 14 and 19.

Hanania, Agnes D. "Churches of the Holy Land: Obligations and Expectations." In *Christians in the Holy Land,* edited by Michael Prior and William Taylor, 205–16. London: World of Islam Festival Trust, 1994.

Handy, Robert T. "American and the Holy Land: Perspectives and Prospectives." in Davis, Moshe (ed.) *With Eyes Toward Zion,* edited by Moshe Davis, 34–56. New York: Arno, 1977.

– "Zion In American Christian Movements." In Moshe Davis. *Israel: Its Role in Civilization,* 284–97. New York: Harper, 1956.

Hanson, Calvin B. *A Gentile with the Heart of a Jew: G. Douglas Young.* Nyack, NY: Parson, 1979.

Harkabi, Y. *Arab Attitudes to Israel.* Jerusalem: Keter, 1972.

Henningsson, Jan. "Contemporary Understandings of Human Rights in Islam" *Al-Liqa' Journal* 5 (July 1995): 27–54.

Henry, Marilyn. "How Pious Was Pius XII?" *Jerusalem Post,* 3 October 1999.

Hero, Alfred O. *American Religious Groups View Foreign Policy.* Durham, NC: Duke University Press, 1973.

Herzl, Theodor. *The Jewish State: An Attempt at a Modern Solution of the Jewish Question.* [1896] London: H. Pordes, 1972.

– *The Complete Diaries of Theodor Herzl*. Edited by Raphael Patai. Translated by Harry Zohn. 5 vols. New York: Herzl Press, 1960.

Herzog, Chaim. *Living History: A Memoir* New York: Pantheon, 1996.

Heschel, Abraham Joseph. *Israel: An Echo of Eternity*. New York: Farrar, Straus and Giroux, 1969.

Hoade, Eugene. *Guide to the Holy Land*. 10th ed. Jerusalem: Franciscan Press, 1979.

Holy Koran. Translated with notes by N.J. Dawood, Harmondsworth: Penguin Books, 1990.

Holy Land in the Monotheistic Faiths. Uppsala: Life and Peace Institute, December 1992.

Holy Land Foundation. *Crisis in the Holy Land*. Pamphlet. Washington, DC: Holy Land Foundation, nd. (c. 1995).

Holy Qur'an. Translation and commentary by A. Yusuf Ali. Brentwood, MD: Amana Corp., 1983.

Hourani, Albert. *A History of the Arab Peoples*. Cambridge, MA: Harvard University Press, 1991.

– "Christians in Muslim Societies." In *Cambridge Encyclopedia of the Middle East and North Africa*, edited by Trevor Mostyn, 190–5. New York: Cambridge University Press, 1988.

Hudson, Darril. *The World Council of Churches in International Affairs*. Leighton Buzzard, UK: Faith Press/Royal Institute of International Affairs. 1977.

Ibrahim, Youssef M. "Palestinian Religious Militants: Why their Ranks Are Growing." *New York Times*, 8 November 1994.

– "Islam's Fury Falls on Egypt's Christians." *New York Times*, 15 March 1993.

International Christian Embassy Jerusalem. *Christians and Israel: Essays on Biblical Zionism and Islamic Fundamentalism*. Jerusalem: International Christian Embassy Jerusalem, 1996.

– *Christian Zionism and Its Biblical Basis*. Jerusalem: International Christian Embassy Jerusalem, 1988.

– *The Ministry of the International Christian Embassy Jerusalem*. Jerusalem: International Christian Embassy Jerusalem, 1992.

Irani, George Emile. *The Papacy and the Middle East: The Role of the Holy See in the Arab-Israeli Conflict*. Notre Dame, IN: University of Notre Dame Press, 1986.

John Paul II, Pope. *Crossing the Threshold of Hope*. Toronto: Knopf, 1994.

Johnson, Donald Bruce, ed. *National Party Platforms*. 2 vols. Urbana, IL: University of Illinois Press, 1978.

Johnson, Paul. *A History of the Jews*. New York: Harper, 1987.

Katz, Samuel. *Battleground: Fact and Fantasy in Palestine*. New York: Bantam, 1977.

Khalidi, Rashid. *Palestinian Identity*. New York: Columbia University Press, 1996.

Khoury, Geries. "Churches and Culture in Palestine: An Historical Overview"; "Contours of Palestinian Contextualized Theology." Both in *The Holy Land in the Monotheistic Faiths*, edited by Roger Wiliamson. Uppsala: Life and Peace Institute, December 1992.

Klaidman, David, and Matt Rees. "Something Rotten in Palestine." *Newsweek* (29 May 2000): 36–8.

Kobler, Franz. *The Vision Was There: A History of the British Movement for the Restoration of the Jews to Palestine*. London: World Jewish Congress/Lincolns-Praeger, 1956.

Koltermann, Ulrike. "Church Heads Accused of Spearheading Anti-Israeli Front." *Jerusalem Times*, 13 June 13 1997.

Kreutz, Andrej. *Vatican Policy on the Palestinian-Israeli Conflict: The Struggle for the Holy Land*. New York: Greenwood, 1990.

Kurtzman, Dan. *Ben-Gurion: Prophet of Fire*. New York: Bantam Books, 1981.

LaHaye, Tim. *The Beginning of the End*. Wheaton, IL: Tyndale, 1972.

Laqueur, Walter. *A History of Zionism*. New York: Schocken, 1989.

Lapide, Pinchas. *The Last Three Popes and the Jews*. London: Souvenir, 1967.

LAW/Palestinian Society for the Protection of Human Rights and the Environment. *The Myth of Christian Persecution by the Palestinian Authority*. Jerusalem: LAW/The Palestinian Society for the Protection of Human Rights and the Environment, May 1998.

Lefever, Ernest W. *Amsterdam to Nairobi: The World Council of Churches and the Third World*. Washington, DC: Georgetown University/Ethics and Public Policy Center, 1979.

– *Nairobi to Vancouver: The World Council of Churches and the World* Washington, DC: Georgetown University/Ethics and Public Policy Center, 1987.

Lewis, Bernard. "The Palestinians and the PLO: An Historical Approach." *Commentary* 59 (January 1975): 32-48.

– *The World of Islam: Faith, People, Culture*. London: Thames, 1975.

– "The Return of Islam." *Commentary* 60 (January 1976): n.p.

– *The Arabs in History*. 4th rev. ed. London: Hutchinson, 1976.

– *Islam and the West*. New York: Oxford University Press, 1993.

– *The Middle East*. London: Phoenix, 1995.

Lewis, David Allen, ed., *Magog 1982-Cancelled*. Harrison, AR: New Leaf Press, 1982.

Lindsell, Harold. *The Gathering Storm: World Events and the Return of Christ*. Wheaton: Tyndale, 1971.

Lindsey, Hal. *The Late Great Planet Earth*. New York: Bantam, 1977.

– *The Rapture*. New York: Bantam, 1983.

Littman, David, and Bat Ye'or. "Protected Peoples Under Islam." Pamphlet. Geneva: Centre d'Information et de Documentation sur le Moyen-Orient, 1976.

Lowdermilk, Walter. *Palestine: Land of Promise.* New York: Harper, 1944.

Malachy, Yona. *American Fundamentalism and Israel.* Jerusalem: Hebrew University Press, 1978.

Malik, Habib C. "Christians in the Land Called Holy." *First Things,* no. 89 (January 1999): 11-12.

Man's Disorder and God's Design: The Amsterdam Assembly Series. New York: Harper/World Council of Churches, 1948.

Marshall, Caroline T. "Some Christian Responses to Jewish and Palestinian Nationalism." *Fides et Historia,* 17, no. 2 (Summer 1985): 53-68.

Manuel, Frank E. *The Realities of American-Palestine Relations.* Washington, DC: Public Affairs Press, 1949.

Maritain, Jacques. "The Mystery of Israel," In *The Social and Political Philsophy of Jacques Maritain,* edited by J.W. Evans and L.R. Ward, 220-41. London: Geoffrey Bles, 1956.

Marshall, Paul. *Their Blood Cries Out.* Dallas: Word, 1997.

Martin, William. *A Prophet with Honor: The Billy Graham Story.* New York: Morrow, 1991.

Mathes, Richard. "Latin Christians in Jerusalem." *Israel Colloquium Bulletin.* Ramat Hasharon, Israel. Autumn 1996.

Mawdudi, Sayyid Abul a'la. *Towards Understanding Islam.* Translated and edited by Khurshid Ahmad. Lahore: Islamic Foundation, 1988.

McLeod, N. Bruce. "Isaac and Ishmael: 1967." *Christian Century* 84 (26 July 1967): 959-61.

Meier, Andreas. "Conference on Palestinian-Israeli Context." *Al-Liqa' Journal* 1 (May 1992): 65-78.

Meir, Golda. *My Life.* New York: Putnam's, 1975.

Melman, Yossi, and Dan Raviv. *Friends in Deed: Inside the US-Israel Alliance.* New York: Hyperion, 1994.

Merkley, Paul C. *Reinhold Niebuhr: A Political Account.* Montreal: McGill-Queen's University Press, 1974.

– *The Politics of Christian Zionism, 1891-1948.* London: Frank Cass, 1998.

Middle East Council of Churches. *The MECC: An Introduction to the Middle East Council of Churches.* Limassol, Cyprus: Middle East Council of Churches, 1995.

– *What Is Western Fundamentalist Christian Zionism?* Limassol, Cyprus: Middle East Council of Churches, 1988.

Miller, Judith. *God Has Ninety-Nine Names: Reporting from a Militant Middle East.* New York: Simon and Schuster, 1996.

Minerbi, Sergio I. *The Vatican and Zionism.* New York: Oxford University Press. 1990.

Moffett, Samuel Hugh. *A History of Christianity in Asia.* Vol. 1: *Beginnings to 1500.* San Francisco: HarperSanFrancisco, 1992.

Morey, Robert. *The Islamic Invasion: Confronting the World's Fastest Growing Religion.* Eugene, OR: Harvest House, 1992.

Morgan, Timothy. "Jerusalem's Living Stones: Will Christianity's Oldest Church Survive the Peace Process? *Christianity Today* 40 (20 May 1996): 58-62.

Morris, Benny. *Righteous Victims: A History of the Zionist-Arab Conflict, 1881-1999.* New York: Knopf, 1999.

Mouly, Ruth W. *US-Arab Relations: The Evangelical Dimension.* New York: National Council on US-Arab Relations/Americans for Middle East Understanding, 1985.

Munayer, Salim J. *Ministry of Reconciliation: In the Footsteps of Our Father Abraham.* Jerusalem: Musalaha, 1993.

"Muslim-Christian Tensions in the Arab-Israeli Community." Middle East Media and Research Institute Special Dispatch No. 41 (Internet newsletter), 2 August 1999.

Nellhaus, Alvin. "Go Tell It on the Mountain." *Jerusalem Post Magazine,* 9 October 1972.

Nelson, F.B. "Zionism and American Christianity." In *Dictionary of Christianity in America,* edited by Daniel G. Reid. Downers Grove, IL: Intervarsity, 1991.

Newman, David. "Who is a Palestinian?" *Jerusalem Post,* 28 July 1999.

Netanyahu, Benjamin. *A Place among the Nations: Israel and the World.* New York: Bantam, 1993.

Nettler, Ronald L. "Islam and the Minorities: Background to the Arab-Israel Conflict." Pamphlet. Jerusalem: Israel Academic Committee on the Middle East, 1979.

Niebuhr, Reinhold. "Jews After the War." *Nation* 154 (21 February 1942): 214-16; (28 February 1942): 253-5.

– *Essays in Applied Christianity.* New York: Meridian, 1959.

– "Our Stake in the State of Israel." *New Republic* 136, no. 4 (4 February 1957): 9-12.

– "The Situation in the Middle East." *Christianity and Crisis* 17 (15 April 1957): 48-9.

– "David and Goliath." *Christianity and Crisis.* 27 (26 June 1967) 141-2).

Nixon, Richard. *In The Arena.* New York: Simon and Schuster, 1990.

– *Leaders.* New York: Touchstone, 1990.

Norman, Edward. *Christianity and World Order.* New York: Oxford University Press, 1979.

O'Brien, Conor Cruise. *On the Eve of the Millennium.* Concord, ON: Anansi, 1994.

– *The Seige.* New York: Simon & Schuster, 1986.

O'Brien, Darcy. *The Hidden Pope.* New York: Daybreak/Rodale, 1998.

O'Neill, Dan, and Don Wagner. *Peace or Armageddon? The Unfolding Drama of the Middle East Accord.* Grand Rapids: Zondervan, 1993.

Oesterreicher, John M. *Internationalization of Jerusalem.* South Orange, NJ: Seton Hall University, 1971.

Orme, William A. "Succoth in Israel, and Here Come the Evangelicals." *New York Times*, 29 September 1999.

Osband, Linda. *Famous Travellers to the Hold Land*. London: Multimedia/Prion, 1989.

Oxtoby, Willard G. "Christians and the Mideast Crisis." *Christian Century* 84 (26 July 1967): 961-5.

Palestine Academic Society for the Study of International Affairs (PASSIA). *Palestine, Jordan, Israel: Building a Base for Common Scholarship and Understanding in the New Era of the Middle East*. Jerusalem: Palestine Academic Society for the Study of International Affairs. 1997.

– *PASSIA Annual Report, 1997*. Jerusalem: Palestine Academic Society for the Study of International Affairs, 1998.

– *PASSIA Diary, 1998*. Jerusalem: Palestine Academic Society for the Study of International Affairs, 1998.

Parkes, James. *A History of Palestine, From 135 AD to Modern Times*. London: Gollancz, 1949.

– *End of an Exile: Israel, the Jews, and the Gentile World*. Marblehead, MA: Micah Publications, 1982.

Paton, David M., ed. *Breaking Barriers: Nairobi, 1975*. Grand Rapids: Eerdmans, 1976.

Pawel, Ernst. *The Labyrinthe of Exile: A Life of Theodor Herzl*. New York: Farrar, Straus and Giroux, 1989.

Pentecost, Dwight. *Things to Come: A Study in Biblical Eschatology*. Grand Rapids: Zondervan, 1958.

Peres, Shimon. *The New Middle East*. New York: Henry Holt, 1993.

Peters, Joan. *From Time Immemorial: The Origins of the Arab-Jewish Conflict Over Palestine*. London: Michael Joseph, 1985.

Peters, Rudolph. *Islam and Colonialism: The Doctrine of Jihad in Modern History*. The Hague: Mouton, 1979.

Pista, Sister. *The Guilt of Christianity towards the Jewish People*. Booklet. Darmstadt, 1997.

Podhoretz, Norman. "In the Matter of Pat Robertson." *Commentary* 100 (August 1995): 27-32.

Polish, David. "Why American Jews are Disillusioned." *Christian Century* 84 (26 July 1967): 965-7.

Pragai, Michael. *Faith and Fulfilment: Christians and the Return to the Promised Land*. London: Vallentine, Mitchell, 1985.

Prior, Michael, and William Taylor, eds. *Christians in the Holy Land*. London: World of Islam Festival Trust, 1994.

"The Priority of Human Need in the Middle East." Editorial. *Christian Century* (2 August 1967).

Pryce-Jones, David. *The Closed Circle: An Interpretation of the Arabs*. New York: Harper, 1989.

Purcell, Julius. "Fighting on Two Fronts." *Jerusalem Times*, 30 January 1998.

Quandt, William B., Fuad Jabber, and Ann Moslely Lesch. *The Politics of Palestinian Nationalism*. Berkeley: University of California Press, 1973.

Qur'an. See Holy Qur'an.

Ra'uf, Muhammed Abdul. "Judaism and Christianity in the Perspective of Islam." In *Trialogue of the Abrahamic Faiths*, edited by Isma'il Raji al-Faruqi, 23–9. Alexandria, VA: Al Sadawi Publications/United Arab Bureau, 1991.

Ragheb, Maraya. "Christians under Fire." *Jerusalem Times*, 31 October 1997.

Raheb, Mitri. *I Am a Palestinian Christian*. Minneapolis: Augsburg/ Fortress, 1995.

Raphael, Chaim. *Chaim Weizmann: The Revelation of the Letters*. Pamphlet. London: Anglo-Israel Association. 1974.

Rausch, David. "Evangelical Protestant Americans." In *With Eyes Toward Zion*, edited by Moshe Davis, 323–32. New York: Arno, 1977.

Reed, Ralph. *Active Faith*. New York: Free Press, 1996.

Reid, Daniel C., ed. *Dictionary of Christianity in America*. Downer's Grove, IL: Intervarsity, 1991.

– *Religious Life in Israel*. Jerusalem: Keter Publishing House, 1974.

Rolef, Susan Hattis, ed. *Political Dictionary of the State of Israel*. New York: Macmillan, 1987.

Rokach, Lidia. *The Catholic Church and the Question of Palestine*. London: Saqi Books, 1987.

Rodan, Steve, and Mohammed Najib. "At the Boiling Point." *Jerusalem Post Magazine*, 11 October 1997.

Rodinson, Maxime. *Mohammed*. English translation. New York: Pantheon, 1971.

Rose, Norman. *Chaim Weizmann*. New York: Viking, 1986.

Rosenthal, A.M. "Cruelty and Silence," *New York Times*, 13 April 1993.

Ross, Robert W. *So It Was True: The American Protestant Press and the Nazi Persecution of the Jews*. Minneapolis: University of Minnesota Press, 1980.

Rottenberg, Isaac C. *The Turbulent Triangle: Christians-Jews-Israel*. Hawley, PA: Red Mountain Associates, 1989.

Rouse, Ruth, and Stephen C. Neill, eds. *A History of the Ecumenical Movement, 1517-1948*. Philadelphia: Westminster Press, 1954.

Rubin, Barry. *Revolution Until Victory? The Politics and History of the PLO*. Cambridge, MA: Harvard University Press, 1994.

Runciman, Steven. *The Great Church in Captivity*. Cambridge: Cambridge University Press, 1968.

Running, Leona G. and David Noel Freedman. *William Foxwell Albright: A Twentieth-Century Genius*. New York: Two Continents/Morgan, 1975.

Sabella, Bernard. "Palestinian Christians: Challenges and Hopes." In Albert Aghazarian et al. *Christian Voices from the Holy Land: Out of Jerusalem?* 5–21. Palestinian General Delegation to the United Kingdom Office of Representation of the PLO to the Holy See, December 1997

Sachar, Abram Leon. *A History of the Jews.* New York: Knopf, 1975.

Sachar, Howard M. *A History of Israel: From the Rise of Zionism to Our Time.* New York: Knopf, 1979.

– *A History of the Jews in America.* New York: Knopf, 1992.

– *Israel and Europe: An Appraisal in History.* New York: Knopf, 1999.

Sanders, J.A. "Urbis and Orbis: Jerusalem Today." *Christian Century* 84 (26 July 1967): 967-70.

Schlink, Basilea M. *Israel, My Chosen People.* [1958] Radlett, UK: Kanaan Publications, 1995.

Schneider, Peter. *Dialogue of Christians and Jews.* New York: Scribner's, 1967.

Schoenbaum, David. *The United States and the State of Israel.* New York: Oxford University Press, 1993.

Schulz, Helena Lindholm. *One Year into Self-Government: Perceptions of the Palestinian Political Elite.* 2d ed. Jerusalem: Palestine Academic Society for the Study of International Affairs, 1995.

Schwartz, William. "Towards Understanding Churches in the Middle East: A Western Evangelical Perspective." MECC Perspective. Quoted in *Christians in the Holy Land,* edited by Michael Prior and William Taylor, 205. London: World of Islam Festival Trust, 1994.

Sfeir, Jacqueline. "Education in the Hold Land." In *Christians in the Holy Land,* edited by Michael Prior and William Taylor, 75–88. London: World of Islam Festival Trust, 1994.

Shafaat, Ahmad. *Islam, Christianity and the State of Israel: As Fulfilment of Old Testament Prophecy.* Indianapolis: American Trust Publication, 1989.

Sharif, Regina S. *Non-Jewish Zionism: Its Roots in Eastern History.* London: Zed Press, 1983.

Shea, Nina. *In the Lion's Den.* Nashville: Broadman and Holman, 1996.

Sherman, A.J. *Mandate Days: British Lives in Palestine, 1918-1948.* London: Thames and Hamilton, 1997.

Sidey, Ken. "For the Love of Zion." *Christianity Today* 36 (9 March 1992): 46-50.

Smith, Bernard. *Fraudulent Gospel: Politics and the World Council of Churches.* 2d ed. Worthington, UK: Bernard Smith, 1979.

Sokolow, Nahum. *History of Zionism.* London: Longhams, Green, 1919.

Solomon, Norman. "The Christian Churches on Israel and the Jews." In *Anti-Zionism and Anti-Semitism in the Contemporary World,* edited by Robert S. Wistricht. New York: New York University Press, 1990.

Stevens, Richard P. *American Zionism and US Foreign Policy, 1941-1947.* New York: Pageant Press, 1962.

Sudilovsky, Judith. "Crossing the Line." *Jerusalem Post Internet Edition,* 16 September 1997.

Suermann, Harold. "Palestinian Contextual Theology." *Al-Liqa' Journal* 5 (July 1995): 7-26.

Szulc, Tad. *Pope John Paul II*. New York: Scribner's, 1995.

Tal, Eliyahu. *Whose Jerusalem?* Jerusalem: International Forum for a United Jerusalem, 1994.

Teveth, Shabta. *Ben-Gurion: The Burning Ground, 1886-1948*. Boston: Houghton, Mifflin, 1987.

Theology and the Local Church in the Holy Land. Nazareth: Al-Hakim Press/Al Liqa' Centre, n.d. [1987 or 1988?]

Tivna, Edward. *The Lobby*. New York: Simon and Schuster, 1987.

Torat Eretz Yisrael: The Teachings of HaRav Zvi Yehuda Hacohen Kook. Jerusalem: Torat Eretz Yisrael Publications, 1991.

Tuchman, Barbara. *The Bible and the Sword*. 1956 ed. New York: Ballantine, 1984.

Van der Hoeven, Jan Willem. *Babylon Or Jerusalem?* Shippensburg, PA: Image, 1983.

Vermaat, J.A. Emerson. "The World Council of Churches and the PLO," *Midstream* 30 (November 1984): 3-9.

Wagner, Donald E. *Anxious for Armageddon*. Scottdale, PA: Herald Press, 1994.

– "Evangelicals and Israel: Theological Roots of a Political Alliance." *Christian Century* 115 (4 November 1998).

Wall, James M. "The View from Bethlehem." *Christian Century* 114 (19 and 26 March 1997): 283-5.

Wallach, Janet and John Wallach. *Arafat: In the Eyes of the Beholder*. Rocklin, CA: Prima, 1992.

Walvoord, John F. *Armageddon, Oil, and the Middle East*. Grand Rapids: Zondervan, 1990.

Watt, W. Montgomery. *Muhammad at Medina*. Oxford: Clarendon Press, 1956.

– *Muhammad: Prophet and Statesman*. New York: Oxford University Press, 1961.

Weber, Timothy P. *Living in the Shadow of the Second Coming: American Premillennialism, 1875-1982*. Grand Rapids: Zondervan/Academie, 1983.

– "How Evangelicals Became Israel's Best Friend." *Christianity Today* 42 (5 October 1998): 38-49.

Weigel, George. *Witness To Hope: The Biography of Pope John Paul II*. New York: HarperCollins/Cliff Street, 1999.

– "With John Paul in the Holy Land." *First Things* 104 (June/July 2000): 27-34.

Weinstein, Allen and Moshe Ma'oz, eds. *Truman and the American Commitment to Israel*. Jerusalem: Magnes Press/Hebrew University, 1981.

Weizman, Ezer. *The Battle for Peace*. New York: Bantam Books, 1981.

Weizmann, Chaim. *Trial and Error: The Autobiography of Chaim Weizmann*. London: East and West Library, 1950.

What Do American Jews Believe? A Symposium. *Commentary* 102 (August 1996): 18-96.

Wikstrom, Lester. "The Return of the Jews and the Return of Jesus: Christian Zionism in the 1970s and 1980s." *Al-Liqa' Journal* 3 (May 1994): 71-9.

Wilken, Louis. "The Jews as the Christians Saw Them." *First Things*, no. 73 (May 1997): 28-32.

Williamson, Roger, ed. *The Holy Land in the Monotheistic Faiths.* Uppsala: Life and Peace Institute, 1992.

Wise, Ruth R. *If I Am Not For Myself: The Liberal Betrayal of the Jews.* New York: MacMillan, 1992.

"Wolves in Sheep's Clothing: Identifying the Coming of Jesus with the 'Intifada of Heaven.'" Pamphlet. Jerusalem: International Christian Embassy Jerusalem, n.d.

Wistricht, Robert S., ed. *Anti-Zionism and Anti-Semitism in the Contemporary World.* New York: New York University Press, 1990.

Woodward, Kenneth. "The Way the World Ends." *Newsweek* 134 (1 November 1999): 66–70.

World Council of Churches. The Church and the International Disorder: Reports of the World Council of Churches. London: SCM Press, 1948.

Ye'or. See Bat Ye'or.

Younan, Munib A. "Palestinian Local Theology." *Al-Liqa Journal* 1 (May 1992): 56-63.

Zipperer, John. "Palestinian Christians Hopeful after Accord." *Christianity Today* 37 (25 October 1993): 80.

Index